THE
IDEA OF THE HOLY

AN INQUIRY
INTO THE NON-RATIONAL FACTOR IN THE IDEA
OF THE DIVINE AND ITS RELATION TO
THE RATIONAL

BY

RUDOLF OTTO

PROFESSOR OF THEOLOGY IN THE UNIVERSITY OF MARBURG

TRANSLATED BY

JOHN W. HARVEY

LECTURER IN PHILOSOPHY IN THE UNIVERSITY OF BIRMINGHAM

Das Schaudern ist der Menschheit bestes Teil.
Wie auch die Welt ihm das Gefühl verteuere,
Ergriffen fühlt er tief das Ungeheuere.

Martino Publishing
Mansfield Centre, CT
2010

Martino Publishing
P.O. Box 373,
Mansfield Centre, CT 06250 USA

www.martinopublishing.com

ISBN 1-57898-861-6

© 2010 Martino Publishing

Cover design by T. Matarazzo

Printed in the United States of America On 100% Acid-Free Paper

THE
IDEA OF THE HOLY

AN INQUIRY
INTO THE NON-RATIONAL FACTOR IN THE IDEA
OF THE DIVINE AND ITS RELATION TO
THE RATIONAL

BY

RUDOLF OTTO

PROFESSOR OF THEOLOGY IN THE UNIVERSITY OF MARBURG

TRANSLATED BY

JOHN W. HARVEY

LECTURER IN PHILOSOPHY IN THE UNIVERSITY OF BIRMINGHAM

Das Schaudern ist der Menschheit bestes Teil.
Wie auch die Welt ihm das Gefühl verteuere,
Ergriffen fühlt er tief das Ungeheuere.

HUMPHREY MILFORD
OXFORD UNIVERSITY PRESS
London   Edinburgh   Glasgow   Copenhagen
New York   Toronto   Melbourne   Cape Town
Bombay   Calcutta   Madras   Shanghai
1923

CONTENTS

TRANSLATOR'S PREFACE

THIS translation of Dr. Rudolf Otto's *Das Heilige* has been made from the ninth German edition, but certain passages, mostly additions to the book in its first form, have been omitted with the concurrence of the author. The chief of these are certain of the appendixes, especially a long one upon 'Myth and Religion in Wundt's *Völkerpsychologie*', and some citations in the text from German and other hymns and liturgies which, besides defying adequate translation, appeared to be of less interest to the English than to the German reader. On the other hand, I would refer the English reader to the brief appendix (No. X) that I have ventured to add, in which I have noted some points relevant to the subject discussed in the book suggested by the usage of English words, and added one or two illustrative passages from English writers.

My warmest thanks are due to the author, not only for the many corrections he has made in the text of the translation, the whole of which he read in manuscript, but more for his generous and patient encouragement, without which it would have been neither undertaken nor completed. My best thanks are also due to the readers of the Oxford University Press for many helpful suggestions and corrections in my English text.

*　　*　　*

In the six years since its first publication in 1917, *Das Heilige* has already passed through ten editions. At a time when circumstances are as adverse to writers and purchasers of serious books as they have been for the last few years in Germany, this fact would alone suggest that the author's work has met a genuine need in his own land; and any one who has followed the movement of religious thought abroad during this period is aware that the success of his book is much more

than a mere vogue, and that it is exerting no little influence
upon religious thought in Germany and North Europe at
the present time. It may be of interest to consider briefly
where its chief significance may be found from the point
of view of the English reader.

One of the most unmistakable points of contrast between
the thought of to-day and that of the later nineteenth century
is the increased comprehensiveness and adequacy with which
the study of religion is being pursued. Not only has the older,
harder, more dogmatic tone on all sides given place to one
more tolerant and sympathetic, but the study of religion has
come to claim a much wider reference and to draw material
from far more diverse sources than would at one time have
been recognized ; and the frontiers of the subject have been
enormously extended in consequence. Anthropology, Sociology,
Psychology, and the history and comparative study of religious
forms and institutions, if they have at once modified and com-
plicated the problems of religious inquiry, have definitely
increased the range of observations likely to throw light upon
them.

If we consider only the English-speaking countries, a future
generation may perhaps judge that no writer did more to
introduce or render more effective this new spirit in the study
of religion than William James in his famous Gifford lectures
on *The Varieties of Religious Experience*, published just over
twenty years ago (1902). In any case the title of that book
might be taken as giving the chief characteristics of that spirit,
the preoccupation with religion in all its manifold forms as a
specific experience, rather than as either the vehicle of a system
of dogma or metaphysics on the one hand or as simply the
emotional 'heightening' of morality on the other. This latter
view is well represented by Matthew Arnold, himself in many
respects a very typical child of his age; and Arnold's well-
known phrase that 'the true meaning of religion is "morality
touched by emotion"' is a fair expression of the limita-

tions and bias of the nineteenth-century mind. It suggests the fundamentally 'rational' temper ('rational' even when attacking 'rationalism') of an age interested almost wholly in practice and conduct, which, rightly reacting against views tending to identify religion with creed and dogma, was content to correct them by one that practically reduced it to an ethic. It has been justly noted[1] that such an account leaves unanswered the question, which to-day so obviously needs asking and which is in part the theme of this book, what *sort* of feelings or emotions it is by which morality is enkindled into religion.

For to-day this almost purely rational and ethical approach to the study of religion has been abandoned. Modern inquiries into the nature of religious experience have indeed tended to overweight the opposite scale. Feeling has, perhaps, something more than come into its own. Instinct, emotion, intuition, the more obscure and the more subjective aspects of religious experience—it is these that are to-day the main centre of interest. The vogue (perhaps now already declining) of M. Bergson's philosophy, in which instinct and intuition are put in fundamental contrast to, if not actually opposed to, rationality and the needs of practical life, has been one, but only one, of the influences making in this direction. Equally significant is the quite modern interest in Mysticism, which owes so much to the admirable works of such writers as Dean Inge, Miss Evelyn Underhill, and Baron von Hügel in this country, and Professor Rufus M. Jones in America. In Germany, where the popular interest in Mysticism is even more recent than it is with us, the same tendency is marked by a special leaning towards the study of oriental, and especially of Indian, religions. There, as here, a constant stream of books indicates how widely held is the conviction that there are essential elements in religion which are not to be comprised in

[1] C. C. J. Webb, *Problems in the Relations of God and Man* (1911), p. 4.

any systematically thought-out fabric of ideas, nor wholly
exhausted in practice and conduct—elements which, if they
admit of expression at all, can find it only in symbolism and
imagery.

If, as one suspects, there are already signs of a new reaction
against the possible over-emphasis of what may be called, for
want of a better single term, the elements of 'feeling' in
religion, such a movement of criticism need not be regretted.
We may note at any rate two points in which it may prove
salutary.

In the first place, it has been urged, not altogether unjustly,
that some modern students of religion, and especially of religion
in its 'mystical' forms, have been misled by their interest in
the experiences of exceptional men into a distorted account of
religion as a whole.   They do not see the wood for the trees;
or, more accurately, they fail to get a true view of the common
nature of the trees in their structure and growth through
an undue preoccupation with certain particularly striking
examples.   It is easy (so it may be urged) to pursue the
varieties so far as to neglect the identities of religious experience, those fundamental elements which distinguish it as
religious from experience of other kinds.   Mystical experience
is surely after all something exceptional.   Religion is something wider than Mysticism.   Yet sometimes one gets the
impression that the non-mystic is only rather grudgingly
and half-heartedly admitted to have any first-hand genuine
religious experience at all.   The abnormal is often the more
interesting, the more fascinating study, but it ought not on
that account to be allowed to usurp the place of the normal;
and this, it may be suggested, is one mistake to which the
modern comprehensive, fertile, and far-casting study of religion
is prone.

This is one possible point of criticism.   A second would
emphasize the danger of subjectivism.   It is possible to devote
our attention to religious 'experience' in a sense which would

almost leave out of account the object of which it is an experience. We may so concentrate upon the 'feeling', that the objective cause of it may fall altogether out of sight. Is religious experience essentially just a state of mind, a feeling, whether of oppression or of exaltation, a sense of 'sin' or an assurance of 'salvation'; or is it not rather our apprehension of 'the divine', meaning by that term at least something independent of the mental and emotional state of the moment of experience? In short, it is suggested that by a one-sided over-emphasis of the subjective aspect of it the matter of our study may cease to be 'religion' and come to be merely 'religiosity', to employ a word which, commoner in German than in English, might well be better acclimatized in our language.

The enlarged and emancipated study of religion characteristic of to-day has sometimes given just ground for these two criticisms. It has not always avoided exaggerating the exceptional experience at the expense of the normal; and it has perhaps not infrequently allowed itself to become so far absorbed in the subjective states of mind manifested in religious experience as to ignore or half ignore the objective significance of them.

It is not least in reference to these two points that the value of Dr. Otto's volume lies. He is concerned to examine the nature of those elements in the religious experience which lie outside and beyond the scope of reason—which cannot be comprised in ethical or 'rational' conceptions, but which none the less as 'feelings' cannot be disregarded by any honest inquiry. And his argument shows in the first place that in all the forms which religious experience may assume and has assumed, so far as these can be re-interpreted—in polytheistic and monotheistic cults, non-mystical and mystical worship alike—certain basic 'moments' of feeling (again a word of which our language might well make fuller use) are always found to recur. All genuine religion exhibits these characteristic reactions in consciousness. They are seen emerging as religion itself emerges, and we are shown their antecedents in the crude and savage stages of 'pre-religion', in magic and in the world of primitive superstition. For this inquiry the author not only draws upon his long familiarity with the theories of the anthropologists and the literature of Naturalism,[1] but also lays under contribution his great erudition in the history of religious development in all its varieties. He has 'ransacked the ages, spoiled the climes'. The remote Mosaic and pre-Mosaic religion of Israel, the Hebrew prophets, and modern Judaism; the religions of Greece and Rome and Islam, of China and of India; the New Testament, the Fathers, the medieval mystics, the reformers, and modern Protestantism: the author calls them all as witnesses. He makes particularly effective use of examples drawn from India through his familiarity with Sanskrit and the great classics of Hinduism. His argument, while laying due stress on the essential differences between religions, emphasizes and establishes their no less fundamental kinship on the side of feeling; and Mysticism, especially, falls into its proper place as neither a morbid freak nor the sole true fruit of religion, but as differing from other forms of religious experience not so much in its essential nature as in the degree in which it 'stresses and overstresses' certain common elements shared with them.

But of still more significance is the author's argument in relation to the second of the two points already mentioned—the question of subjectivism. Here we are shown that the religious 'feeling' properly involves a unique kind of apprehension, *sui generis*, not to be reduced to ordinary intellectual or rational 'knowing' with its terminology of notions and concepts, and yet—and this is the paradox of the matter—itself a genuine 'knowing', the growing awareness of an object,

---

[1] His book, *Naturalistische und religiöse Weltansicht* (The Naturalistic and the Religious View of the World), has been translated into English under the title *Naturalism and Religion*, 1907.

deity. All the 'feelings' and emotions that recur the same through all their diversities of manifestation in different religions are shown to be just the reflection in human feeling of this awareness, as it changes and grows richer and more unmistakable; a response, so to speak, to the impact upon the human mind of 'the divine', as it reveals itself whether obscurely or clearly. The primary fact is the confrontation of the human mind with a Something, whose character is only gradually learned, but which is from the first felt as a transcendent presence, 'the beyond', even where it is also felt as 'the within' man. Hence the author shows that Schleiermacher, who did so much to emphasize the function of 'feeling' in religion, is wrong in starting his account with the 'sense of absolute dependence', for that is to start from what is after all secondary and derivative, the reflection in self-feeling of this felt presence of the divine.

The 'feeling' element in religion involves, then, a genuine 'knowing' or awareness, though, in contrast to that knowing which can express itself in concepts, it may be termed 'non-rational'. The feeling of the 'uncanny', the thrill of awe or reverence, the sense of dependence, of impotence, or of nothingness, or again the feelings of religious rapture and exaltation, —all these are attempted designations of the mental states which attend the awareness of certain aspects of 'the divine'. In some religions one may be more prominent and in some another; and different individuals will vary widely in their susceptibility to these feelings, or, in Dr. Otto's terminology, in the degree and character of their faculty of 'divination'. But all of these feelings have a necessary and some a permanent place in the developing recognition of the divine nature. The particular aspect of it, glimpsed, as it were, in each of them, he tries to isolate the better by having recourse to a Latin terminology: but such terms as 'mysterium', 'maiestas', 'fascinans', are confessedly, like 'fear', 'awe', 'love', in their religious application, not so much precise and definable concepts as what he calls 'ideograms', hinting at meanings which elude exact formulation.

A word of explanation and defence (for the English reader does not take kindly to fresh word-coinages) may be offered in respect to the chief new word introduced by the author. Dr. Otto is maintaining the autonomy and uniqueness of a particular sort of 'knowing'. Just as the recognition and appreciation of beauty cannot be reduced to that of moral goodness, just as 'the beautiful' and 'the good' are, in the philosopher's phrase, 'categories' in their own right, so, too, it is with religion. There, too, we have to deal with a peculiar and irreducible kind of apprehension—we employ or apply a distinct 'category'. The natural term for this would be that which stands in the title of this book : 'the holy', or else 'the sacred'. But the meaning of these words is at once too lofty and too narrow. 'Holiness', 'sanctity', are words which are charged with *ethical* import.[1] A large part, perhaps the chief part, of their meaning is moral. This, as the author maintains, is necessarily the case, inasmuch as, the better the character of deity and the divine becomes known, the more intimately it absorbs within itself all the highest moral and 'rational' attributes. But though, in our final experience of God's 'Holiness', *perfect goodness* has an absolutely essential and central place, yet there remains a something beyond. Holiness or sanctity has an element in it independent of the category of the good. And to this the author gives the name of the 'numinous' element, from the Latin *numen*, the most general Latin word for supernatural divine power. 'Numinous' feeling is, then, just this unique apprehension of a Something, whose character may at first seem to have little connexion with our ordinary moral terms, but which later 'becomes charged' with the highest and deepest moral significance. And 'the holy' will be, in Dr. Otto's language, a complex category of the 'numinous' and the 'moral', or, in

[1] See, further, Appendix X.

one of his favourite metaphors, a fabric in which we have the non-rational numinous experience as the woof and the rational and ethical as the warp.

'Numinous' and 'Numen' will, then, be words which bear no moral import, but which stand for the specific non-rational religious apprehension and its object, at all its levels, from the first dim stirrings where religion can hardly yet be said to exist to the most exalted forms of spiritual experience. And then we can keep the words 'holy' and 'sacred', 'holiness' and 'sanctity', to their more usual meaning.

Dr. Otto is concerned in this volume primarily to establish the autonomy and uniqueness of this 'numinous' experience— to show its essential place in religion and its significance in religious development. But so far from claiming that this is all,—that, for example, mystic 'intuition' can dispense with the knowledge that comes through human reason and moral experience,—he asserts emphatically the contrary. And in his later chapters he makes it clear that for him the supremacy of Christianity over all other religions lies in the unique degree in which (as he holds) in Christianity the numinous elements, such as the sense of awe and reverence before infinite mystery and infinite majesty, are yet combined and made one with the rational elements, assuring us that God is an all-righteous, all-provident, and all-loving Person, with whom a man may enter into the most intimate relationship.

What is maintained in this book is, in fact, that religion is something not only natural but also, in the strict sense of the word, paradoxical. It is a real knowledge of, and real personal communion with, a Being whose nature is yet above knowledge and transcends personality. This apparent contradiction cannot be evaded by concentrating upon one aspect of it and ignoring the other, without doing a real injury to religion. It must be faced directly in the experience of worship, and there, and only there, it ceases to be a contradiction and becomes a harmony. And many who are grateful

to Dr. Otto for his clear exposition of the unity of Religion
through all the diversity of religions, and for his emphasis
upon the objective significance of religious feeling, will be perhaps still more grateful to him for insisting that both elements
in the harmony must be preserved.

For in this, too, the argument of this book has something to
offer to the thought of to-day.   It would hardly be denied that
the dominant movement of thought in this nearly completed
first quarter of the twentieth century has been what has
been called 'humanistic', and what might better be termed
'anthropocentric'.   In religion, as in other domains, we have
learned to view things, in the phrase of a brilliant exponent of
this way of thinking,[1] 'from the human end'; man, an ideal
humanity, has come to be increasingly our measure.   We see
one example of this in such a popular religious philosophy
as that of Mr. H. G. Wells, with its virtual apotheosis of
the spirit of striving mankind and the sharp antagonism it
introduces between the ' God in man ' and the Veiled Being, the
mysterious Power in Nature.   It is only the former who has
any religious significance for Mr. Wells.   In such cases
a standard less merely ethical may be employed than that
which the moralistic tendency of the nineteenth century
demanded, but it is far more a purely human standard.   We
need not repeat the taunt of the later nineteenth-century
agnosticism which finds nothing in the God of traditional
orthodoxy but 'man's giant shadow, hailed divine'.[2]   To say
that religious thought to-day is too anthropocentric does not
mean that it is thus crudely anthropomorphic.   But it does
suggest that by *undue* preoccupation with the human and the
personal we may blind ourselves to that transcendent and
supra-personal character of the deity which cannot be
surrendered without a real loss to religion.

Is it possible that once more in this too anthropocentric

[1] Dr. L. P. Jacks.
[2] Sir William Watson, *The Unknown God.*

trend in religious thought the tide is on the turn, and that men are beginning to feel it insufficient to think of God in wellnigh exclusively human terms? One suspects that it may be so, and that at any rate a religion which sets God as Person and Friend of Man at scarcely disguised enmity with the inscrutable power and mysterious tremendousness of nature will not for long satisfy the demands of the soul. And those who think thus will value all the more an exposition which recalls us, as this volume does, to the unsearchable 'otherness' as well as to the human likeness of deity.

*   *   *

In this book there are certain features that may be puzzling and unfamiliar to some readers. Those unaccustomed to such terms may find words like 'category', 'a priori', 'schematize', repellent to them. To the general reader the quasi-Kantian treatment of this matter or that may be a stumbling-block, and to the mystic perhaps foolishness. Again, some may find the argument too much of an analysis ; others, too much of an apologetic. To some it may seem too logical ; to others, too theological. But it is good that our incurable propensity to think in compartments, to keep, if we admit them at all, our philosophy and theology strangers, should receive a shock now and then. And, for the rest, it is surely good that a book upon religion should be written by a man who feels that religion stands at the very centre and basis of life—that ' the divine' in man is, in Plato's phrase, the head and the root of him—and who can make no pretence of viewing his own religion from without, as though it meant no more to him than any other. For though in so many departments in life it is the detached and unprejudiced observer who can best pronounce judgement, in this one the paradox must hold that he who professes to stand outside religion and view all the religions of the world in impartial detachment will never wholly under-stand any one of them.

J. W. H.

March 1923.

CHAPTER I

THE RATIONAL AND THE NON-RATIONAL

IT is essential to every theistic conception of God, and most of all to the Christian, that it designates and precisely characterizes Deity by the attributes Spirit, Reason, Purpose, Good Will, Supreme Power, Unity, Selfhood. The nature of God is thus thought of by analogy with our human nature of reason and personality; only, whereas in ourselves we are aware of this as qualified by restriction and limitation, as applied to God the attributes we use are 'completed', i, e. thought as absolute and unqualified. Now all these attributes constitute clear and definite *concepts*: they can be grasped by the intellect; they can be analysed by thought; they even admit of definition. An object that can thus be thought conceptually may be termed *rational*. The nature of deity described in the attributes above mentioned is, then, a rational nature; and a religion which recognizes and maintains such a view of God is in so far a 'rational' religion. Only on such terms is Belief possible in contrast to mere *feeling*. And of Christianity at least it is false that 'feeling is all, the name but sound and smoke'[1];—where 'name' stands for conception or thought. Rather we count this the very mark and criterion of a religion's high rank and superior value—that it should have no lack of *conceptions* about God; that it should admit knowledge—the knowledge that comes by faith—of the transcendent in terms of conceptual thought, whether those already mentioned or others which continue and develop them. Christianity not only possesses such conceptions but possesses them in unique clarity and abundance, and this is, though not the sole or even the chief, yet a very real sign of its superiority over religions of other forms and at other levels. This must be asserted at the outset and with the most positive emphasis,

[1] Goethe, *Faust*.

But, when this is granted, we have to be on our guard against an error which would lead to a wrong and one-sided interpretation of religion. This is the view that the essence of deity can be given completely and exhaustively in such 'rational' attributions as have been referred to above and in others like them. It is not an unnatural misconception. We are prompted to it by the traditional language of edification, with its characteristic phraseology and ideas; by the learned treatment of religious themes in sermon and theological instruction; and further even by our Holy Scriptures themselves. In all these cases the 'rational' element occupies the foreground, and often nothing else seems to be present at all. But this is after all to be expected. All language, in so far as it consists of words, purports to convey ideas or concepts;— that is what language means;—and the more clearly and unequivocally it does so, the better the language. And hence expositions of religious truth in language inevitably tend to stress the 'rational' attributes of God.

But though the above mistake is thus a natural one enough, it is none the less seriously misleading. For so far are these 'rational' attributes from exhausting the idea of deity, that they in fact imply a non-rational or supra-rational Subject of which they are predicates. They are 'essential' (and not merely 'accidental') attributes of that subject, but they are also, it is important to notice, *synthetic* essential attributes. That is to say, we have to predicate them of a subject which they qualify, but which in its deeper essence is not, nor indeed can be, comprehended in them; which rather requires comprehension of a quite different kind. Yet, though it eludes the conceptual way of understanding, it must be in some way or other within our grasp, else absolutely nothing could be asserted of it. And even Mysticism, in speaking of it as τὸ ἄρρητον, the ineffable, does not really mean to imply that absolutely nothing can be asserted of the object of the religious consciousness; otherwise, Mysticism could exist only in unbroken silence, whereas what has generally been a characteristic of the mystics is their copious eloquence.

Here for the first time we come up against the contrast

between Rationalism and profounder religion, and with this contrast and its signs we shall be repeatedly concerned in what follows. We have here in fact the first and most distinctive mark of Rationalism, with which all the rest are bound up. It is not that which is commonly asserted, that Rationalism is the denial, and its opposite the affirmation, of the miraculous. That is manifestly a wrong or at least a very superficial distinction. For the traditional theory of the miraculous as the occasional breach in the causal nexus in nature by a Being who himself instituted and must therefore be master of it— this theory is itself as massively ' rational ' as it is possible to be. Rationalists have often enough acquiesced in the possibility of the miraculous in this sense ; they have even themselves contributed to frame a theory of it ;—whereas anti-Rationalists have been often indifferent to the whole controversy about miracles. The difference between Rationalism and its opposite is to be found elsewhere. It resolves itself rather into a peculiar difference of *quality* in the mental attitude and emotional content of the religious life itself. All depends upon this : in our idea of God is the non-rational overborne, even perhaps wholly excluded, by the rational ? Or conversely, does the non-rational itself preponderate over the rational ? Looking at the matter thus, we see that the common dictum, that Orthodoxy itself has been the mother of Rationalism, is in some measure well founded. It is not simply that Orthodoxy was dissipated in doctrine and the framing of dogma, for these have been no less a concern of the wildest mystics. It is rather that Orthodoxy found in the construction of dogma and doctrine no way to do justice to the non-rational aspect of its subject. So far from keeping the non-rational element in religion alive in the heart of the religious experience, orthodox Christianity manifestly failed to recognize its value, and by this failure gave to the idea of God a one-sidedly intellectualistic and rationalistic interpretation.

This bias to rationalization still prevails, not only in theology but in the science of comparative religion in general, and from top to bottom of it. The modern students of mythology, and those who pursue research into the religion of ' primitive man ' and attempt to reconstruct the 'bases' or 'sources' of religion, are all victims to it. Men do not, of course, in these cases employ those lofty 'rational' concepts which we took as our point of departure; but they tend to take these concepts and their gradual 'evolution' as setting the main problem of their inquiry, and fashion ideas and notions of lower value, which they regard as paving the way for them. It is always in terms of concepts and ideas that the subject is pursued, 'natural' ones, moreover, such as have a place in the general sphere of man's ideational life, and are not specifically 'religious'. And then with a resolution and cunning which one can hardly help admiring, men shut their eyes to that which is quite unique in the religious experience, even in its most primitive manifestations. But it is rather a matter for astonishment than for admiration! For if there be any single domain of human experience that presents us with something unmistakably specific and unique, peculiar to itself, assuredly it is that of the religious life. In truth the enemy has often a keener vision in this matter than either the champion of religion or the neutral and professedly impartial theorist. For the adversaries on their side know very well that the entire 'mystical unrest' has nothing to do with 'reason' and 'rationality'.

And so it is salutary that we should be incited to notice that Religion is not exclusively contained and exhaustively comprised in any series of 'rational' assertions; and it is well worth while to attempt to bring the relation of the different 'moments' of religion to one another clearly before the mind, so that its nature may become more manifest.

This attempt we are now to make with respect to the quite distinctive category of the holy or sacred.

CHAPTER II

'NUMEN' AND THE 'NUMINOUS'

'HOLINESS'—'the holy'—is a category of interpretation and valuation peculiar to the sphere of religion. It is, indeed, applied by transference to another sphere—that of Ethics—but it is not itself derived from this. While it is complex, it contains a quite specific element or 'moment', which sets it apart from 'the Rational' in the meaning we gave to that word above, and which remains inexpressible—an ἄρρητον or *ineffabile*—in the sense that it completely eludes apprehension in terms of concepts. The same thing is true (to take a quite different region of experience) of the category of the beautiful.

Now these statements would be untrue from the outset if 'the holy' were merely what is meant by the word, not only in common parlance, but in philosophical, and generally even in theological usage. The fact is we have come to use the words *holy, sacred* (heilig) in an entirely derivative sense, quite different from that which they originally bore. We generally take 'holy' as meaning 'completely good'; it is the absolute moral attribute, denoting the consummation of moral goodness. In this sense Kant calls the will which remains unwaveringly obedient to the moral law from the motive of duty a 'holy' will; here clearly we have simply the *perfectly moral* will. In the same way we may speak of the holiness or sanctity of Duty or Law, meaning merely that they are imperative upon conduct and universally obligatory.

But this common usage of the term is inaccurate. It is true that all this moral significance is contained in the word 'holy', but it includes in addition—as even we cannot but feel—a clear overplus of meaning, and this it is now our task to isolate. Nor is this merely a later or acquired meaning; rather, 'holy', or at least the equivalent words in Latin and

Greek, in Semitic and other ancient languages, denoted first
and foremost *only* this overplus: if the ethical element was
present at all, at any rate it was not original and never con-
stituted the whole meaning of the word.   Any one who uses it
to-day does undoubtedly always feel 'the morally good' to be
implied in 'holy'; and accordingly in our inquiry into that
element which is separate and peculiar to the idea of the holy
it will be useful, at least for the temporary purpose of the
investigation, to invent a special term to stand for 'the holy'
minus its moral factor or 'moment', and, as we can now add,
minus its 'rational' aspect altogether.

It will be our endeavour to suggest this unnamed Something
to the reader as far as we may, so that he may himself feel it.
There is no religion in which it does not live as the real innermost core, and without it no religion would be worthy of the
name. It is pre-eminently a living force in the Semitic religions,
and of these again in none has it such vigour as in that of the
Bible.   Here, too, it has a name of its own, viz. the Hebrew
qādôsh, to which the Greek ἄγιος and the Latin *sanctus*, and,
more accurately still, *sacer*, are the corresponding terms.   It is
not, of course, disputed, that these terms in all three languages
connote, as part of their meaning, *good, absolute goodness*,
when, that is, the notion has ripened and reached the highest
stage in its development.   And we then use the word 'holy'
to translate them.   But this 'holy' then represents the
gradual shaping and filling in with ethical meaning, or what
we shall call the 'schematization', of what was a unique
original feeling-response, which can be in itself ethically
neutral and claims consideration in its own right.   And when
this moment or element first emerges and begins its long
development, all those expressions (*qādôsh*, ἄγιος, *sacer*, &c.)
mean beyond all question something quite other than 'the
good'.   This is universally agreed by contemporary criticism,
which rightly explains the rendering of *qādôsh* by 'good' as
a mistranslation   and   unwarranted   'rationalization'   or
'moralization' of the term.

Accordingly, it is worth while, as we have said, to find
a word to stand for this element in isolation, this 'extra' in

the meaning of 'holy' above and beyond the meaning of goodness. By means of a special term we shall the better be able, first, to keep the meaning clearly apart and distinct, and second, to apprehend and classify connectedly whatever subordinate forms or stages of development it may show. For this purpose I adopt a word coined from the Latin *numen*. *Omen* has given us *ominous*, and there is no reason why from *numen* we should not similarly form a word '*numinous*'. I shall speak then of a unique 'numinous' category of value and of a definitely 'numinous' state of mind, which is always found wherever the category is applied. This mental state is perfectly *sui generis* and irreducible to any other; and therefore, like every absolutely primary and elementary datum, while it admits of being discussed, it cannot be strictly defined. There is only one way to help another to an understanding of it. He must be guided and led on by consideration and discussion of the matter through the ways of his own mind, until he reach the point at which 'the numinous' in him perforce begins to stir, to start into life and into consciousness. We can co-operate in this process by bringing before his notice all that can be found in other regions of the mind, already known and familiar, to resemble, or again to afford some special contrast to, the particular experience we wish to elucidate. Then we must add: 'This *X* of ours is not precisely *this* experience, but akin to this one and the opposite of that other. Cannot you now realize for yourself what it is?' In other words our *X* cannot, strictly speaking, be taught, it can only be evoked, awakened in the mind; as everything that comes 'of the spirit' must be awakened.

CHAPTER III

THE ELEMENTS IN THE 'NUMINOUS'

Creature-Feeling.

THE reader is invited to direct his mind to a moment of deeply-felt religious experience, as little as possible qualified by other forms of consciousness. Whoever cannot do this, whoever knows no such moments in his experience, is requested to read no further; for it is not easy to discuss questions of religious psychology with one who can recollect the emotions of his adolescence, the discomforts of indigestion, or, say, social feelings, but cannot recall any intrinsically religious feelings. We do not blame such an one, when he tries for himself to advance as far as he can with the help of such principles of explanation as he knows, interpreting 'Aesthetics' in terms of sensuous pleasure, and 'Religion' as a function of the gregarious instinct and social standards, or as something more primitive still. But the artist, who for his part has an intimate personal knowledge of the distinctive element in the aesthetic experience, will decline his theories with thanks, and the religious man will reject them even more uncompromisingly.

Next, in the probing and analysis of such states of the soul as that of solemn worship, it will be well if regard be paid to what is unique in them rather than to what they have in common with other similar states. To be *rapt* in worship is one thing; to be morally *uplifted* by the contemplation of a good deed is another; and it is not to their common features, but to those elements of emotional content peculiar to the first that we would have attention directed as precisely as possible. As Christians we undoubtedly here first meet with feelings familiar enough in a weaker form in other departments of experience, such as feelings of gratitude, trust, love, reliance, humble submission, and dedication. But this does not by any means exhaust the content of religious worship. Not in any of these have we got the special features of the quite unique and incomparable experience of solemn worship. In what does this consist ?

Schleiermacher has the credit of isolating a very important element in such an experience. This is the 'feeling of dependence'. But this important discovery of Schleiermacher is open to criticism in more than one respect.

In the first place, the feeling or emotion which he really has in mind in this phrase is in its specific quality not a 'feeling of dependence' in the 'natural' sense of the word. As such, other domains of life and other regions of experience than the religious occasion the feeling, as a sense of personal insufficiency and impotence, a consciousness of being determined by circumstances and environment. The feeling of which Schleiermacher wrote has an undeniable analogy with these states of mind : they serve as an indication to it, and its nature may be elucidated by them, so that, by following the direction in which they point, the feeling itself may be spontaneously felt. But the feeling is at the same time also qualitatively different from such analogous states of mind. Schleiermacher himself, in a way, recognizes this by distinguishing the feeling of pious or religious dependence from all other feelings of dependence. His mistake is in making the distinction merely that between 'absolute' and 'relative' dependence, and therefore a difference of degree and not of intrinsic quality. What he overlooks is that, in giving the feeling the name 'feeling of dependence' at all, we are really employing what is no more than a very close analogy. Any one who compares and contrasts the two states of mind introspectively will find out, I think, what I mean. It cannot be expressed by means of anything else, just because it is so primary and elementary a datum in our psychical life, and therefore only definable through itself. It may perhaps help him if I cite a well-known example, in which the precise 'moment' or element of religious feeling of which we are speaking is most actively present. When Abraham ventures to plead with God for the men of Sodom, he says (Genesis xviii. 27) : ' Behold now, I have taken upon

me to speak unto the Lord, which am but dust and ashes.'
There you have a self-confessed 'feeling of dependence', which
is yet at the same time far more than, and something other than,
merely a feeling of dependence.   Desiring to give it a name of
its own, I propose to call it ' creature-consciousness' or creature-
feeling. It is the emotion of a creature, abased and overwhelmed
by its own nothingness in contrast to that which is supreme
above all creatures.

It is easily seen that, once again, this phrase, whatever it is,
is not a *conceptual* explanation of the matter.   All that this
new term, ' creature-feeling', can express, is the note of self-
abasement into nothingness before an overpowering, absolute
might of some kind; whereas everything turns upon the
character of this overpowering might, a character which
cannot be expressed verbally, and can only be suggested
indirectly through the tone and content of a man's feeling-
response to it.   And this response must be directly experienced
in oneself to be understood.

We have now to note a second defect in the formulation of
Schleiermacher's principle.   The religious category discovered
by him, by whose means he professes to determine the real
content of the religious emotion, is merely a category of *self*-
valuation, in the sense of self-depreciation.   According to him
the religious emotion would be directly and primarily a sort
of *self*-consciousness, a feeling concerning one's self in a special,
determined relation, viz. one's dependence.   Thus, according
to Schleiermacher, I can only come upon the very fact of God
as the result of an inference, that is, by reasoning to a cause
beyond myself to account for my 'feeling of dependence'.
But this is entirely opposed to the psychological facts of the
case.   Rather, the 'creature-feeling' is itself a first subjective
concomitant and effect of another feeling-element, which casts
it like a shadow, but which in itself indubitably has immediate
and primary reference to an object outside the self.[1]

---

[1] This is so manifestly borne out by experience that it must be about
the first thing to force itself upon the notice of psychologists analysing
the facts of religion.   There is a certain naïveté in the following
passage from William James's *Varieties of Religious Experience* (p. 58),

But this object is just what we have already spoken of as
'the numinous'. For the 'creature-feeling' and the sense of
dependence to arise in the mind the 'numen' must be
experienced as present, a 'numen praesens', as in the case of
Abraham. There must be felt a something 'numinous',
something bearing the character of a 'numen', to which the
mind turns spontaneously; or (which is the same thing in
other words) these feelings can only arise in the mind as
accompanying emotions when the category of 'the numinous'
is called into play.

The numinous is thus felt as objective and outside the sel .
We have now to inquire more closely into its nature and the
modes of its manifestation.

where, alluding to the origin of the Grecian representations of the gods,
he says : 'As regards the origin of the Greek gods, we need not at present seek an opinion. But the whole array of our instances leads to a
conclusion something like this : It is as if there were in the human consciousness *a sense of reality, a feeling of objective presence, a perception* of
what we may call " *something there* ", more deep and more general than
any of the special and particular " senses " by which the current psychology supposes existent realities to be originally revealed.' (The italics
are James's own.) James is debarred by his empiricist and pragmatist
stand-point from coming to a recognition of faculties of knowledge and
potentialities of thought in the spirit itself, and he is therefore obliged
to have recourse to somewhat singular and mysterious hypotheses to
explain this fact. But he grasps the fact itself clearly enough and is
sufficient of a realist not to explain it away. But this 'feeling of reality',
the feeling of a 'numinous' *object* objectively given, must be posited as
a primary immediate datum of consciousness, and the 'feeling of dependence' is then a consequence, following very closely upon it, viz. a
depreciation of the *subject* in his own eyes   The latter presupposes the
former.

CHAPTER IV

MYSTERIUM TREMENDUM

The Analysis of 'Tremendum'.

WE said above that the nature of the numinous can only be suggested by means of the special way in which it is reflected in the mind in terms of feeling. 'Its nature is such that it grips or stirs the human mind with this and that determinate affective state.' We have now to attempt to give a further indication of these determinate states. We must once again endeavour, by adducing feelings akin to them for the purpose of analogy or contrast, and by the use of metaphor and symbolic expressions, to make the states of mind we are investigating ring out, as it were, of themselves.

Let us consider the deepest and most fundamental element in all strong and sincerely felt religious emotion. Faith unto Salvation, Trust, Love—all these are there. But over and above these is an element which may also on occasion, quite apart from them, profoundly affect us and occupy the mind with a wellnigh bewildering strength. Let us follow it up with every effort of sympathy and imaginative intuition wherever it is to be found, in the lives of those around us, in sudden, strong ebullitions of personal piety and the frames of mind such ebullitions evince, in the fixed and ordered solemnities of rites and liturgies, and again in the atmosphere that clings to old religious monuments and buildings, to temples and to churches. If we do so we shall find we are dealing with something for which there is only one appropriate expression, *mysterium tremendum*. The feeling of it may at times come sweeping like a gentle tide, pervading the mind with a tranquil mood of deepest worship. It may pass over into a more set and lasting attitude of the soul, continuing, as it were, thrillingly vibrant and resonant, until at last it dies away and the soul resumes its 'profane', non-religious mood of everyday experience. It may burst in sudden eruption up from the depths of the soul with spasms and convulsions, or lead to the strangest excitements, to intoxicated frenzy, to transport, and to ecstasy. It has its wild and demonic forms and can sink to an almost grisly horror and shuddering. It has its crude, barbaric antecedents and early manifestations, and again it may be developed into something beautiful and pure and glorious. It may become the hushed, trembling, and speechless humility of the creature in the presence of—whom or what ? In the presence of that which is a *Mystery* inexpressible and above all creatures.

It is again evident at once that here too our attempted formulation by means of a concept is once more a merely negative one. Conceptually 'mysterium' denotes merely that before which the eyes are held closed, that which is hidden and esoteric, that which is beyond conception or understanding, extraordinary and unfamiliar. The term does not define the object more positively in its qualitative character. But though what is enunciated in the word is negative, what is meant is something absolutely and intensely positive. This pure positive we can experience in feelings, feelings which our discussion can help to make clear to us, in so far as it arouses them actually in our hearts.

1. *The Element of Awefulness.*

To get light upon the positive ' quale ' of the object of these feelings, we must analyse more closely our phrase *mysterium tremendum*, and we will begin first with the adjective.

' Tremor ' is in itself merely the perfectly familiar and ' natural ' emotion of *fear*. But here the term is taken, aptly enough but still only by analogy, to denote a quite specific kind of emotional response, wholly distinct from that of being afraid, though it so far resembles it that the analogy of fear may be used to throw light upon its nature. There are in some languages special expressions which denote, either exclusively or in the first instance, this ' fear ' that is more than fear proper. The Hebrew *hiqdīsh* (hallow) is an example. To 'keep a thing holy in the heart' means to mark it off by a feeling of peculiar dread, not to be mistaken for any ordinary dread, that is, to appraise it by the category of the numinous. But the Old Testament throughout is rich in parallel expressions for this feeling. Specially noticeable is the *emāt* of Yahweh ('fear of God'), which Yahweh can pour forth, dispatching almost like a daemon, and which seizes upon a man with paralysing effect. It is closely related to the δεῖμα πανικόν of the Greeks. Compare Exodus xxiii. 27: 'I will send my fear before thee and will destroy all the people to whom thou shalt come . . .'; also Job ix. 34; xiii. 21 ('Let not his fear terrify me'; 'Let not thy dread make me afraid'). Here we have a terror fraught with an inward shuddering such as not even the most menacing and overpowering created thing can instil. It has something spectral in it.

In the Greek language we have a corresponding term in σεβαστός. The early Christians could clearly feel that the title σεβαστός (*augustus*) was one that could not fittingly be given to any creature, not even to the emperor. They felt that to call a man σεβαστός was to give a human being a name proper only to the numen, to rank him by the category proper only to the numen, and that it therefore amounted to a kind of idolatry. Of modern languages English has the words 'awe', 'aweful', which in their deeper and most special sense approximate closely to our meaning. The phrase, 'he stood aghast', is also suggestive in this connexion. On the other hand, German has no native-grown expression of its own for the higher and riper form of the emotion we are considering, unless it be in a word like '*erschauern*', which does suggest it fairly well. It is far otherwise with its cruder and more debased phases, where such terms as '*grausen*' and '*Schauer*', and the more popular and telling '*gruseln*' ('grue'), '*gräsen*', and '*grässlich*' ('grisly'), very clearly designate the numinous element. In my examination of Wundt's Animism I suggested the term 'Scheu' (dread); but the special 'numinous' quality (making it '*awe*' rather than '*dread*' in the ordinary sense) would then of course have to be denoted by inverted commas. 'Religious dread' (or 'awe') would perhaps be a better designation. Its antecedent stage is ' daemonic dread ' (cf. the horror of Pan) with its queer perversion, a sort of abortive off-shoot, the ' dread of ghosts '. It first begins to stir in the feeling of ' something uncanny ', ' eerie ', or ' weird '. It is this feeling which, emerging in the mind of primeval man, forms the starting-point for the entire religious development in history. ' Daemons ' and ' gods ' alike spring from this root, and all the products of ' mythological apperception ' or ' fantasy ' are nothing but different modes in which it has been objectified. And all ostensible explanations of the origin of religion in terms of animism or magic or folk psychology are doomed from the outset to wander astray and miss the real goal of their inquiry, unless they recognize this fact of our nature —primary, unique, underivable from anything else—to be the basic factor and the basic impulse underlying the entire process of religious evolution.[1]

Not only is the saying of Luther that "the natural man cannot fear God" perfectly correct from the stand-point of psychology, but we ought to go further and add that the natural man is quite unable to shudder (*grauen*) or feel horror in the real sense of the word. For ' shuddering ' is something more than ' natural ', ordinary fear. It implies that the mysterious is already beginning to loom before the mind, to touch the feelings. It implies the first application of a category of valuation which has no place in the everyday natural world of ordinary experience, and is only possible to a being in whom has been awakened a mental predisposition, unique in kind and

[1] Cf. my papers in *Theologische Rundschau*, 1910, vol. i, on ' Myth and Religion in Wundt's *Völkerpsychologie* ', and in *Deutsche Literaturzeitung*, 1910, No. 38. I find in more recent investigations, especially those of R. R. Marett and N. Söderblom, a very welcome confirmation of the position I there maintained. It is true that neither of them call attention quite as precisely as, in this matter, psychologists need to do, to the unique character of the religious ' awe ' and its qualitative distinction from all ' natural ' feelings. But Marett more particularly comes within a hair's breadth of what I take to be the truth about the matter. Cf. his *Threshold of Religion* (London, 1909), and N. Söderblom's *Das Werden des Gottesglaubens* (Leipzig, 1915), also my review of the latter in *Theol. Literaturzeitung*, Jan. 1915.

different in a definite way from any 'natural' faculty. And this newly-revealed capacity, even in the crude and violent manifestations which are all it at first evinces, bears witness to a completely new function of experience and standard of valuation, only belonging to the spirit of man.

Before going on to consider the elements which unfold as the 'tremendum' develops, let us give a little further consideration to the first crude, primitive forms in which this 'numinous dread' or *awe* shows itself. It is the mark which really characterizes the so-called 'Religion of Primitive Man', and there it appears as 'daemonic dread'. This crudely naïve and primordial emotional disturbance, and the fantastic images to which it gives rise, are later overborne and ousted by more highly-developed forms of the numinous emotion, with all its mysteriously impelling power. But even when this has long attained its higher and purer mode of expression it is possible for the primitive types of excitation that were formerly a part of it to break out in the soul in all their original naïveté and so to be experienced afresh. That this is so is shown by the potent attraction again and again exercised by the element of horror and 'shudder' in ghost stories, even among persons of high all-round education. It is a remarkable fact that the physical reaction to which this unique 'dread' of the uncanny gives rise is also unique, and is not found in the case of any 'natural' fear or terror. We say: 'my blood ran icy cold', and 'my flesh crept'. The 'cold blood' feeling may be a symptom of ordinary, natural fear, but there is something non-natural or supernatural about the symptom of 'creeping flesh'. And any one who is capable of more precise introspection must recognize that the distinction between such a 'dread' and natural fear is not simply one of degree and intensity. The awe or 'dread' *may* indeed be so overwhelmingly great that it seems to penetrate to the very marrow, making the man's hair bristle and his limbs quake. But it may also steal upon him almost unobserved as the gentlest of agitations, a mere fleeting shadow passing across his mood. It has therefore nothing to do with intensity, and no natural fear passes over into it merely by being intensified. I may be beyond all

measure afraid and terrified without there being even a trace
of the feeling of uncanniness in my emotion.

We should see the facts more clearly if psychology in general
would make a more decisive endeavour to examine and classify
the feelings and emotions according to their qualitative differences. But the far too rough division of elementary feelings
in general into pleasures and pains is still an obstacle to this.
In point of fact ' pleasures ' no more than other feelings are
differentiated merely by degrees of intensity ; they show very
definite and specific differences. It makes a specific difference
to the condition of mind whether the soul is merely in a state
of pleasure, or joy, or aesthetic rapture, or moral exaltation,
or finally in the religious bliss that may come in worship.
Such states certainly show resemblances one to another, and
on that account can legitimately be brought under a common
class-concept ('pleasure '), which serves to cut them off from
other psychical functions, generically different. But this
class-concept, so far from turning the various subordinate
species into merely different degrees of the same thing, can do
nothing at all to throw light upon the essence of each several
state of mind which it includes.

Though the numinous emotion in its completest development
shows a world of difference from the mere ' daemonic dread', yet
not even at the highest level does it belie its pedigree or
kindred. Even when the worship of ' daemons ' has long since
reached the higher level of worship of 'gods ', these gods still
retain as ' numina ' something of the ' ghost ' in the impress
they make on the feelings of the worshipper, viz. the peculiar
quality of the 'uncanny ' and ' awful ', which survives with
the quality of exaltedness and sublimity or is symbolized by
means of it. And this element does not disappear even on the
highest level of all, where the worship of God is at its purest.
Its disappearance would be indeed an essential loss. The
' shudder ' reappears in a form ennobled beyond measure where
the soul, held speechless, trembles inwardly to the furthest
fibre of its being. It invades the mind mightily in Christian
worship with the words: ' Holy, holy, holy '; it breaks forth
from the hymn of Tersteegen:

C

God Himself is present:
Heart, be stilled before Him:
Prostrate inwardly adore Him.

The 'shudder' has here lost its crazy and bewildering note,
but not the ineffable something that holds the mind. It has
become a mystical awe, and sets free as its accompaniment,
reflected in self-consciousness, that 'creature-feeling' that has
already been described as the feeling of personal nothingness
and abasement before the awe-inspiring object directly experienced.

The referring of this feeling of numinous 'tremor' to its
object in the numen brings into relief a 'property' of the
latter which plays an important part in our Holy Scriptures,
and which has been the occasion of many difficulties, both to
commentators and to theologians, from its puzzling and baffling
nature. This is the ὀργή (orgé), the Wrath of Yahweh, which
recurs in the New Testament as ὀργὴ θεοῦ, and which is
clearly analogous to the idea occurring in many religions of a
mysterious 'ira deorum'. To pass through the Indian Pantheon
of Gods is to find deities who seem to be made up altogether
out of such an ὀργή; and even the higher Indian gods of grace
and pardon have frequently, beside their merciful, their 'wrath'
form. But as regards the 'Wrath of Yahweh', the strange
features about it have for long been a matter for constant
remark. In the first place, it is patent from many passages of
the Old Testament that this 'Wrath' has no concern whatever with moral qualities. There is something very baffling
in the way in which it 'is kindled' and manifested. It is, as
has been well said, 'like a hidden force of nature', like stored-
up electricity, discharging itself upon any one who comes too
near. It is 'incalculable' and 'arbitrary'. Any one who is
accustomed to think of deity only by its rational attributes
must see in this 'Wrath' mere caprice and wilful passion.
But such a view would have been emphatically rejected by
the religious men of the Old Covenant, for to them the Wrath
of God, so far from being a diminution of His Godhead, appears
as a natural expression of it, an element of 'holiness' itself,
and a quite indispensable one. And in this they are entirely

right. This ὀργή is nothing but the 'tremendum' itself, apprehended and expressed by the aid of a naïve analogy from the domain of natural experience, in this case from the ordinary passional life of men. But naïve as it may be, the analogy is most disconcertingly apt and striking; so much so that it will always retain its value, and for us no less than for the men of old be an inevitable way of expressing one element in the religious emotion. It cannot be doubted that, despite the protest of Schleiermacher and Ritschl, Christianity also has something to teach of the 'Wrath of God'.

It will be again at once apparent that in the use of this word we are not concerned with a genuine intellectual 'concept', but only with a sort of illustrative substitute for a concept. 'Wrath' here is the 'ideogram' of a unique emotional moment in religious experience, a moment whose singularly *daunting* and awe-inspiring character must be gravely disturbing to those persons who will recognize nothing in the divine nature but goodness, gentleness, love, and a sort of confidential intimacy, in a word, only those aspects of God which turn towards the world of men.

This ὀργή is thus quite wrongly spoken of as 'natural' wrath: rather it is an entirely non- or super-natural, i. e. numinous, quality. The rationalization process takes place when it begins to be filled in with elements derived from the moral reason:—righteousness in requital, and punishment for moral transgression. But it should be noted that the idea of the Wrath of God in the Bible is always a synthesis, in which the original is combined with the later meaning that has come to fill it in. Something supra-rational throbs and gleams, palpable and visible, in the 'Wrath of God', prompting to a sense of 'terror' that no 'natural' anger can arouse.

Beside the Wrath or Anger of Yahweh stands the related expression 'Jealousy of Yahweh'. The state of mind denoted by the phrase 'being jealous *for* Yahweh' is also a numinous state of mind, in which features of the 'tremendum' pass over into the man who has experience of it.

2. *The element of ' Overpoweringness' ('majestas').*

We have been attempting to unfold the implications of that aspect of the 'mysterium tremendum' indicated by the adjective, and the result so far may be summarized in two words, constituting, as before, what may be called an ' ideogram ', rather than a concept proper, viz. ' absolute unapproachability '.

It will be felt at once that there is yet a further element which must be added, that, namely, of 'might ', 'power ', ' absolute overpoweringness'. We will take to represent this the term ' majestas ', majesty—the more readily because any one with a feeling for language must detect a last faint trace of the numinous still clinging to the word. The ' tremendum ' may then be rendered more adequately ' tremenda majestas ', or ' aweful majesty'. This second element of majesty may continue to be vividly preserved, where the first, that of unapproachability, recedes and dies away, as may be seen, for example, in Mysticism. It is especially in relation to this element of majesty or absolute overpoweringness that the creature-consciousness, of which we have already spoken, comes upon the scene, as a sort of shadow or subjective reflection of it. Thus, in contrast to ' the overpowering' of which we are conscious as an object over against the self, there is the feeling of one's own abasement, of being but ' dust and ashes' and nothingness. And this forms the numinous raw material for the feeling of religious humility.[1]

Here we must revert once again to Schleiermacher's expression for what we call ' creature-feeling ', viz. the ' feeling of dependence '. We found fault with this phrase before on the ground that Schleiermacher thereby takes as basis and point of departure what is merely a secondary effect; that he sets out to teach a consciousness of the religious *object* only by way of an inference from the shadow it casts upon *self*-consciousness. We have now a further criticism to bring against it, and it is this. By ' feeling of dependence' Schleiermacher means consciousness of *being conditioned* (as effect by cause), and so he develops the implications of this logically enough

---

[1] Cf. R. R. Marett, 'The Birth of Humility,' in *The Threshold of Religion*, 2nd ed., 1914. [Tr.]

in his sections upon Creation and Preservation. On the side of the deity the correlate to 'dependence' would thus be 'causality', i. e. God's character as all-causing and all-conditioning. But a sense of this does not enter at all into that immediate and first-hand religious emotion which we have in the moment of worship, and which we can recover in a measure for analysis; it belongs on the contrary decidedly to the *rational* side of the idea of God; its implications admit of precise conceptual determination; and it springs from quite a distinct source. The difference between the 'feeling of dependence' of Schleiermacher and that which finds typical utterance in the words of Abraham already cited might be expressed as that between the consciousness of *createdness* (Geschaffenheit) and the consciousness of *creaturehood* (Geschöpflichkeit). In the one case you have the creature as the work of the divine creative act; in the other, impotence and general nothingness as against overpowering might, dust and ashes as against 'majesty'. In the one case you have the fact of having been created; in the other, the status of the creature. And as soon as speculative thought has come to concern itself with this latter type of consciousness—as soon as it has come to analyse this 'majesty'—we are introduced to a set of ideas quite different from those of creation or preservation. We come upon the ideas, first, of the annihilation of self, and then, as its complement, of the transcendent as the sole and entire reality. These are the characteristic notes of Mysticism in all its forms, however otherwise various in content. For one of the chiefest and most general features of Mysticism is just this *self-depreciation* (so plainly parallel to the case of Abraham), the estimation of the self, of the personal 'I', as something not perfectly or essentially real, or even as mere nullity, a self-depreciation which comes to demand its own fulfilment in practice in rejecting the delusion of selfhood, and so makes for the annihilation of the self. And on the other hand Mysticism leads to a valuation of the transcendent object of its reference as that which through plenitude of being stands supreme and absolute, so that the finite self contrasted with it becomes conscious even in its nullity that 'I am nought, Thou

art all '. There is no thought in this of any causal relation
between God, the creator, and the self, the creature. The
point from which speculation starts is not a ' consciousness of
absolute dependence'—of myself as result and effect of a
divine cause—for that would in point of fact lead to insistence
upon the reality of the self; it starts from a consciousness of
the absolute superiority or supremacy of a power other than
myself, and it is only as it falls back upon ontological terms
to achieve its end—terms generally borrowed from natural
science—that that element of the ' tremendum ', originally
apprehended as ' plenitude of power ', becomes transmuted into
' plenitude of being '.

This leads again to the mention of Mysticism. No mere
inquiry into the genesis of a thing can throw any light upon
its essential nature, and it is hence immaterial to us how
Mysticism historically arose. But essentially Mysticism is the
stressing to a very high degree, indeed the overstressing, of
the non-rational or supra-rational elements in religion ; and it
is only intelligible when so understood. The various phases
and factors of the non-rational may receive varying emphasis,
and the type of Mysticism will differ according as some or
others fall into the background. What we have been analysing, however, is a feature that recurs in all forms of Mysticism
everywhere, and it is nothing but the ' creature-consciousness '
stressed to the utmost and to excess, the expression meaning,
if we may repeat the contrast already made, not ' feeling of
our createdness ' but ' feeling of our creaturehood ', that is, the
consciousness of the littleness of every creature in face of that
which is above all creatures.

A characteristic common to all types of Mysticism is the
Identification, in different degrees of completeness, of the
personal self with the transcendent Reality. This identification has a source of its own, with which we are not here
concerned, and springs from ' moments ' of religious experience
which would require separate treatment. ' Identification '
alone, however, is not enough for Mysticism ; it must be Identification with the Something that is at once absolutely
supreme in power and reality and wholly non-rational. And it
is among the mystics that we most encounter this element of

religious consciousness.   Récéjac has noticed this in his *Essai sur les fondements de la connaissance mystique* (Paris, 1897). He writes (p. 90) :

'Le mysticisme commence par la crainte, par le sentiment d'une *domination* universelle, *invincible*, et devient plus tard un désir d'union avec ce qui domine ainsi.'

And some very clear examples of this taken from the religious experience of the present day are to be found in W. James (*op. cit.*, p. 66) :

'The perfect stillness of the night was thrilled by a more solemn silence.   The darkness held a presence that was all the more felt because it was not seen.   I could not any more have doubted that *He* was there than that I was.   Indeed, I felt myself to be, if possible, the less real of the two.'

This example is particularly instructive as to the relation of Mysticism to the 'feelings of Identification', for the experience here recounted was on the point of passing into it.[1]

3. *The Element of 'Energy' or Urgency.*

There is, finally, a third element comprised in those of 'tremendum' and 'majestas', awefulness and majesty, and this I venture to call the *urgency* or *energy* of the numinous object. It is particularly vividly perceptible in the 'ὀργή' or 'Wrath'; and it everywhere clothes itself in symbolical expressions— vitality, passion, emotional temper, will, force, movement,[2] excitement, activity, violence.   These features are typical and recur again and again from the daemonic level up to the idea of the 'living' God.   We have here the factor that has everywhere more than any other prompted the fiercest opposition to the philosophic' God of mere rational speculation, who can be put into a definition.   And for their part the philosophers have condemned these expressions of the energy of the numen, whenever they are brought on to the scene, as sheer anthropomorphism.   In so far as their opponents have for the most part themselves failed to recognize that the terms they have borrowed from the sphere of human conative and affective life have merely value as analogies, the philosophers are right to

---

[1] Compare too the experience on p. 70 : '... What I felt on these occasions was a temporary loss of my own identity.'

[2] The 'mobilitas Dei' of Lactantius.

condemn them.   But they are wrong, in so far as, this error
notwithstanding,'these terms stood for a genuine aspect of the
divine nature—its non-rational aspect—a due consciousness of
which served to protect religion itself from being 'rationalized'
away.

For wherever men have been contending for the 'living'
God and for voluntarism there, we may be sure, have been
non-rationalists fighting rationalists and rationalism.   It was
so with Luther in his controversy with Erasmus; and Luther's
'omnipotentia Dei' in his *De Servo Arbitrio* is nothing but
the union of 'majesty'—in the sense of absolute supremacy—
with this 'energy', in the sense of a force that knows not stint
nor stay, which is urgent, active, compelling, and alive.   In
Mysticism, too, this element of 'energy' is a very living and
vigorous factor, at any rate in the 'voluntaristic' Mysticism,
the Mysticism of love, where it is very forcibly seen in that
'consuming fire' of love whose burning strength the mystic
can hardly bear, but begs that the heat that has scorched him
may be mitigated, lest he be himself destroyed by it.   And in
this urgency and pressure the mystic's 'love' claims a perceptible kinship with the ὀργή itself, the scorching and consuming wrath of God; it is the same 'energy', only differently
directed.   'Love', says one of the mystics, 'is nothing else
than quenched Wrath'.

The element of 'energy' reappears in Fichte's speculations
on the Absolute as the gigantic, never-resting, active world-
stress, and in Schopenhauer's daemonic 'Will'.   At the same
time both these writers are guilty of the same error that
is already found in Myth; they transfer 'natural' attributes,
which ought only to be used as 'ideograms' for what is itself
properly beyond utterance, to the non-rational as real qualifica-
tions of it, and they mistake symbolic expressions of feelings
for adequate concepts upon which a 'scientific' structure of
knowledge may be based.

In Goethe, as we shall see later, the same element of energy
is emphasized in a quite unique way in his strange descriptions
of the experience he calls 'daemonic'.

CHAPTER V

THE ANALYSIS OF 'MYSTERIUM'

Ein begriffener Gott ist kein Gott.
'A God comprehended is no God.' (TERSTEEGEN.)

WE gave to the object to which the numinous consciousness is directed the name 'mysterium tremendum', and we then set ourselves first to determine the meaning of the adjective 'tremendum'—which we found to be itself only justified by analogy—because it is more easily analysed than the substantive idea 'mysterium'. We have now to turn to this, and try, as best we may, by hint and suggestion, to get to a clearer apprehension of what it implies.

4. *The 'Wholly Other'.*

It might be thought that the adjective itself gives an explanation of the substantive; but this is not so. It is not merely analytical; it is a synthetic attribute to it; i.e. 'tremendum' adds something not necessarily inherent in 'mysterium'. It is true that the reactions in consciousness that correspond to the one readily and spontaneously overflow into those that correspond to the other; in fact, any one sensitive to the use of words would commonly feel that the idea of 'mystery' (*mysterium*) is so closely bound up with its synthetic qualifying attribute 'aweful' (*tremendum*) that one can hardly say the former without catching an echo of the latter, 'mystery' almost of itself becoming 'aweful mystery' to us. But the passage from the one idea to the other need not by any means be always so easy. The elements of meaning implied in 'awefulness' and 'mysteriousness' are in themselves definitely different. The latter may so far preponderate in the religious consciousness, may stand out so

vividly, that in comparison with it the former almost sinks out
of sight; a case which again could be clearly exemplified from
some forms of Mysticism. Occasionally, on the other hand,
the reverse happens, and the 'tremendum' may in turn occupy
the mind without the 'mysterium'.

This latter, then, needs special consideration on its own
account. We need an expression for the mental reaction
peculiar to it; and here, too, only one word seems appropriate,
though, as it is strictly applicable only to a 'natural' state of
mind, it has here meaning only by analogy: it is the word
'stupor'. *Stupor* is plainly a different thing from *tremor*; it
signifies blank wonder, an astonishment that strikes us dumb,
amazement absolute.[1] Taken, indeed, in its purely natural
sense, 'mysterium' would first mean merely a secret or a
mystery in the sense of that which is alien to us, uncomprehended and unexplained; and so far 'mysterium' is itself
merely an ideogram, an analogical notion taken from the
natural sphere, illustrating, but incapable of exhaustively
rendering, our real meaning. Taken in the religious sense,
that which is 'mysterious' is—to give it perhaps the most
striking expression—the 'wholly other' (θάτερον, *anyad, alie-
num*), that which is quite beyond the sphere of the usual,
the intelligible, and the familiar, which therefore falls quite
outside the limits of the 'canny', and is contrasted with it,
filling the mind with blank wonder and astonishment.

This is already to be observed on the lowest and earliest
level of the religion of primitive man, where the numinous
consciousness is but an inchoate stirring of the feelings. What
is really characteristic of this stage is *not*—as the theory of

---

[1] Compare also '*obstupefacere*'. Still more exact equivalents are the
Greek θάμβος and θαμβεῖν. The sound θαμβ (*thamb*) excellently depicts this
state of mind of blank, staring wonder. And the difference between the
moments of 'stupor' and 'tremor' is very finely suggested by the passage, Mark x. 32 (cf. *infra*, p. 163). On the other hand, what was said above
of the facility and rapidity with which the two moments merge and
blend is also markedly true of θάμβος, which then becomes a classical
term for the (ennobled) awe of the numinous in general. So Mark xvi.
5 is rightly translated by Luther 'und sie entsetzten sich', and by the
English Authorized Version 'and they were affrighted'.

Animism would have us believe—that men are here concerned with curious entities, called 'souls' or 'spirits', which happen to be invisible. Representations of spirits and similar conceptions are rather one and all early modes of 'rationalizing' a precedent experience, to which they are subsidiary. They are attempts in some way or other, it little matters how, to guess the riddle it propounds, and their effect is at the same time always to weaken and deaden the experience itself. They are the source from which springs, not religion, but the rationalization of religion, which often ends by constructing such a massive structure of theory and such a plausible fabric of interpretation, that the 'mystery' is frankly excluded.[1] Both imaginative 'Myth', when developed into a system, and intellectualist Scholasticism, when worked out to its completion, are methods by which the fundamental fact of religious experience is, as it were, simply rolled out so thin and flat as to be finally eliminated altogether.

Even on the lowest level of religious development the essential characteristic is therefore to be sought elsewhere than in the appearance of 'spirit' representations. It lies rather, we repeat, in a peculiar 'moment' of consciousness, to wit, the *stupor* before something 'wholly other', whether such an other be named 'spirit' or 'daemon' or 'deva', or be left without any name. Nor does it make any difference in this respect whether, to interpret and preserve their apprehension of this 'other', men coin original imagery of their own or adapt imaginations drawn from the world of legend, the fabrications of fancy apart from and prior to any stirrings of daemonic dread.

In accordance with laws of which we shall have to speak again later, this feeling or consciousness of the 'wholly other' will attach itself to, or sometimes be indirectly aroused by means of, objects which are already puzzling upon the 'natural' plane, or are of a surprising or astounding character; such as extraordinary phenomena or astonishing occurrences or things

---

[1] A spirit or soul that has been conceived and comprehended no longer prompts to 'shuddering', as is proved by Spiritualism. But it thereby ceases to be of interest for the psychology of religion.

in inanimate nature, in the animal world, or among men. But
here once more we are dealing with a case of association
between things specifically different—the 'numinous' and the
'natural' moment of consciousness—and not merely with
the gradual enhancement of one of them—the 'natural'—till
it becomes the other. As in the case of 'natural fear' and
'daemonic dread' already considered, so here the transition
from natural to daemonic amazement is not a mere matter of
degree. But it is only with the latter that the complementary
expression 'mysterium' perfectly harmonizes, as will be felt
perhaps more clearly in the case of the adjectival form
'mysterious'. No one says, strictly and in earnest, of a piece
of clockwork that is beyond his grasp, or of a science that he
cannot understand: 'That is "mysterious" to me.'

It might be objected that the mysterious is something
which is and remains absolutely and invariably beyond our
understanding, whereas that which merely eludes our understanding for a time but is perfectly intelligible in principle
should be called, not a 'mystery', but merely a 'problem'.
But this is by no means an adequate account of the matter.
The truly 'mysterious' object is beyond our apprehension and
comprehension, not only because our knowledge has certain
irremovable limits, but because in it we come upon something
inherently 'wholly other', whose kind and character are incommensurable with our own, and before which we therefore
recoil in a wonder that strikes us chill and numb.[1]

This may be made still clearer by a consideration of that
degraded offshoot and travesty of the genuine 'numinous'
dread or awe, the fear of ghosts. Let us try to analyse this
experience. We have already specified the peculiar feeling-

[1] In *Confessions*, ii. 9. 1, Augustine very strikingly suggests this stiffen-
ing, benumbing element of the 'wholly other' and its contrast to the
rational aspect of the numen ; the 'dissimile' and the 'simile'.

'Quid est illud, quod interlucet mihi et percutit cor meum sine laesione ?
Et inhorresco et inardesco. *Inhorresco*, in quantum *dissimilis* ei sum.
Inardesco, in quantum similis ei sum.'

('What is that which gleams through me and smites my heart without
wounding it ? I am both a-shudder and a-glow. A-shudder, in so far as
I am unlike it, a-glow in so far as I am like it.')

element of 'dread' aroused by the ghost as that of 'grue', grisly horror (*gruseln, grüsen*). Now this 'grue' obviously contributes something to the attraction which ghost-stories exercise, in so far, namely, as the relaxation of tension ensuing upon our release from it relieves the mind in a pleasant and agreeable way. So far, however, it is not really the ghost itself that gives us pleasure, but the fact that we are rid of it. But obviously this is quite insufficient to explain the ensnaring attraction of the ghost-story. The ghost's real attraction rather consists in this, that of itself and in an uncommon degree it entices the imagination, awakening strong interest and curiosity; it is the weird thing itself that allures the fancy. But it does this, not because it is 'something long and white' (as some one once defined a ghost), nor yet through any of the positive and conceptual attributes which fancies about ghosts have invented, but because it is a thing that 'doesn't really exist at all', the 'wholly other', something which has no place in our scheme of reality but belongs to an absolutely different one, and which at the same time arouses an irrepressible interest in the mind.

But that which is perceptibly true in the fear of ghosts, which is, after all, only a caricature of the genuine thing, is in a far stronger sense true of the 'daemonic' experience itself, of which the fear of ghosts is a mere off-shoot. And while, following this main line of development, this element in the numinous consciousness, the feeling of the 'wholly other', is heightened and clarified, its higher modes of manifestation come into being, which set the numinous object in contrast not only to everything wonted and familiar (i.e., in the end, to nature in general), thereby turning it into the 'supernatural', but finally to the world itself, and thereby exalt it to the 'supramundane', that which is above the whole world-order.

In Mysticism we have in the 'Beyond' (ἐπέκεινα) again the strongest stressing and over-stressing of those non-rational elements which are already inherent in all religion. Mysticism continues to its extreme point this contrasting of the numinous object (the numen), as the 'wholly other', with ordinary experience. Not content with contrasting it with all that is of nature or this world, Mysticism concludes by contrasting it with Being itself and all that 'is', and finally actually calls it 'that which is nothing'. By this 'nothing' is meant not only that of which nothing can be predicated, but that which is absolutely and intrinsically other than and opposite of everything that is and can be thought. But while exaggerating to the point of paradox this *negation* and contrast—the only means open to conceptual thought to apprehend the 'mysterium'—Mysticism at the same time retains the *positive quality* of the 'wholly other' as a very living factor in its over-brimming religious emotion.

But what is true of the strange 'nothingness' of our mystics holds good equally of the 'sūnyam' and the 'sūnyatā', the 'void' and 'emptiness' of the Buddhist mystics. This aspiration for the 'void' and for becoming void, no less than the aspiration of our western mystics for 'nothing' and for becoming nothing, must seem a kind of lunacy to any one who has no inner sympathy for the esoteric language and ideograms of Mysticism, and lacks the matrix from which these come necessarily to birth. To such an one Buddhism itself will be simply a morbid sort of pessimism. But in fact the 'void' of the eastern, like the 'nothing' of the western, mystic is a numinous ideogram of the 'wholly other'.

These terms, 'supernatural' and 'transcendent' (literally, supramundane: *überweltlich*), give the appearance of positive attributes, and, as applied to the mysterious, they appear to divest the 'mysterium' of its originally negative meaning and to turn it into an affirmation. On the side of conceptual thought this is nothing more than appearance, for it is obvious that the two terms in question are merely negative and exclusive attributes with reference to 'nature' and the 'world' or cosmos respectively. But on the side of the feeling-content it is otherwise; that *is* in very truth positive in the highest degree, though here too, as before, it cannot be rendered explicit in conceptual terms. It is through this positive feeling-content that the concepts of the 'transcendent' and 'supernatural' become forthwith designations for a unique 'wholly other' reality and quality, something of whose special character we can *feel*, without being able to give it clear conceptual expression.

CHAPTER VI

5. THE ELEMENT OF FASCINATION

THE qualitative *content* of the numinous experience, to which 'the mysterious' stands as *form*, is in one of its aspects the element of daunting 'awefulness' and 'majesty', which has already been dealt with in detail; but it is clear that it has at the same time another aspect, in which it shows itself as something uniquely attractive and *fascinating*.

These two qualities, the daunting and the fascinating, now combine in a strange harmony of contrasts, and the resultant dual character of the numinous consciousness, to which the entire religious development bears witness, at any rate from the level of the 'daemonic dread' onwards, is at once the strangest and most noteworthy phenomenon in the whole history of religion. The daemonic-divine object may appear to the mind an object of horror and dread, but at the same time it is no less something that allures with a potent charm, and the creature, who trembles before it, utterly cowed and cast down, has always at the same time the impulse to turn to it, nay even to make it somehow his own. The 'mystery' is for him not merely something to be wondered at but something that entrances him; and beside that in it which bewilders and confounds, he feels a something that captivates and transports him with a strange ravishment, rising often enough to the pitch of dizzy intoxication; it is the Dionysiac-element in the numen.

The ideas and concepts which are the parallels or 'schemata' on the rational side of this non-rational element of 'fascination' are Love, Mercy, Pity, Comfort; these are all 'natural' elements of the common psychical life, only they are here thought as absolute and in completeness. But important as these are for the experience of religious bliss or felicity, they do not by any means exhaust it. It is just the same as with the opposite experience of religious infelicity—the experience of the ὀργή or Wrath of God:—both alike contain fundamentally non-rational elements. Bliss or beatitude is more, far more, than the mere natural feeling of being comforted, of reliance, of the joy of love, however these may be heightened and enhanced. Just as ' Wrath ', taken in a purely rational or a purely ethical sense, does not exhaust that profound element of *awefulness* which is locked in the mystery of deity, so neither does ' Graciousness ' exhaust the profound element of *wonderfulness* and rapture which lies in the mysterious beatific experience of deity. The term ' grace ' may indeed be taken as its aptest designation, but then only in the sense in which it is really applied in the language of the mystics, and in which not only the ' gracious intent ' but ' something more ' is meant by the word. This ' something more ' has its antecedent phases very far back in the history of religions.

It may well be possible, it is even probable, that in the first stage of its development the religious consciousness started with only one of its poles—the ' daunting ' aspect of the numen —and so at first took shape only as ' daemonic dread '. But if this did not point to something beyond itself, if it were not but one ' moment ' of a completer experience, pressing up gradually into consciousness, then no transition would be possible to the feelings of positive self-surrender to the numen. The only type of worship that could result from this ' dread ' alone would be that of ' ἀπαιτεῖσθαι ' and ' ἀποτρέπειν ', taking the form of expiation and propitiation, the averting or the appeasement of the ' wrath ' of the numen. It can never explain how it is that ' the numinous ' is the object of search and desire and yearning, and that too for its own sake and not only for the sake of the aid and backing that men expect from it in the natural sphere. It can never explain how this takes place, not only in the forms of ' rational ' religious worship, but in those queer ' sacramental ' observances and rituals and procedures of communion in which the human being seeks to get the numen into his possession.

Religious practice may manifest itself in those normal and easily intelligible forms which occupy so prominent a place in the history of religion, such forms as Propitiation, Petition, Sacrifice, Thanksgiving, &c.   But besides these there is a series of strange proceedings which are constantly attracting greater and greater attention, and in which it is claimed that we may recognize, besides mere religion in general, the particular roots of Mysticism.   I refer to those numerous curious modes of manipulation and fantastic forms of mediation, by means of which the primitive religious man attempts to master 'the mysterious', and to fill himself and even to identify himself with it.   These modes of manipulation fall apart into two classes.   On the one hand the 'magical' identification of the self with the numen proceeds by means of various transactions, at once magical and devotional in character—by formula, ordination, adjuration, consecration, exorcism, &c.: on the other hand are the 'shamanistic' ways of procedure, possession, indwelling, self-imbuement with the numen in exaltation and ecstasy.   All these have, indeed, their starting-points simply in magic, and their intention at first was certainly simply to appropriate the prodigious force of the numen for the natural ends of man. But the process does not rest there.   Possession of and by the numen becomes an end in itself ; it begins to be sought for its own sake ; and the wildest and most artificial methods of asceticism are put into practice to attain it.   In a word, the 'vita religiosa' begins; and to remain in these strange and bizarre states of numinous possession becomes a good in itself, even a way of salvation, wholly different from the profane goods pursued by means of magic.   Here, too, commences the process of development by which the experience is matured and purified, till finally it reaches its consummation in the sublimest and purest states of the 'life within the Spirit' and in the noblest Mysticism.   Widely various as these states are in themselves, yet they have this element in common, that in them the 'mysterium' is experienced in its essential, positive, and specific character, as something that bestows upon man a beatitude beyond compare, but one whose real nature he can neither proclaim in speech nor conceive in thought, but may know only by a direct and living experience. It is a bliss which embraces all those blessings that are indicated or suggested in positive fashion by any 'doctrine of Salvation', and it quickens all of them through and through; but these do not exhaust it. Rather by its all-pervading, penetrating glow it makes of these very blessings more than the intellect can conceive in them or affirm of them. It gives the Peace that passes understanding, and of which the tongue can only stammer brokenly. Only from afar, by metaphors and analogies, do we come to apprehend what it is in itself, and even so our notion is but inadequate and confused.

'Eye hath not seen, nor ear heard, neither have entered into the heart of man, the things which God hath prepared for them that love Him.' Who does not feel the exalted sound of these words and the 'Dionysiac' element of transport and fervour in them? It is instructive that in such phrases as these, in which consciousness would fain put its highest consummation into words, 'all images fall away' and the mind turns from them to grasp expressions that are purely negative. And it is still more instructive that in reading and hearing such words their merely negative character simply is not noticed; that we can let whole chains of such negations enrapture, even intoxicate us, and that entire hymns—and deeply impressive hymns—have been composed, in which there is really nothing positive at all! All this teaches us the independence of the positive content of this experience from the implications of its overt conceptual expression, and how it can be firmly grasped, thoroughly understood, and profoundly appreciated, purely in, with, and from the feeling itself.

Mere love, mere trust, for all the glory and happiness they bring, do not explain to us that moment of rapture that breathes in our tenderest and most heart-felt hymns of salvation, as also in such eschatological hymns of longing as that Rhyme of St. Bernard in which the very verses seem to dance.

Urbs Sion unica, mansio mystica, condita caelo,
Nunc tibi gaudeo, nunc tibi lugeo, tristor, anhelo,
Te, quia corpore non queo, pectore saepe penetro;
Sed caro terrea, terraque carnea, mox cado retro.

Nemo retexere, nemoque promere sustinet ore,
Quo tua moenia, quo capitolia plena nitore.
Id queo dicere, quo modo tangere pollice coelum,
Ut mare currere, sicut in aere figere telum.
Opprimit omne cor ille tuus decor, O Sion, O Pax.
Urbs sine tempore, nulla potest fore laus tibi mendax.
O nova mansio, te pia concio, gens pia munit,
Provehit, excitat, auget, identitat, efficit, unit.[1]

This is where the living 'something more' of the 'fascinans',
the element of fascination, is to be found. It lives no less
in those tense extollings of the blessing of salvation, which
recur in all religions of salvation, and stand in such remarkable
contrast to the relatively meagre and frequently childish
import of that which is revealed in them by concept or by
image. Everywhere Salvation is something whose meaning
is often very little apparent, is even wholly obscure, to the
'natural' man; on the contrary, *so far as he understands it*,
he tends to find it highly tedious and uninteresting, sometimes
downright distasteful and repugnant to his nature, as he
would, for instance, find the beatific vision of God in our
own doctrine of Salvation, or the 'Henosis' of 'God all in all'
among the mystics. 'So far as he understands', be it noted;
but then he does not understand it in the least. Because he
lacks the inward teaching of the Spirit, he must needs confound
what is offered him as an expression for the experience of
salvation—a mere ideogram of what is felt, whose import
it hints at by analogy—with 'natural' concepts, as though it
were itself just such an one. And so he 'wanders ever
further from the goal'.

[1] 'O Zion, thou city sole and single, mystic mansion hidden away in the
heavens, now I rejoice in thee, now I moan for thee and mourn and
yearn for thee; Thee often I pass through in the heart, as I cannot in the
body, but being but earthly flesh and fleshly earth soon I fall back.
None can disclose or utter in speech what plenary radiance fills thy walls
and thy citadels. I can as little tell of it as I can touch the skies with
my finger, or run upon the sea or make a dart stand still in the air.
This thy splendour overwhelms every heart, O Sion, O Peace! O time-
less City, no praise can belie thee. O new dwelling-place, thee the
concourse and people of the faithful erects and exalts, inspires and increases, joins to itself, and makes complete and one.'

It is not only in the religious feeling of longing that the moment of fascination is a living factor.   It is already alive and present in the moment of ' solemnity ', both in the gathered concentration and humble abasement of private devotion, when the mind is exalted to the holy, and in the common worship of the congregation, where this is practised with earnestness and deep sincerity, as, it is to be feared, is with us a thing rather desired than realized.   It is this and nothing else that in the solemn moment can fill the soul so full and keep it so inexpressibly tranquil.   Schleiermacher's assertion [1] is perhaps true of it, as of the numinous consciousness in general, viz. that it cannot really occur alone on its own account, or except combined and penetrated with rational elements.   But, if this be admitted, it is upon other grounds than those adduced by Schleiermacher; while, on the other hand, it may occupy a more or less predominant place and lead to states of calm ($\dot{\eta}\sigma\upsilon\chi\acute{\iota}\alpha$) as well as of transport, in which it *almost* of itself wholly fills the soul.   But in all the manifold forms in which it is aroused in us, whether in eschatological promise of the coming kingdom of God and the transcendent bliss of Paradise, or in the guise of an entry into that beatific Reality that is ' above the world '; whether it come first in expectancy or preintimation or in a present experience ('When I but *have* Thee, I ask no question of heaven and earth '); in all these forms, outwardly diverse but inwardly akin, it appears as a strange and mighty propulsion toward an ideal good known only to religion and in its nature fundamentally non-rational, which the mind knows of in yearning and presentiment, recognizing it for what it is behind the obscure and inadequate symbols which are its only expression.   And this shows that above and beyond our rational being lies hidden the ultimate and highest part of our nature, which can find no satisfaction in the mere allaying of the needs of our sensuous, psychical, or intellectual impulses and cravings.   The mystics called it the basis or ground of the soul.

We saw that in the case of the element of the mysterious the

[1] *Glaubenslehre*, § 5.

'wholly other' led on to the supernatural and transcendent, and that above these appeared the 'beyond' (ἐπέκεινα) of Mysticism, through the non-rational side of religion being raised to its highest power and stressed to excess. It is the same in the case of the element of 'fascination'; here, too, is possible a transition into Mysticism. At its highest point of stress the fascinating becomes the 'overabounding',[1] the mystical 'moment' which exactly corresponds upon this line to the ἐπέκεινα upon the other line of approach, and which is to be understood accordingly. But while this feeling of the 'overabounding' is specially characteristic of Mysticism, a trace of it survives in all truly felt states of religious beatitude, however restrained and kept within measure by other factors. This is seen most clearly from the psychology of those great experiences—of grace, conversion, second birth—in which the religious experience appears in its pure intrinsic nature and in heightened activity, so as to be more clearly grasped than in the less typical form of tranquil, ordinary piety. The hard core of such experiences in their Christian form consists of the redemption from guilt and bondage to sin, and we shall have presently to see that this also does not occur without a participation of non-rational elements. But leaving this out of account, what we have here to point out is the unutterableness of what has been yet genuinely experienced, and how such an experience may pass into blissful excitement, rapture, and exaltation verging often on the bizarre and the abnormal.[2] This is vouched for by the autobiographical testimony of the 'converted' from St. Paul onward. William James has collected a great number of these, without, however,

---

[1] *Das Überschwengliche.*

[2] This may be found fatal to the attempt to construct a 'Religion within the limits of pure reason or 'of humanity'; but, none the less, the matter is as we have described it, as far as concerns the psychological inquiry into religion, which asks, not what it is within the aforementioned limits, but what it is in its own essential nature. And for that matter this proceeding of constructing a 'humanity' prior to and apart from the most central and potent of human capacities is like nothing so much as the attempt to frame a standard idea of the human body after having previously cut off the head.

himself noticing the non-rational element that thrills in them.

Thus, one writes:

'. . . For the moment nothing but an ineffable joy and exaltation remained. It is impossible fully to describe the experience. It was like the effect of some great orchestra, when all the separate notes have melted into one swelling harmony, that leaves the listener conscious of nothing save that his soul is being wafted upwards and almost bursting with its own emotion.' (*Varieties*, &c., p. 66.)

And another :

'. . . The more I seek words to express this intimate inter-course, the more I feel the impossibility of describing the thing by any of our usual images.' (Ibid., p. 68.)

And almost with the precision of dogma, a third (Jonathan Edwards) indicates the qualitative difference of the experience of beatitude from other 'rational' joy :

'The conceptions which the saints have of the loveliness of God and that kind of delight which they experience in it are quite peculiar and entirely different from anything which a natural man can possess or of which he can form any proper notion.' (Ibid., p. 229.)

Cf. also pp. 192, 225; and the testimony of Jacob Boehme, given on p. 417. Also this of Boehme :

' But I can neither write nor tell of what sort of Exaltation the triumphing in the Spirit is. It can be compared with nought, but that when in the midst of death life is born, and it is like the resurrection of the dead.'

With the mystics these experiences pass up wholly into the 'over-abounding'. 'O that I could tell you what the heart feels, how it burns and is consumed inwardly! Only, I find no words to express it. I can but say: Might but one little drop of what I feel fall into Hell, Hell would be transformed into a Paradise.' So says St. Catherine of Genoa ; and all the multitude of her spiritual kindred testify to the same effect.

What we Christians know as the experiences of grace and the second birth have their parallels also in the religions of high spiritual rank beyond the borders of Christianity. Such are the breaking out of the saving ' Bodhi ', the opening of the 'heavenly eye', the *Jñāna* by *Iśvaras prasāda*, which is victorious over the darkness of nescience and shines out in an experience with which no other can be measured. And in all these the entirely non-rational and specific element in the beatific experience is immediately noticeable. The qualitative character of it varies widely in all these cases, and is again in them all very different from its parallels in Christianity; still in all it is very similar in intensity, and in all it is a 'salvation' and an absolute 'fascination', which in contrast to all that admits of 'natural' expression or comparison is deeply imbued with the 'over-abounding' nature of the numen.

And this is also entirely true of the rapture of Nirvana, which is only in appearance a cold and negative state. It is only conceptually that 'Nirvana' is a negation; it is felt in consciousness as in the strongest degree positive; it exercises a 'fascination' by which its votaries are as much carried away as are the Hindu or the Christian by the corresponding objects of their worship. I recall vividly a conversation I had with a Buddhist monk. He had been putting before me methodically and pertinaciously the arguments for the Buddhist 'theology of negation', the doctrine of Anātman and 'entire emptiness'. When he had made an end, I asked him, what then Nirvana itself is; and after a long pause came at last the single answer, low and restrained: 'Bliss—unspeakable'. And the hushed restraint of that answer, the solemnity of his voice, demeanour, and gesture, made more clear what was meant than the words themselves.

And so we maintain, on the one hand, following the 'via eminentiae et causalitatis', that the divine is indeed the highest, strongest, best, loveliest, and dearest that man can think of; but we assert on the other, following the 'via negationis', that God is not *merely* the ground and superlative of all that can be thought; He is in Himself a subject on His own account and in Himself.

*   *   *

In the adjective δεινός the Greek language possesses a word peculiarly difficult to translate, and standing for an idea peculiarly difficult to grasp in all its strange variations. And if we ask whence this difficulty arises, the answer is plain; it is because δεινός is simply the numinous (mostly of course at a lower level, in an arrested form, attenuated by rhetorical or poetic usage).   Consequently δεινός is the equivalent of 'dirus' and 'tremendus'. It may mean evil or imposing, potent and strange, queer and marvellous, horrifying and fascinating, divine and daemonic, and a source of 'energy'. Sophocles means to awaken the feeling of 'numinous awe' through the whole gamut of its phases at the contemplation of man, the creature of marvel, in the choric song of the *Antigone*:

πολλὰ τὰ δεινὰ, κοὐδὲν ἀνθρώπου δεινότερον πέλει.

This line defies translation, just because our language has no term that can isolate distinctly and gather into one word the total numinous impression a thing may make on the mind. The nearest that German can get to it is in the expression '*das Ungeheuere*' (monstrous), while in English 'weird' is perhaps the closest rendering possible. The mood and attitude represented in the foregoing verse might then be fairly well rendered by such a translation as :

'Much there is that is weird ; but nought is weirder than man.'

The German *ungeheuer* is not by derivation simply 'huge', in quantity or quality ;—this, its common meaning, is in fact a rationalizing interpretation of the real idea; it is that which is not '*geheuer*', i. e., approximately, the *uncanny*—in a word, the numinous.   And it is just this element of the uncanny in man that Sophocles has in mind.   If this, its fundamental meaning, be really and thoroughly felt in consciousness, then the word could be taken as a fairly exact expression for the numinous in its aspects of mystery, awefulness, majesty, augustness, and 'energy'; nay, even the aspect of fascination is dimly felt in it.

The variations of meaning in the German word *ungeheuer* can be well illustrated from Goethe.[1]   He, too, uses the word

---

[1] Cf. *Wilhelm Meisters Wanderjahre*, Bk. I, ch. 10; *Wahlverwandtschaften*, 2. 15 ; *Dichtung und Wahrheit*, 2. 9 ; 4. 20.

first to denote the huge in size—what is too vast for our faculty of space-perception, such as the immeasurable vault of the night sky.   In other passages the word retains its original non-rational colour more markedly; it comes to mean the uncanny, the fearful, the dauntingly 'other' and incomprehensible, that which arouses in us 'stupor' and '$\theta\acute{a}\mu\beta os$'; and finally, in the wonderful words of Faust which I have put upon my title-page, it becomes an almost exact synonym for our 'numinous' under all its aspects.

> Das Schaudern ist der Menschheit bestes Teil.
> Wie auch die Welt ihm das Gefühl verteuere,
> Ergriffen fühlt er tief das Ungeheuere.[1]

[1] Awe is the best of man : howe'er the world's
 Misprizing of the feeling would prevent us,
 Deeply we feel, once gripped, the weird Portentous.
                    (GOETHE, *Faust*, Second Part, Act I, Sc. v.)

CHAPTER VII

ANALOGIES AND ASSOCIATED FEELINGS

In order to give an adequate account of this second aspect
of the numinous, we were led to add to its original designation
as ' mysterium tremendum ' that it at the same time exercises a
supreme ' fascination '. And this its dual character, as at once
an object of boundless awe and boundless wonder, quelling and
yet entrancing the soul, constitutes the proper *positive* content
of the ' mysterium ' as it manifests itself in conscious feeling.
No attempt of ours to describe this harmony of contrasts in
the import of the mysterium can really succeed ; but it may
perhaps be adumbrated, as it were from a distance, by taking
an analogy from a region belonging not to religion but to
aesthetics. In the category and feeling of the *sublime* we
have a counterpart to it, though it is true it is but a pale
reflexion, and moreover involves difficulties of analysis all its
own. The analogies between the consciousness of the sublime
and of the numinous may be easily grasped.[1] To begin with,
' the sublime ', like ' the numinous ', is in Kantian language an
idea or concept ' that cannot be unfolded ' or explicated (*unaus-
wickelbar*). Certainly we can tabulate some general ' rational '
signs that uniformly recur as soon as we call an object sublime ;
as, for instance, that it must approach, or threaten to overpass,
the bounds of our understanding by some ' dynamic ' or
' mathematic ' greatness, by potent manifestations of force

---

[1] We are often prone to resort to this familiar feeling-content to fill
out the negative concept 'transcendent', explaining frankly God's 'tran-
cendence' by His 'sublimity'. As a figurative analogical description
this is perfectly allowable, but it would be an error if we meant it literally
and in earnest. Religious feelings are not the same as aesthetic feelings,
and ' the sublime ' is as definitely an aesthetic term as ' the beautiful ',
however widely different may be the facts denoted by the words.

or magnitude in spatial extent.   But these are obviously
only conditions of, not the essence of, the impression of sublimity.   A thing does not become sublime merely by being
great.   The concept itself remains unexplicated; it has in
it something mysterious, and in this it is like that of
'the numinous'.   A second point of resemblance is that the
sublime exhibits the same peculiar dual character as the
numinous; it is at once daunting, and yet again singularly
attracting, in its impress upon the mind.   It humbles and at
the same time exalts us, circumscribes and extends us beyond
ourselves, on the one hand releasing in us a feeling analogous
to fear, and on the other rejoicing us.   So the idea of the
sublime is closely similar to that of the numinous, and is well
adapted to excite it and to be excited by it, while each tends
to pass over into the other.

The Law of the Association of Feelings.

As these expressions 'excite' and 'pass over' will later
assume importance, and as the latter in particular is hedged
about with misconceptions which are prominent in the modern
doctrines of Evolution and give rise to quite erroneous conclusions, we will enter at once upon a closer consideration of
them.

It is a well-known and fundamental psychological law that
ideas 'attract' one another, and that one will excite another and
call it into consciousness, if it resembles it.   An entirely similar
law holds good with regard to feelings.   A feeling, no less
than an idea, can arouse its like in the mind; and the
presence of the one in my consciousness may be the occasion
for my entertaining the other at the same time.   Further,
just as in the case of ideas the law of reproduction by similarity
leads to an exchange and replacement of ideas, so that I come
to entertain an idea x, when y would have been the appropriate one, so we may be led to exchanges and replacements
of feelings, and I may react with a feeling x to an impression
to which the feeling y would normally correspond.   Finally,
I can pass from one feeling to another by an imperceptibly
gradual transition, the one feeling x dying away little by

little, while the other, y, excited together with it, increases and strengthens in a corresponding degree. But it is important here to recognize the true account of the phenomenon. What passes over—undergoes transition—is not the feeling itself. It is not that the actual feeling gradually changes in quality or ' evolves ', i. e. transmutes itself into a quite different one, but rather that I pass over or make the transition from one feeling to another as my circumstances change, by the gradual decrease of the one and increase of the other. A transition of the actual feeling into another would be a real ' transmutation ', and would be a psychological counterpart to the alchemist's production of gold by the transmutation of metals.

And yet it is this transmutation that is assumed by the modern ' Evolutionism '—more properly to be called ' Transmutationism '—by the introduction of the equivocal phrase, 'gradually evolve' (i. e. from a thing of a certain quality to something qualitatively different), or the no less equivocal words ' Epigenesis ', ' Heterogony ',[1] and their like. In this way, they would have us believe, the feeling, e. g. of moral obligation, ' evolves ' or develops. At first, so it is said, all that exists is the simple constraint of uniform custom, as seen in the community of the clan. Then, out of that, it is said, ' arises ' the idea of a universally obligatory ' ought '. How the idea can do so is not disclosed. Now such a theory misses the fact that in moral obligation we have something *qualitatively* quite different from constraint by custom. The finer and more penetrating psychological analysis that can apprehend differences in quality is rudely ignored and in consequence the whole problem is misconceived. Or, if something of the essential difference is felt, it is covered up and glozed over by the phrase 'gradually evolve', and the one thing is made to turn into the other ' par la durée ', much as milk grows sour from standing. But ' ought ' is a primary and unique meaning, as little derivable from another as blue from bitter, and there are not ' transmutations ' in the psychological any more than in the

---

[1] Neither Heterogony nor Epigenesis is genuine Evolution. They are rather just what the biologists call 'generatio equivoca', and therefore mere formation of an aggregate by addition and accumulation.

physical world. The idea 'ought' is only 'evolvable' out of the spirit of man itself, and then in the sense of being 'arousable', because it is already potentially implanted in him. Were it not so, no 'evolution' could effect an introduction for it.

The evolutionists may be quite correct in reconstructing the kind of historical process that took place, viz. the gradual and successive entry upon the scene of different 'moments' of feeling-consciousness in historical sequence, and the order of entry itself may have been correctly discovered. But the explanation of this process is quite different from that which they intend; it is, namely, the law of the excitation and arousing of feelings and ideas according to the measure of their resemblance. There is in point of fact a very strong analogy between constraint by custom and constraint by moral obligation, as both are constraints upon conduct. Consequently the former can *arouse* the latter in the mind if it— the latter—was already potentially planted there; the feeling of 'ought' may start into consciousness at the presence of the other feeling, and the man may gradually effect a transition to it from that other. But what we are concerned with is the *replacement* of the one by the other, and not the *transmutation* of the one into the other.

Now it is just the same with the feeling of the numinous as with that of moral obligation. It too is not to be derived from any other feeling, and is in this sense 'unevolvable'. It is a content of feeling that is qualitatively *sui generis*, yet at the same time one that has numerous analogies with others, and therefore it and they may reciprocally excite or stimulate one another and cause one another to appear in the mind. Instead of framing 'epigenetic' and other fabrications of the course the evolution of religion has taken, it is our task to inquire into these 'stimuli' or 'excitations', these elements that cause the numinous feeling to appear in consciousness, to intimate by virtue of what analogies they came to be able to do so, and so to discover the series or chain of these stimuli by whose operation the numinous feeling was awakened in us.

Such a power of stimulation characterizes the feeling of the sublime, in accordance with the law we found, and through the analogies it bears to the numinous feeling. But this is indubitably a stimulus that only makes its appearance late in the excitation-series, and it is probable that the feeling of the sublime is itself first aroused and disengaged by the precedent religious feeling—not from itself, but from the rational spirit of man and its *a priori* capacity.

Schematization.

The 'Association of Ideas' does not simply cause the idea y to reappear in consciousness with the given idea x occasionally only, it also sets up under certain circumstances lasting combinations and connexions between the two. And this is no less true of the association of feelings. Accordingly, we see religious feeling in permanent connexion with other feelings which are conjoined to it in accordance with this principle of Association. It is, indeed, more accurate to say 'conjoined' than really 'connected', for such mere conjunctions or chance connexions according to laws of purely external analogy are to be distinguished from necessary connexions according to principles of true inward affinity and cohesion. An instance of a connexion of this latter kind—an example, indeed, of an inner *a priori* principle—is (following the theory of Kant) the connexion of the Category of Causality with its temporal 'schema', the temporal sequence of two successive events, which by being brought into connexion with the Category of Causality is *known* and recognized as a causal relation of the two. In this case analogy between the two—the category and the schema—has also a place, but it is not chance external resemblance but essential correspondence, and the fact that the two belong together is here a necessity of our reason. On the basis of such a necessity the temporal sequence 'schematizes' the category.

Now the relation of the rational to the non-rational element in the idea of the holy or sacred is just such a one of 'schematization', and the non-rational numinous fact, schematized by the rational concepts we have suggested above, yields us the complex category of 'holy' itself, richly charged and complete and in its fullest meaning. And that the schematism

is a genuine one, and not a mere combination of analogies, may
be distinctly seen from the fact that it does not fall to
pieces, and cannot be cut out as the development of the
consciousness of religious truth proceeds onwards and upwards, but is only recognized with greater definiteness and
certainty.   And it is for the same reason inherently probable
that there is more, too, in the combination of 'the holy' with
'the sublime' than a mere association of feelings; and perhaps we may say that, while as a matter of historical genesis
such an association was the means whereby this combination
was awakened in the mind and the occasion for it, yet the inward and lasting character of the connexion in all the higher
religions does prove that 'the sublime' too is an authentic
'scheme' of 'the holy'.

The intimate interpenetration of the non-rational with the
rational elements of the religious consciousness, like the interweaving of warp and woof in a fabric, may be elucidated by
taking another familiar case, in which a universal human
feeling, that of personal affection, is similarly interpene-
trated by a likewise thoroughly non-rational and separate
element, namely, the sex instinct.   It goes without saying
that this latter lies just on the opposite side of 'reason' to the
numinous consciousness; for, while this is 'above all reason',
the sex impulse is below it, an element in our instinctive life.
'The numinous' infuses the rational from above, 'the sexual'
presses up from beneath, quite wholesomely and normally
out of the nature which the human being shares with the
general animal world, into the higher realm of the specifically
'humane'.   But though the two things I am comparing are
thus manifestly opposite extremes, they have a closely corresponding relation to that which lies between them, viz. the
reason.   For the quite special domain of the 'erotic' is only
brought into existence as the reproductive instinct passes up
out of the merely instinctive life, penetrates the higher humane
life of mind and feeling, and infuses wishes, cravings, and
longings in personal liking, friendship, and love, in song and
poetry and imaginative creation in general.   Whatever falls
within the sphere of the erotic is therefore always a composite

product, made up of two factors : the one something that
occurs also in the general sphere of human behaviour as such,
as friendship and liking, the feeling of companionship, the
mood of poetic inspiration or joyful exaltation, and the like;
and the other an infusion of a quite special kind, which is not
to be classed with these, and of which no one can have any
inkling, let alone understand it, who has not learnt from the
actual inward experience of 'eros' or love. Another point
in which the 'erotic' is analogous to the 'holy' is in
having in the main no means of linguistic expression but
terms drawn from other fields of mental life, which only cease
to be ' innocuous ' (i. e. only become genuinely 'erotic' terms)
when it is realized that the lover, like the orator, bard, or singer,
expresses himself not so much by the actual words he uses as
by the accent, tone, and imitative gesture which reinforce
them.

The phrase ' he loves me' is verbally identical, whether it is
said by a child of its father or by a girl of her lover.   But in
the second case a ' love ' is meant which is at the same time
' something more ' (viz. *sexual* love), and something more not
only in quantity but in quality.   So, too, the phrase ' We
ought to fear, love, and trust him ' [1] is verbally identical,
whether it refers to the relation of child to father or to that
of man to God.   But again in the second case these ideas are
infused with a meaning of which none but the religious-
minded man can have any comprehension or indeed any
inkling, whose presence makes, e. g., the ' fear of God ' ' something more ' than any fear of a man, qualitatively, not merely
quantitatively, though retaining the essence of the most
genuine reverence felt by the child for its father.   And Suso
means in the same way to distinguish ' love ' and ' love of
God ', when he says :

' There was never a string so dulcet-toned but ceased to
sound if stretched to a withered frame ; a heart poor in love
can no more understand speech rich in love than a German
can an Italian.' [2]

[1] Luther's amplification of the First Commandment.
[2] Works, ed. Denifle, p. 309.

There is another kind of experience in which we may find
an example of the way in which rational elements in our
feeling-consciousness may be thus penetrated by quite non-
rational ones, and an example even more proximate to the
complex feeling of the holy than that just described—'erotic'
experience;—in so far as the non-rational element is, like the
'numinous' feeling but unlike the sexual impulse, at the same
time *supra*-rational.   I refer to the state of mind induced
in us by a song set to music.   The verbal text of the song
expresses feelings that are 'natural', homesickness perhaps,
or confidence in time of danger, hope for a future good, or joy
in a present possession—all concrete elements in our 'natural'
human lot, and capable of being described in conceptual terms.
But it is otherwise with the music, purely as music.   It
releases a blissful rejoicing in us, and we are conscious of a
glimmering, billowy agitation occupying our minds, without
being able to express or explain in concepts what it really is
that moves us so deeply.   And to say that the music is mourn-
ful or exultant, that it incites or restrains, is merely to use
signs by analogy, choosing them for their resemblance to the
matter in hand out of other regions of our mental life ; and at
any rate we cannot say what the object or ground of this
mourning or exulting may be.   Music, in short, arouses in us
an experience and vibrations of mood that are quite specific in
kind and must simply be called 'musical' ; but the rise and
fall and manifold variations of this experience exhibit—
though again only in part—definite, if fugitive, analogies and
correspondences with our ordinary non-musical emotional
states, and so can call these into consciousness and blend with
them.   If this happens, the specific 'music-consciousness' is
thereby 'schematized' and rationalized, and the resultant
complex mood is, as it were, a fabric, in which the general
human feelings and emotional states constitute the warp, and
the non-rational music-feelings the woof.   The total song is
therefore music 'rationalized'.

Now here is illustrated the contrast between the legitimate
and the illegitimate processes of 'rationalization'.   For, if the
song may be called music 'rationalized' in the legitimate sense,

in programme-music we have a musical 'rationalism' in the bad sense. Programme-music, that is to say, misinterprets and perverts the idea of music by its implication that the inner content of music is not—as in fact it is—something unique and mysterious, but just the incidental experiences—joy and grief, expansion and repression—familiar to the human heart. And in its attempt to make of musical tones a language to recount the fortunes of men programme-music abolishes the autonomy of music, and is deceived by a mere resemblance into employing as a means what is an end and substantive content in its own right. It is just the same mistake as when the ' august ' aspect of the numinous is allowed to evaporate into the 'morally good', instead of merely being 'schematized' by it, or as when we let 'the holy' be identified with ' the perfectly good' will. And not only programme-music is at fault here. The 'music-drama' of Wagner, by attempting a thoroughgoing unification of the musical and the dramatic, commits the same offence against both the non-rational spirit of the former and the autonomy of either. We can only succeed in very partial and fragmentary fashion in 'schematizing' the non-rational factor in music by means of the familiar incidents of human experience. And the reason is just this, that the real content of music is not drawn from the ordinary human emotions at all, and that it is in no way merely a second language, alongside the usual one, by which these emotions find expression. Musical feeling is rather (like numinous feeling) something 'wholly other', which, while it affords analogies and here and there will run parallel to the ordinary emotions of life, cannot be made to coincide with them by a detailed point-to-point correspondence. It is, of course, from those places where the correspondence holds that the spell of a composed song arises by a blending of verbal and musical expression. But the very fact that we attribute to it a spell, an enchantment, points in itself to that ' woof' in the fabric of music of which we spoke, the woof of the unconceived and non-rational.[1]

[1] This is the point of view from which to estimate both the excellent and the inadequate features of E. Hanslick's book, *Vom Musicalisch-Schönen.*

But we must beware of confounding in any way the non-rational of music and the non-rational of the numinous itself, as Schopenhauer, for example, does.   Each is something in its own right, independently of the other.   We shall discuss later whether, and how far, the former may become a means of expression for the latter.

CHAPTER VIII

THE HOLY AS A CATEGORY OF VALUE

Sin and Atonement

WE have already met that strange and profound mental reaction to the numinous which we proposed to call 'creature-feeling' or creature-consciousness, with its concomitant feelings of abasement and prostration and of the diminution of the self into nothingness; bearing always in mind that these expressions do not hit with precision, but merely hint at what is really meant,[1] inasmuch as this 'diminution of the self', &c., is something very different from the littleness, weakness, or dependence of which we may become aware under other conditions than that of numinous feeling. And we had to notice that this experience marks a definite depreciation or disvaluation of the self in respect, so to speak, of its reality and very existence. We have now to put alongside of this another sort of self-disvaluation, which has long been a matter of common observation, and only needs to be suggested in order to be recognized. 'I am a man of *unclean* lips and dwell among a people of unclean lips.' 'Depart from me, for I am a *sinful* man, O Lord.' So say respectively Isaiah and Peter, when the numinous reality encounters them as a present fact of consciousness. In both cases this self-depreciating feeling-response is marked by an immediate, almost instinctive, spontaneity. It is not based on deliberation, nor does it follow any rule, but breaks, as it were, palpitant from the soul—like a direct reflex movement at the stimulation of the numinous. It does not spring from

---

[1] Cf. Hugo of St. Victor's words : 'Sumpta sunt vocabula, ut intellegi aliquatenus posset quod comprehendi non poterat'. ('These words were chosen, that that which could not be comprehended might yet in some measure be understood.')

the consciousness of some committed transgression, but rather
is an immediate datum given with the feeling of the numen :
it proceeds to 'disvalue' together with the self the tribe to
which the person belongs, and indeed together with that,
all existence in general. Now it is to-day pretty generally
agreed that, all this being the case, these outbursts of feeling
are not simply, and probably at first not at all, *moral* deprecia-
tions, but belong to a quite special category of valuation and
appraisement. The feeling is beyond question not that of the
transgression of the moral law, however evident it may be that
such a transgression, where it has occurred, will involve it as
a consequence : it is the feeling of absolute 'profaneness'.

But what is this ? Again something which the 'natural'
man cannot, as such, know or even imagine. He, only, who is
'in the Spirit' knows and feels what this 'profaneness' is ; but
to such an one it comes with piercing acuteness, and is accompanied by the most uncompromising judgement of self-depreciation, a judgement passed, not upon his character, because of
individual 'profane' actions of his, but upon his own very
existence as creature before that which is supreme above all
creatures. And at the same moment he passes upon the
numen a judgement of *appreciation* of a unique kind by the
category diametrically contrary to 'the profane', the category
'holy', which is proper to the numen alone, but to it in an
absolute degree ; he says : '*Tu solus sanctus*'. This 'sanctus'
is not merely 'perfect' or 'beautiful' or 'sublime' or 'good',
though, being like these concepts also a *value*, objective
and ultimate, it has a definite, perceptible analogy with them.
It is the positive *numinous* value or worth, and to it corresponds on the side of the creature a numinous *disvalue* or
'unworth'.

In every highly-developed religion the appreciation of moral
obligation and duty, ranking as a claim of the deity upon man,
has been developed side by side with the religious feeling
itself. None the less a profoundly humble and heartfelt
recognition of 'the holy' may occur in particular experiences
without being always or definitely charged or infused with the
sense of moral demands. The 'holy' will then be recognized as

that which commands our respect, as that whose real value is to be acknowledged inwardly. It is not that the awe of holiness is itself simply ' fear ' in face of what is absolutely overpowering, before which there is no alternative to blind, awe-struck obedience. 'Tu solus sanctus' is rather a paean of *praise*, which, so far from being merely a faltering confession of the divine supremacy, recognizes and extols a value, precious beyond all conceiving. The object of such praise is not simply absolute Might, making its claims and compelling their fulfilment, but a might that has at the same time the supremest *right* to make the highest claim to service, and receives praise because it is in an absolute sense worthy to be praised. ' Thou art *worthy* to receive praise and honour and power' (Rev. iv. 11).

When once it has been grasped that *qādósh* or *sanctus* is not originally a *moral* category at all, the most obvious rendering of the words is ' transcendent ' ('supramundane', *überweltlich*). The one-sided character of this rendering to which we had to take exception has been supplemented by the more detailed exposition of the numinous and its implications. But its most essential defect remains to be noted: ' transcendent' is a purely ontological attribute and not an attribute of *value*; it denotes a character that can, if need be, abash us, but cannot inspire us with *respect*. It might once again, therefore, be an advantage to introduce another term to underline this side of the numinous, and the words *augustus* and σεμνός suggest themselves for the purpose. ' Augustus', ' august ', no less than σεμνός, is really appropriate only to numinous objects —to rulers only as offspring or descendants of gods. Then, while σεβαστός indicates the *being* of the numen, σεμνός or *augustus* would refer rather to its supreme worth or *value*, its illustriousness. There will, then, in fact be two values to distinguish in the numen ; its 'fascination' (fascinans) will be that element in it whereby it is of *subjective* value (= beatitude) to man; but it is 'august' (augustum) in so far as it is recognized as possessing in itself *objective* value that claims our homage.

Mere ' unlawfulness ' only becomes ' sin ', ' impiety', ' sacrilege ', when the character of *numinous unworthiness* or *disvalue* goes on to be transferred to and centred in *moral* delinquency.   And only when the mind feels it as ' sin ' does the transgression of law become a matter of such dreadful gravity for the conscience, a catastrophe that leads it to despair of its own power.   The meaning of ' sin ' is not understood by the ' natural ', nor even by the merely moral, man ; and the theory of certain dogmatists, that the demand of morality as such urged man on to an inner collapse and then obliged him to look round for some deliverance, is palpably incorrect.   There are serious-minded men of sincere moral endeavour who cannot understand what such a ' deliverance ' or ' redemption ' may be, and dismiss it with a shrug of the shoulders.   They are aware that they are erring and imperfect men, but they know and put into practice the methods of self-discipline, and so labour onward upon their way with sturdy resolution.   The morally robust older Rationalism was lacking neither in a sincere and respectful recognition of the moral law nor in honest endeavour to conform to it.   It knew well and sternly condemned what was ' wrong ', and the aim of its exhortations and instruction was that men should realize better and take more in earnest the facts of moral right and wrong. But no ' downfall ' or ' collapse ' and no ' need of redemption ' came within its scheme, because the objection brought against it by its opponents was in fact just ; Rationalism lacked understanding of what ' sin ' is.[1]   Mere morality is not the soil from which grows either the need of ' redemption ' and deliverance or the need for that other unique good which is likewise

[1] Cf. the testimony of Theodore Parker—certainly a man of far from crude mental development — as to his own experience, given by W. James, *Varieties*, p. 81 :

'They (sc. the heathen of classical antiquity) were conscious of wrath, of cruelty, avarice, drunkenness, lust, sloth, cowardice, and other actual vices, and struggled and got rid of the deformities ; but they were not conscious of " enmity against God " and didn't sit down and whine and groan against non-existent evil. I have done wrong things enough in my life, and do them now : I miss the mark, draw bow, and try again. But . . . I know there is much "health in me" ; and in my body, even now, there dwelleth many a good thing, spite of consumption and Saint Paul.'

If there is nothing crude about such a statement, it is at any rate *superficial*.   The depths of the non-rational consciousness must be stirred to find with Anselm ' quanti ponderis sit peccatum '.

altogether and specifically numinous in character, 'covering', and 'atonement'. There would perhaps be less disputing as to the warrant and value of these latter in Christian doctrine if dogmatic theology itself had not transferred them from their mystical sphere into that of rational ethics and attenuated them into moral concepts. They were thus taken from a sphere where they have an authentic and necessary place to one where their validity is most disputable.

We meet the 'moment' of 'covering' in specially clear form in the religion of Yahweh, in its rites and the emotion they excite; but it is contained also, though more obscurely, in many other religions. It comprises, first, a manifestation of the numinous awe, viz. the feeling that the 'profane' creature cannot forthwith approach the numen, but has need of a covering or shield against the ὀργή of the numen. Such a 'covering' is then a 'consecration', i.e. a procedure that renders the approacher himself 'numinous', frees him from his 'profane' being and fits him for intercourse with the numen. The means of 'consecration', however—'means of grace' in the proper sense—are derived from, or conferred and appointed by, the numen itself, which bestows something of its own quality to make man capable of communion with it. And this act is something very different from the 'annulment of mistrust', the phrase in which Ritschl seeks to rationalize these relations between God and man.

'Atonement', following our view, is a 'sheltering' or 'covering', but a profounder form of it. It springs directly from the idea of numinous value or worth and numinous disvalue or unworth as soon as these have been developed. Mere awe, mere need of shelter from the 'tremendum', has here been elevated to the feeling that man in his 'profaneness' is not *worthy* to stand in the presence of the holy one, and that his own entire personal unworthiness might defile even holiness itself. This is obviously the case in the vision of the call of Isaiah; and the same note recurs, less emphatically but quite unmistakably, in the story of the centurion of Capernaum (St. Luke vii. 1–10), and his words: 'I am not worthy that thou shouldest enter under my roof'. Here we have both the light thrill of awe before the

' tremendum' of the numen and also, and more especially, the
feeling of this unique disvalue or unworth of the profane
confronted by the numen, which suggests to the man that even
holiness itself may be tainted and tarnished by his presence.

Here, then, comes in the felt necessity and longing for
' atonement ', and all the more strongly when the close presence
of the numen, intercourse with it, and enduring possession of
it, becomes an object of craving, is even desired as the *summum
bonum*.   It amounts to a longing to transcend this sundering
unworthiness, given with the self's existence as ' creature ' and
profane natural being.   It is an element in the religious consciousness, which, so far from vanishing in the measure in
which religion is deepened and heightened, grows on the
contrary continually stronger and more marked. Belonging,
as it does, wholly to the non-rational side of religion, it may
remain latent while, in the course of religious evolution, the
rational side at first unfolds and assumes vigorous and definite
form ;   it may retire for a time behind other elements and
apparently die away, but only to return more powerfully and
insistently than before.   And again it may grow to be the sole,
one-sided, exclusive interest, a cry that drowns all other notes,
so that the religious consciousness is distorted and disfigured ;
as may readily happen where through long periods of time the
rational aspects of religion have been fostered unduly and at
the cost of the non-rational.

The special character of this consciousness of need for
atonement may perhaps be brought home more clearly by an
analogy from our 'natural' emotional life ; but at the same
time it is important that the religious feeling we are considering should itself be kept distinct from its analogue, as the
two are frequently confounded. The analogy is with the
feeling arising from moral transgression. There, too, we
practise a kind of self-depreciation which is clear and familiar
and perfectly intelligible to us, when we esteem ourselves
guilty of a bad action and the action itself as morally evil.
The evil of the action *weighs upon us* and deprives us of our
self-respect.   We *accuse* ourselves and *remorse* sets in.   But
alongside this self-depreciation stands a second one, which

while it may have reference to the same action as the other,
yet avails itself of definitely different categories. The same
perverse action that before weighed upon us now *pollutes* us;
we do not accuse ourselves, we are defiled in our own
eyes. And the characteristic form of emotional reaction is
no longer remorse but *loathing*. The man feels a need,
to express which he has recourse to images of *washing*
and cleansing. The two kinds of self-depreciation proceed
on parallel lines and may relate to the same action; but
none the less it is obvious that they are, inwardly and in
their essence, determinately different. Now the second of
them has a plain analogy with the need for 'atonement', and
so can fairly be drawn upon for its elucidation; while at the
same time it is yet nothing more than an analogy from another
sphere, viz. that of morality.

No religion has brought the mystery of the need for
atonement or expiation to so complete, so profound, or so
powerful expression as Christianity. And in this, too, it
shows its superiority over others. It is a more perfect religion
and more perfectly religion than they, in so far as what is
potential in religion in general becomes in Christianity a pure
actuality. And the distrust and suspicion which so widely
obtains with regard to this mystery is only to be explained
from the general custom—for which our theoretical cult of
homiletics, liturgy, and catechism is largely responsible—of
taking into account only the rational side of religion. Yet
this atonement mystery is a 'moment' which no Christian
teaching that purports to represent the religious experience
of the Christian and biblical tradition can afford to surrender.
The teacher will have to make explicit, by an analysis of the
Christian religious experience, how the 'very numen', by
imparting itself to the worshipper, becomes itself the means of
'atonement'. And in this regard it does not matter so
very much what the decisions of the commentators are
as to what, if anything, Paul or Peter wrote on the subject of expiation and atonement, or whether, indeed, there
is any 'scriptural authority' for the thing at all. Were
there in scripture no word written about it, it might still

be written to-day from our own experience. But it would indeed be extraordinary if it had not long ago been written of. For the God of the New Testament is not less holy than the God of the Old Testament, but more holy. The interval between the creature and Him is not diminished but made absolute; the unworthiness of the profane in contrast to Him is not extenuated but enhanced. That God none the less admits access to Himself and intimacy with Himself is not a mere matter of course; it is a grace beyond our power to apprehend, a prodigious paradox. To take this paradox out of Christianity is to make it shallow and superficial beyond recognition. But if this is so, the intuitions concerning, and the need felt for, 'Covering' and 'Atonement' result immediately. And the divinely appointed means of God's self-revelation, where experienced and appraised as such—'the Word', 'the Spirit', 'the Person of Christ',—become that to which the man 'flees', in which he finds refuge, and in which he 'locks' himself, in order that, consecrated and cleansed of his 'profaneness' thereby, he may come into the presence of Holiness itself.

That these ideas are viewed with a certain distrust may be traced to two causes. One is, that what is a specifically religious element is distortingly moralized. If we start from mere morality and in relation to a God understood as being the personification of the moral order endowed with love, then all these things are wholly inapplicable and a source of genuine difficulty. But we are concerned with *religious* (not merely moral) intuitions, and it is impossible to dispute how right or wrong they are with a man whose interest is wholly in morality and not in religion, and who is therefore quite incapable of appreciating them. Whoever, on the other hand, penetrates to the unique centre of the religious experience, so that it starts awake in his own consciousness, finds that the truth of these intuitions is experienced directly, as soon as he penetrates into their depths.

The other ground of distrust is that usually in our theological systems an attempt is made to develop conceptual *theories* of these ideas, which are all pure intuitions, emotional rather than conceptual in character. They are thus made objects of speculation, and the final outcome is the quasi-mathematical ' Doctrine of Imputation' and its drastic ascription to the credit of the 'sinner' of the 'merit' of Christ, not to mention the learned inquiry whether this transaction involves an ' analytic' or a 'synthetic' judgement of God.

       *   *   *   *

Let us look back once more from the point we have reached over the course our inquiry has so far taken. As the sub-title of this book suggests, we were to investigate the non-rational element in the idea of the divine. The words 'non-rational' and 'irrational' are to-day used almost at random. The non-rational is sought over the most widely different regions, and writers generally shirk the trouble of putting down precisely what they intend by the term, giving it often the most multifarious meanings or applying it with such vague generality that it admits of the most diverse interpretations. Pure fact in contrast to law, the empirical in contrast to reason, the contingent in contrast to the necessary, the psychological in contrast to transcendental fact, that which is known *a posteriori* in contrast to that which is determinable *a priori*; power, will, and arbitrary choice in contrast to reason, knowledge, and determination by value; impulse, instinct, and the obscure forces of the subconscious in contrast to insight, reflection, and intelligible plan; mystical depths and stirrings in the soul, surmise, presentiment, intuition, prophecy, and finally the 'occult' powers also; or, in general, the uneasy stress and universal fermentation of the time, with its groping after the thing never yet heard or seen in poetry or the plastic arts—all these and more may claim the names 'non-rational', 'irrational', and according to circumstances are extolled or condemned as modern 'irrationalism'. Whoever makes use of the word 'non-rational' to-day ought to say what he actually means by it. This we did in our intro-ductory chapter. We began with the 'rational' in the idea of God and the divine, meaning by the term that in it which is clearly to be grasped by our power of conceiving, and enters the domain of familiar and definable conceptions. We went on to maintain that beneath this sphere of clarity and lucidity lies a hidden depth, inaccessible to our conceptual thought, which we in so far call the 'non-rational'. So that this name is for us a purely formal one, merely connoting a contrast and hence merely provisional. It has no longer any particular aptness when once we have succeeded in coming to an understanding of the way in which this hidden deep affects religion. This we attempted to hint and suggest in the ideograms of the numinous.

CHAPTER IX

MEANS OF EXPRESSION OF THE NUMINOUS

1. *Direct Means*

IT may serve to make the essential nature of the numinous consciousness clearer if we call to mind the manner in which it expresses itself outwardly, and how it spreads and is transmitted from mind to mind. There is, of course, no 'transmission' of it in the proper sense of the word; it cannot be 'taught', it must be 'awakened' from the spirit. And this could not justly be asserted, as it often is, of religion as a whole and in general, for in religion there *is* very much that *can* be taught—that is, handed down in concepts and passed on in school instruction. What is incapable of being so handed down is this numinous basis and background to religion, which can only be induced, incited, and aroused. This is least of all possible by mere verbal phrase or external symbol; rather we must have recourse to the way all other moods and feelings are transmitted, to a penetrative imaginative sympathy with what passes in the other person's mind. More of the experience lives in reverent attitude and gesture, in tone and voice and demeanour, expressing its momentousness, and in the solemn devotional assembly of a congregation at prayer, than in all the phrases and negative nomenclature which we have found to designate it. Indeed, these never give a positive suggestion of the object to which the religious consciousness refers; they are only of assistance in so far as they profess to indicate *an* object, which they at the same time contrast with another, at once distinct from and inferior to it, e. g. 'the invisible', 'the eternal' (non-temporal), 'the supernatural', 'the transcendent'. Or they are simply ideograms for the unique content of feeling, ideograms to understand which a man must already have had the experience himself. Far the best means are actual ' holy ' situations or their representation in description. If a man does not *feel* what the numinous is, when he reads the sixth chapter of Isaiah, then no ' preaching, singing, telling ', in Luther's phrase, can avail him. Little of it can usually be noticed in theory and dogma, or even in exhortation, unless it is actually *heard*. Indeed no element in religion needs so much as this the ' viva vox ', transmission by living fellowship and the inspiration of personal contact.[1]

But the mere word, even when it comes as a living voice, is powerless without the ' Spirit in the heart ' of the hearer to move him to apprehension. And this Spirit, this inborn capacity to receive and understand, is the essential thing. If that is there, very often only a very small incitement, a very remote stimulus, is needed to arouse the numinous conscious-ness. It is indeed astonishing to see how small a stimulus suffices—and that too coming sometimes only in clumsy and bewildered guise—to raise the Spirit of itself to the strongest pitch of the most definitely religious excitement. But where the wind of the Spirit blows, there the mere ' rational ' terms themselves are indued with power to arouse the feeling of the ' non-rational ', and become adequate to tune the mood at once to the right tone. Here ' schematization ' starts at once and needs no prompting. He who ' in the Spirit ' reads the written word lives in the numinous, though he may have neither notion of it nor name for it, nay, though he may be unable to analyse any feeling of his own and so make explicit

---

[1] Suso says of the transmission of the mystical experience : ' One thing there may be known ; unlike as it is, when a man heareth himself a dulcet instrument of strings sweetly sounding, compared to whoso but heareth tell thereof, even so are the words which are received in the purity of grace and flow forth out of a living heart by a living mouth unlike to those same words if they are beheld upon the dead parchment. . . . For there they grow cold, I know not how, and wither away like roses that have been plucked. For the lovely melody that above all toucheth the heart is then quenched to silence ; and in the waste places of the withered heart are they then received.'

to himself the nature of that numinous strand running through
the religious experience.

2. *Indirect Means*

For the rest, the methods by which the numinous
feeling is presented and evoked are indirect; i.e. they
consist in those means by which we express kindred and
similar feelings belonging to the 'natural' sphere. We have
already become acquainted with these feelings, and we shall
recognize them at once if we consider what are the means of
expression which religion has employed in all ages and in
every land.

One of the most primitive of these—which is later
more and more felt to be inadequate, until it is finally
altogether discarded as 'unworthy'—is quite naturally the
'fearful' and horrible, and even at times the revolting and
the loathsome. Inasmuch as the corresponding feelings are
closely analogous to that of the 'tremendum', their outlets
and means of expression may become indirect modes of
expressing the specific 'numinous awe' that cannot be
expressed directly. And so it comes about that the horrible
and dreadful character of primitive images and pictures of
gods, which seems to us to-day frequently so repellent, has
even yet among naïve and primitive natures—nay, occasionally
even among ourselves—the effect of arousing genuine feelings
of authentic religious awe. And, vice versa, this awe operates
as a supremely potent stimulus to express the element of
terror in different forms of imaginative representation. The
hard, stern, and somewhat grim pictures of the Madonna in
ancient Byzantine art attract the worship of many Catholics
more than the tender charm of the Madonnas of Raphael.
This trait is most signally evident in the case of certain figures
of gods in the Indian pantheon. Durgā, the 'great Mother' of
Bengal, whose worship can appear steeped in an atmosphere
of profoundest devotional awe, is represented in the orthodox
tradition with the visage of a fiend. And this same blending of appalling frightfulness and most exalted holiness
can perhaps be even more clearly studied in the eleventh book

of the Bhagavad-Gītā,[1] in which Vishnu—who is yet to his
votaries the very principle of goodness—displays himself to
Aryuna in the true height of his divinity. Here, too, the
mind has recourse for mode of expression first to the fearful
and dreadful, though this is at the same time permeated with
that element of 'the grand' to which we next turn.

This mode of expression, by way of 'grandeur' or 'sublimity', is found on higher levels, where it replaces mere
'terror' and 'dread'. We meet it in an unsurpassable form
in the sixth chapter of Isaiah, where there is sublimity alike
in the lofty throne and the sovereign figure of God, the skirts
of His raiment 'filling the temple' and the solemn majesty of
the attendant angels about Him. While the element of
'dread' is gradually overborne, the connexion of 'the sublime' and 'the holy' becomes firmly established as a legitimate schematization and is carried on into the highest
forms of religious consciousness—a proof that there exists
a hidden kinship between the numinous and the sublime
which is something more than a mere analogy, and to which
Kant's *Critique of Judgement* bears distant witness.

So far we have been concerned with that element or factor of
the numinous which was the first our analysis noted and which
we proposed to name symbolically 'the aweful' (*tremendum*).
We pass now to consider the means by which the second—the
element of 'the mysterious' (*mysterium*)—is expressed. Here
we light upon the analogical mode of manifestation that in every
religion occupies a foremost and extraordinary place, and the
theory of which we are now in a position to give. I refer to
miracle. 'Miracle is the dearest child of Faith'; if the
history of religions had not already taught us the truth of
Schiller's saying, we might have reached it by anticipation
a priori from the element of 'the mysterious', as already
shown. Nothing can be found in all the world of 'natural'
feelings bearing so immediate an analogy—*mutatis mutandis*—
to the religious consciousness of ineffable, unutterable mystery,

---

[1] See Appendix II. Nowhere can the non-rational element of ὀργή be
better studied than in this chapter, one of the perfectly classical passages
for the theory of Religion.

the 'absolute other', as the incomprehensible, unwonted, enigmatic thing, in whatever place or guise it may confront us. This will be all the more true if the uncomprehended thing is something at once *mighty* and *fearful*, for then there is a twofold analogy with the numinous—that is to say, an analogy not only with the 'mysterium' aspect of it, but with the 'tremendum' aspect, and the latter again in the two directions already suggested of *fearfulness* proper and *sublimity*. This exemplifies the general truth already considered that any form of the numinous consciousness may be stirred by means of feelings analogous to it of a 'natural' kind, and then itself pass over into these, or, more properly, be replaced by them. And in fact this is everywhere manifest in the experience of man. Whatever has loomed upon the world of his ordinary concerns as something terrifying and baffling to the intellect; whatever among natural occurrences or events in the human, animal, or vegetable kingdoms has set him astare in wonder and astonishment—such things have ever aroused in man, and become endued with, the 'daemonic dread' and 'numinous' feeling, so as to become 'portents', 'prodigies', and 'marvels'. Thus and only thus is it that 'the miraculous' arose. And, in the reverse direction, the feeling of the *numen* as 'the mysterious' worked as a potent stimulus on the naïve imagination, inciting it to expect miracles, to invent them, to 'experience' them, to recount them, just as before the felt awefulness of the numen became a stimulus to select or fashion inventively, as a means of religious expression, images of fear and dread. 'The mysterious' became an untiring impulse, prompting to inexhaustible invention in folk-tale and myth, saga and legend, permeating ritual and the forms of worship, and remaining till to-day to naïve minds, whether in the form of narrative or sacrament, the most powerful factor that keeps the religious consciousness alive. But here too, as in the case of the fearful and terrible, progress to a higher stage of development shows the gradual elimination of this merely external analogue to the numinous, viz. the miraculous; and so we see how, on the more enlightened levels, 'miracle' begins to fade away; how Christ is at one with Mohammed and Buddha in declining the rôle of mere 'wonder-worker'; how Luther dismisses the 'outward miracles' disparagingly as 'jugglery' or 'apples and nuts for children'; and finally how the 'supernaturalism' of miracle is purged from religion as something that is only an imperfect analogue and no genuine 'schema' of the numinous.

There are other manifestations of this tendency of the feeling of the 'mysterious' to be attracted to objects and aspects of experience analogous to it in being 'uncomprehended'. It finds its most unqualified expression in the spell exercised by the only half intelligible or wholly unintelligible language of devotion, and in the unquestionably real enhancement of the awe of the worshipper which this produces. Instances of this are—the ancient traditional expressions, still retained despite their obscurity, in our Bible and hymnals; the special emotional virtue attaching to words like Hallelujah, Kyrie eleison, Selah, just because they are 'wholly other' and convey no clear meaning; the Latin in the service of the Mass, felt by the Catholic to be, not a necessary evil, but something especially holy; the Sanskrit in the Buddhist Mass of China and Japan; the 'language of the gods' in the ritual of sacrifice in Homer; and many similar cases. Especially noticeable in this connexion are the half-revealed, half-concealed and esoteric elements in the Communion Service, in the Greek Church liturgy, and so many others; we can see here one factor that justifies and warrants them. And the same is true of the remaining portions of the old Mass which recur in the Lutheran ritual. Just because their design shows but little of regularity or conceptual arrangement, they preserve in themselves far more of the spirit of worship than the proposed recastings of the service put forward by the most recent practical reformers. In these we find carefully arranged schemes worked out with the balance and coherence of an essay, but nothing unaccountable, and for that very reason suggestive; nothing accidental, and for that very reason pregnant in meaning; nothing that rises from the deeps below consciousness to break the rounded unity of the wonted disposition, and thereby point to a unity of a higher order—

in a word, little that is really spiritual.   All the cases cited,
then, have one and the same point of agreement; they are all
instances of the analogy to 'the mysterious' afforded by that
which is not wholly understood, unwonted and at the same
time venerable through age; and in the resemblance they
present to the 'mysterious' they arouse it in the mind by
a sort of 'anamnesis' or reminder, and at the same time constitute its outward analogical representation.

3. *Means by which the Numinous is expressed in Art*

In the arts nearly everywhere the most effective means of
representing the numinous is 'the sublime'.   This is especially
true of architecture, in which it would appear to have first
been realized.   One can hardly escape the idea that this feeling
for expression must have begun to awaken far back in the
remote Stone Age.   The motive underlying the erection of those
gigantic blocks of rock, hewn or unworked, single monoliths
or titanic rings of stone, as at Stonehenge, may have well been
originally to localize and preserve and, as it were, to store up
the numen in solid presence by magic; but the change to the
motive of *expression* must have been from the outset far too
vividly stimulated not to occur at a very early date.   In fact
the bare feeling for solemn and imposing magnitude and for the
pomp of sublime pose and gesture is a fairly elementary one,
and we cannot doubt that this stage had been reached when
the *mastabas*, obelisks and pyramids were built in Egypt.   It
is indeed beyond question that the builders of these Temples,
and of the Sphinx of Gizeh, which set the feeling of the
sublime, and together with and through it that of the numinous,
throbbing in the soul almost like a mechanical reflex, must
themselves have been conscious of this effect and have intended it.

Further, we often say of a building, or indeed of a song,
a formula, a succession of gestures or musical notes, and in
particular of certain manifestations of ornamental and decora-
tive art, symbols, and emblems, that they make a 'downright
magical' impression, and we feel we can detect the special
characteristic of this 'magical' note in art with fair assurance

even under the most varying conditions and in the most diverse relationships. The art of China, Japan, and Tibet, whose specific character has been determined by Taoism and Buddhism, surpasses all others in the unusual richness and depth of such impressions of the 'magical', and even an inexpert observer responds to them readily. The designation 'magical' is here correct even from the historical point of view, since the origin of this language of form was properly magical representations, emblems, formularies, and contrivances. But the actual impression of 'magic' is quite independent of this historical bond of connexion with magical practices. It occurs even when nothing is known of the latter; nay, in that case it comes out most strongly and unbrokenly. Beyond dispute art has here a means of creating a unique impression—that of the magical—apart from and independent of reflection. Now the magical is nothing but a suppressed and blurred form of the numinous, a crude form of it which great art purifies and ennobles. In great art the point is reached at which we may no longer speak of the 'magical', but rather are confronted with the numinous itself, with all its impelling motive power, transcending reason, expressed in sweeping lines and rhythm. In no art, perhaps, is this more fully realized than in the great landscape painting and religious painting of China in the classical period of the T'ang and Sung dynasties. It has been said of this great art:

'These works are to be classed with the profoundest and sublimest of the creations of human art. The spectator who, as it were, immerses himself in them feels behind these waters and clouds and mountains the mysterious breath of the primeval Tao, the pulse of innermost being. Many a mystery lies half-concealed and half-revealed in these pictures. They contain the knowledge of the "nothingness" and the "void", of the "Tao" of heaven and earth, which is also the Tao of the human heart. And so, despite their perpetual agitation, they seem as remotely distant and as profoundly calm as though they drew secret breath at the bottom of a sea.'[1]

[1] From an article by Otto Fischer on Chinese landscape painting in *Das Kunstblatt*, Jan. 1920.

To us of the West the Gothic appears as the most numinous of all types of art. This is due in the first place to its sublimity ; but Worringer in his work *Probleme der Gothik* has done a real service in showing that the peculiar impressiveness of Gothic does not consist in its sublimity alone, but draws upon a strain inherited from primitive magic, of which he tries to show the historical derivation. To Worringer, then, the impression Gothic makes is one of magic ; and, whatever may be said of his historical account of the matter, it is certain that in this at least he is on the right track. Gothic *does* instil a spell that is more than the effect of sublimity. But ' magic ' is too low a word : the tower of the Cathedral of Ulm is emphatically not ' magical ', it is *numinous*. And the difference between the numinous and the merely magical can nowhere be felt more clearly than in the splendid plate Worringer gives in his book of this marvellous work of architecture. But when this is said, we may still keep the word ' magic ' in use to denote the style and means of artistic expression by which the impression of the numinous comes into being.

But in neither the sublime nor the magical, effective as they are, has art more than an indirect means of representing the numinous. Of directer methods our Western art has only two, and they are in a noteworthy way *negative*, viz. *darkness* and *silence*. The darkness must be such as is enhanced and made all the more perceptible by contrast with some last vestige of brightness, which it is, as it were, on the point of extinguishing ; hence the ' mystical ' effect begins with semi-darkness. Its impression is rendered complete if the factor of the ' sublime ' comes to unite with and supplement it. The semi-darkness that glimmers in vaulted halls, or beneath the branches of a lofty forest glade, strangely quickened and stirred by the mysterious play of half-lights, has always spoken eloquently to the soul, and the builders of temples, mosques, and churches have made full use of it.

Silence is what corresponds to this in the language of musical sounds. ' Yahweh is in His holy Temple, let all the earth keep silence before Him.' (Habakkuk, ii. 20.)   Neither we nor (probably) the prophet any longer bear in mind that this 'keeping silence' (as εὐφημεῖν in Greek), if regarded from the historical, 'genetic' standpoint, springs from the fear of using words of evil omen, which therefore prefers to be altogether speechless. It is the same with Tersteegen in his 'God is present, let all in us be silent'. With prophet and psalmist and poet we feel the necessity of silence from another and quite independent motive. It is a spontaneous reaction to the feeling of the actual 'numen praesens'. Once again, what is found coming upon the scene at a higher level of evolution cannot be explained by merely interpolating links in a 'historico-genetic' chain of development; and the Psalmist and Tersteegen and even we ourselves are at least as interesting subjects for the analysis of the psychologist of religion as are the 'Primitives', with their habitual practice of εὐφημία, the silence that merely avoids words of ill augury.

Besides Silence and Darkness oriental art knows a third direct means for producing a strongly numinous impression, to wit, *emptiness* and *empty distances*. Empty distance, remote vacancy, is, as it were, the sublime in the horizontal. The wide-stretching desert, the boundless uniformity of the steppe, have real sublimity, and even in us Westerners they set vibrating chords of the numinous along with the note of the sublime, according to the principle of the association of feelings. Chinese architecture, which is essentially an art in the laying out and grouping of buildings, makes a wise and very striking use of this fact. It does not achieve the impression of solemnity by lofty vaulted halls or imposing altitudes, but nothing could well be more solemn than the silent amplitude of the enclosed spaces, courtyards, and vestibules which it employs. The imperial tombs of the Ming emperors at Nanking and Peking are, perhaps, the strongest example of this, including, as they do, in their plan the empty distances of an entire landscape. Still more interesting is the part played by the factor of void or emptiness in Chinese painting. There it has almost become a special art to paint empty space, to make it palpable, and to develop variations upon this singular theme. Not only are there pictures upon which 'almost nothing' is painted, not only is it an essential feature of their style to make the strongest impression with the fewest strokes and the scantiest means, but there are very many pictures—especially such as are connected with contemplation—which impress the observer with the feeling that the void itself is depicted as a subject, is indeed the main subject of the picture. We can only understand this by recalling what was said above on the 'nothingness' and the 'void' of the mystics and on the enchantment and spell exercised by the 'negative hymns'. For 'Void' is, like Darkness and Silence, a negation, but a negation that does away with every 'this' and 'here', in order that the 'wholly other' may become actual.

Not even music, which else can give such manifold expression to all the feelings of the mind, has any positive way to express 'the holy'. Even the most consummate Mass-music can only give utterance to the holiest, most 'numinous' moment in the Mass—the moment of transubstantiation—by sinking into stillness: no mere momentary pause, but an absolute cessation of sound long enough for us to 'hear the Silence' itself; and no devotional moment in the whole Mass approximates in impressiveness to this 'keeping silence before the Lord'. It is instructive to submit Bach's Mass in B minor to the test in this matter. Its mystical portion is the 'Incarnatus' in the Credo, and there the effect is due to the faint, whispering, lingering sequence in the fugue structure, dying away pianissimo. The held breath and hushed sound of the passage, its weird cadences, sinking away in lessened thirds, its pauses and syncopations, and its rise and fall in astonishing semi-tones, which render so well the sense of awe-struck wonder—all this serves to express the mysterium by way of intimation, rather than in forthright utterance. And by this means Bach attains his aim here far better than in the 'Sanctus'. This latter is indeed an incomparably successful expression of Him, whose is 'the power and the glory', an enraptured and triumphant choric hymn to perfect and absolute sovereignty. But it is very far distant from the mood of the text that accompanies the music, which is taken from Isaiah vi, and which the composer should have interpreted in accordance with that passage as a whole.   No one would gather from this magnificent chorus that the Seraphim covered their faces with two of their wings.[1] In this point Mendelssohn shows very fine sensibility in his musical setting of Psalm ii at the words (v. 11) : ' Serve the Lord with fear, and rejoice with trembling.' And here too the matter is expressed less in the music itself than in the way the music is restrained and repressed—one might almost say, abashed—as the Cathedral choir at Berlin so well knows how to render it.   And, if a final example may be cited, the ' Popule meus ' of Thomas Luiz gets as near to the heart of the matter as any music can. In this the first chorus sings the first words of the 'Trisagion': ' Hagios, ho theos, hagios ischyros, hagios athanatos ', and the second chorus sings in response the Latin rendering of the words : ' Sanctus deus, sanctus fortis, sanctus immortalis', each chorus thrilling with a sort of muffled tremor.   But the Trisagion itself, sung pianissimo by singers kept out of sight far at the back, is like a whisper floating down through space, and is assuredly a consummate reproduction of the scene in the vision of Isaiah.

[1] The Jewish tradition has been, however, very well aware of the import of the matter.   In the splendid New Year's day Hymn of Melek Elyōn the words run: ' All the mighty ones on high *whisper low :* Yahweh is King.'

CHAPTER X

THE NUMINOUS IN THE OLD TESTAMENT

WHILE the feelings of the non-rational and numinous constitute a vital factor in every form religion may take, they are pre-eminently in evidence in Semitic religion and most of all in the religion of the Bible. Here Mystery lives and moves in all its potency. It is present in the ideas of the daemonic and angelic world, which, as a 'wholly other', surrounds, transcends, and permeates this world of ours; it is potent in the Biblical eschatology and the ideal of a 'kingdom of God' contrasted with the natural order, now as being future in time, now as being eternal, but always as the downright marvellous and 'other'; and finally it impresses itself on the character of Yahweh and Elohim—that God who is nevertheless the 'Heavenly Father' of Jesus and as such 'fulfils', not loses, his character as Yahweh.

The lower stage of numinous consciousness, viz. daemonic dread, has already been long superseded by the time we reach the Prophets and Psalmists. But there are not wanting occasional echoes of it, found especially in the earlier narrative literature. The story in Exodus iv. 24, of how Yahweh in his ὀργή met Moses by the way 'and sought to kill him', still bears this 'daemonic' character strongly, and the tale leaves us almost with the suggestion of a ghostly apparition. And from the standpoint of the more highly developed 'fear of God' one might easily get from this and similar stories the impression that this is not yet religion at all, but a sort of pre-religious, vulgar fear of demons or the like. That would, however, be a misconception; a 'vulgar fear of demons' would refer to a 'demon' in the narrower sense of the word, in which it is a synonym for devil, fiend, or goblin, and is *contrasted* with the divine. But 'demon' in this sense has

not been, any more than ' ghost ' or ' spectre ', a point in the
transition, or, if it be preferred, a link in the chain of development which religious consciousness has undergone.   Both
' demon ' (= fiend) and ' spectre ' are, so to speak, offshoots
from the true line of progress, spurious fabrications of the
fancy accompanying the numinous feeling.   We must carefully
distinguish from such a ' demon ' the δαίμων or ' daemon ' in
the more general sense of the word, which, if it is not yet
itself a ' god ', is still less an anti-god, but must be termed
a ' pre-god ', the numen at a lower stage, in which it is still
trammelled and suppressed, but out of which the ' god '
gradually grows to more and more lofty manifestations.   *This*
is the phase whose after-effects can be detected in these
ancient stories.

It will be worth while to consider this matter further.
Two things may help to an understanding of the real relation
with which we are here concerned.   First, we may refer back
to what was said on an earlier page upon the capacity of ' the
dreadful ' and ' terrible ' in general to attract and arouse, and
also to express, the true ' numinous ' consciousness or emotion.
In the second place, we may refer to the parallel case of
music.   A man with a pronounced musical faculty, so long as
he is a mere raw tyro, may be enraptured by the sound of the
bagpipes or the hurdy-gurdy, though perhaps both become
intolerable to him when his musical education has been completed.   But, if he then recalls the qualitative character of his
earlier musical experience and compares it with his present
one, he will have to admit that, in both, one and the same side
of his mind is functioning, and that what has taken place in
the rise of his feeling for music to a more elevated form
is no transition to something different in kind, but a process
which we may call ' development ' or ' growth to maturity ',
but can hardly further specify.   Were we to hear to-day
the music of Confucius, it would probably be to us merely
a succession of queer noises.   Yet already Confucius speaks
of the power of music on the mind in a way we moderns
cannot better, and touches upon just those elements which we
also must recognize in the experience of music.   But the most

striking consideration in this regard is the way in which some savage tribes are endowed with a capacity for a ready appreciation of our music, which they grasp quickly, practise assiduously, and enjoy intensely, when it is brought before them.   This endowment did not first enter their minds at the moment they heard the music by a ' heterogony ', ' epigenesis ', or other miracle ; it simply existed all the time as a natural predisposition or latent capacity.   It was aroused and began to develop as soon as the proper incitement came to stimulate it, but to the end it was yet *the selfsame* disposition that had been formerly excited to such primitive and crude manifestations.   This ' crude ', ' primitive ' form of music is often almost or wholly unrecognizable as real music by our developed musical taste, although it was the manifestation of the same impulse and the same element of our psychical nature.   Now it is exactly a parallel case when the ' God-fearing ' man of to-day finds it hard to detect in the narrative of Exodus iv that which is akin to his own religious experience, or misjudges it altogether.   All this involves a point of view which should be taken into consideration more generally with respect to the religion of ' primitive man ', though naturally great caution should be used in applying it, seeing that very mistaken conclusions can be drawn from it and there is a real danger of confounding the lower with the higher levels of development and of making too little of the interval between them.   However, it is still more dangerous to exclude this point of view altogether, as is unfortunately very commonly done.[1]

Recent research has sought to discover a difference in character between Yahweh, the austere and stern, and Elohim, the familiar, patriarchal God, and there is something very illuminating in the suggestion.   Söderblom's supposition[2] is that the notion of Yahweh had its point of origin in earlier ' animistic ' ideas.   I do not dispute the importance of such ' animistic ' ideas in the religious evolutionary process ; in

[1] In this regard Mr. Marett in particular has important and novel considerations to offer.

[2] Söderblom, *Das Werden des Gottesglaubens*, 1916, pp. 297 ff.

fact, I should go even farther than Söderblom in that respect, for he would explain them as a sort of primitive 'philosophy', and therefore has to exclude them altogether from the domain of genuinely *religious* imagination. It would be perfectly compatible with my own view to hold that where ideas of an animistic character had been framed they could serve as an important link in the 'chain of stimulation' by which true numinous consciousness is aroused (namely, in so far as they served to disengage and free the obscure feeling-element of 'existent being', latent in it). But what distinguishes Yahweh from El-Shaddai-Elohim is not that the former is an 'anima', but (and the distinction may be applied to differentiate all god-types) that, whereas in Yahweh the numinous preponderates over the familiar 'rational' character, in Elohim the rational aspect outweighs the numinous. 'Outweighs' is as much as we can say, for in Elohim too the numinous element is certainly present; Elohim is, for instance, the subject of the genuinely numinous narrative of the theophany in the burning bush, with the characteristic verse (Exodus iii. 6): 'And Moses hid his face; for he was afraid to look upon God.'

For the copious and diverse characteristics of the idea of God of the ancient Israelites which might be instanced here the reader is referred to works upon the history of religion.[1] The noble religion of Moses marks the beginning of a process which from that point onward proceeds with ever increasing momentum, by which 'the numinous' is throughout rationalized and moralized, i.e. charged with ethical import, until it becomes 'the holy' in the fullest sense of the word. The culmination of the process is found in the Prophets and in the Gospels. And it is in this that the special nobility of the religion revealed to us by the Bible is to be found, which, when the stage represented by the deutero-Isaiah is reached, justifies its claim to be a universal world-religion. Here is to be found its manifest superiority over, e. g., Islam, in which Allah is mere 'numen', and is in fact precisely Yahweh in his pre-Mosaic form and upon a larger scale. But this moralizing

[1] They are given exhaustively in the Encyclopaedia *Die Religion in Geschichte und Gegenwart*, vol. ii, pp. 1530, 2036.

and rationalizing process does not mean that the numinous itself has been overcome, but merely that its preponderance has been overcome. The numinous is at once the basis upon which and the setting within which the ethical and rational meaning is consummated.

The capital instance of the intimate mutual interpenetration of the numinous with the rational and moral is Isaiah. The note struck in the vision of his call is the keynote of his entire prophecy. And nothing is in this regard more significant than the fact that it is in Isaiah that the expression 'the Holy One of Israel' first becomes established as the expression, *par excellence*, for the deity, prevailing over all others by its mysterious potency. This remains so in the writings of the 'deutero-Isaiah', who follows the tradition of the earlier Isaiah. Assuredly in deutero-Isaiah, if in any writer, we have to do with a God whose attributes are clear to conceptual thought: omnipotence, goodness, wisdom, truth; and yet all the time these are attributes of 'the Holy One', whose strange name deutero-Isaiah too repeats no less than fifteen times and always in passages where it has a special impressiveness.

Related expressions akin to the 'holiness' of Yahweh are His 'fury', His 'jealousy', His 'wrath', the 'consuming fire', and the like. The import of them all is not only the all-requiting righteousness of God, not even merely His susceptibility to strong and living emotions, but all this ever enclosed in and permeated with the 'awefulness' and the 'majesty', the 'mystery' and the 'augustness', of His non-rational divine nature.

And this holds good, also, of the expression 'the living God'. God's 'livingness' is perceptibly akin to His 'jealousy' and is manifested in and through this, as in His other 'passions' generally.[1] It is by His 'life' that this God is differ-

---

[1] Cf. Deut. v. 26: 'For who is there of all flesh, that hath heard the voice of the *living* God speaking out of the midst of the fire, as we have, *and lived*?' Cf. also Josh. iii. 10; 1 Sam. xvii. 26, 36; 2 Kings xix. 4; Isa. xxxvii. 4, 17; Jer. x. 10: 'He is the *living* God: ... at His *wrath* the earth shall tremble and the nations shall not be able to abide His *indigna-*

entiated from all mere ' World Reason ', and becomes this ultimately non-rational essence, that eludes all philosophic treatment. This is the God that lives in the consciousness of all prophets and apostles of the Old and the New Dispensation alike. And all those who later championed against the ' God of philosophy ' the ' living God ' and the God of anger and love and the emotions have unwittingly been defending the non-rational core of the Biblical conception of God from all excessive rationalization. And so far they were right. Where they were wrong and sank into ' anthropomorphism ' was in defending, not figurative ' anger ' and ' emotion ', but literal anger and emotion, misconceiving the numinous character of the attributes in question and holding them simply to be ' natural ' attributes, taken absolutely, instead of realizing that they can only be admitted as figurative indications of something essentially non-rational by means of symbols drawn from feelings that have analogy to it.

We find the power of the numinous—in its phase of the mysterious—to excite and intensify the imagination displayed with particular vividness in Ezekiel. Here are to be classed Ezekiel's dreams and parables and fanciful delineation of God's being and sovereign state, which are, as it were, an example by anticipation of the later more spurious sort of excitement of the religious impulse to the mysterious, leading (in accordance with analogies already expounded) to the merely strange, the extraordinary, the marvellous, and the fantastic. When such an operation of the religious consciousness works itself out in accordance with a wrong analogy, the way is prepared for miracle and legend and the whole dream-

tion '; Jer. xxiii. 36 ; 2 Macc. vii. 33 ; Matt. xxvi. 63 (the adjuration ' by the *living* God ', the God of terror and dread); and Heb. x. 31: 'It is a fearful thing to fall into the hands of the *living* God.' The Old Testament idea of the terrible ' living ' God reaches its completion in the ideas of the 'avenging God', of which the most ruthless expression is in the almost appalling image of the treader of the wine-press, Isa. lxiii. 3 : 'I will tread them in mine anger, and trample them in my fury ; and their blood shall be sprinkled upon my garments and I will stain all my raiment.' The dreadful image recurs in the New Testament in Rev. xix. 15 : ' He treadeth the wine-press of the fierceness and wrath of Almighty God.'

world of pseudo-mysticism ; and, though these are all truly
enough emanations from the genuine religious experience, they
are emanations broken by the opaque, dull medium through
which they pass, a mere substitute for the genuine thing, and
they end in a vulgar rankness of growth that overspreads
the pure feeling of the 'mysterium' as it really is and chokes
its direct and forthright emotional expression.

But, if Ezekiel hardly shows the numinous moment apart
from an admixture of excessive fantasy and imagination, the
same is not true of the Book of Job.   In the 38th chapter of
Job we have the element of the mysterious displayed in
rare purity and completeness, and this chapter may well rank
among the most remarkable in the history of religion.   Job
has been reasoning with his friends against Elohim, and—as
far as concerns them—he has been obviously in the right.
They are compelled to be dumb before him.   And then Elohim
Himself appears to conduct His own defence in person.   And
He conducts it to such effect that Job avows himself to be
overpowered, truly and rightly overpowered, not merely
silenced by superior strength.   Then he confesses : ' Therefore I abhor myself and *repent* in dust and ashes.'   That
is an admission of inward *convincement* and conviction,
not of impotent collapse and submission to merely superior
power.   Nor is there here at all the frame of mind to which
St. Paul now and then gives utterance ; e.g. Rom. ix. 20 :
' Shall the thing formed say to him that formed it, Why hast
thou made me thus ?   Hath not the potter power over the
clay, of the same lump to make one vessel unto honour, and
another unto dishonour ? '   To interpret the passage in Job
thus would be a misunderstanding of it.   This chapter does
not proclaim, as Paul does, the renunciation of, the realization
of the impossibility of, a ' theodicy ' ; rather, it aims at putting
forward a real theodicy of its own, and a better one than that
of Job's friends ; a theodicy able to convict even a Job, and
not only to convict him, but utterly to still every inward
doubt that assailed his soul.   For latent in the weird experience that Job underwent in the revelation of Elohim is
at once an inward relaxing of his soul's anguish and an

appeasement, an appeasement which would alone and in itself perfectly suffice as the solution of the problem of the Book of Job, even without Job's rehabilitation in chapter xlii, which is merely a later addition to the real narrative. But what is this strange 'moment' of experience that here operates at once as a vindication of God to Job and a reconciliation of Job to God?

In the words put into the mouth of Elohim nearly every note is sounded which the situation may prepare one to expect *a priori*: the summons to Job, and the demonstration of God's overwhelming power, His sublimity and greatness, and His surpassing wisdom. This last would yield forthwith a plausible and rational solution of the whole problem, if only the argument were here completed with some such sentences as: 'My ways are higher than your ways; in my deeds and my actions I have ends that you understand not'; viz. the testing or purification of the godly man, or ends that concern the whole universe as such, into which the single man must fit himself with all his sufferings. If you start from rational ideas and concepts, you absolutely *thirst* for such a conclusion to the discourse. But nothing of the kind follows; nor does the chapter intend at all to suggest such teleological reflections or solutions. In the last resort it relies on something quite different from anything that can be exhaustively rendered in rational concepts, namely, on the sheer absolute wondrousness that transcends thought, on the *mysterium*, presented in its pure, non-rational form. All the glorious examples from nature speak very plainly in this sense. The eagle, that 'dwelleth and abideth on the rock, upon the crag of the rock, and the strong place', whose 'eyes behold afar off' her prey, and whose 'young ones also suck up blood, and where the slain are, there is she'—this eagle is in truth no evidence for the *teleological* wisdom that 'prepares all cunningly and well', but is rather the creature of *strangeness* and *marvel*, in whom the wondrousness of its creator becomes apparent. And the same is true of the ostrich (xxxix. 13–18) with its *inexplicable* instincts. The ostrich is indeed, as here depicted, and 'rationally' considered, a crucial difficulty rather than an evidence of

G

wisdom, and it affords singularly little help if we are seeking
purpose in nature: 'which leaveth her eggs in the earth,
and warmeth them in the dust, and forgetteth that the foot
may crush them or that the wild beast may break them.
She is hardened against her young ones as though they were
not hers: her labour is in vain without fear; because God
hath *deprived her of wisdom*, neither hath he imparted to her
understanding.'

It is the same with the 'wild ass' (verse 5) and the unicorn
(verse 9). These are beasts whose complete 'dysteleology'
or negation of purposiveness is truly magnificently depicted;
but, nevertheless, with their mysterious instincts and the
riddle of their generation, this very negation of purpose
becomes a thing of baffling significance, as in the case of the
'wild goat' (verse 1) and the hind. The 'wisdom' of the inward parts (xxxviii. 36), and the 'knowledge' of dayspring,
winds, and clouds, with the mysterious ways in which they
come and go, arise and vanish, shift and veer and re-form;
and the wonderful Pleiades aloft in heaven, with Orion and
'Arcturus and his sons'—these serve but to emphasize the
same lesson. It is conjectured that the descriptions of the
hippopotamus (behemoth) and crocodile (leviathan) in xl. 15 ff.
are a later interpolation. This may well be the fact; but,
if so, it must be admitted that the interpolator has felt the
point of the entire section extraordinarily well. He only
brings to its grossest expression the thought intended by
all the other examples of animals; they gave portents only,
he gives us 'monsters'—but 'the monstrous' is just the
'mysterious' in a gross form. Assuredly these beasts would
be the most unfortunate examples that one could hit upon
if searching for evidences of the purposefulness of the divine
'wisdom'. But they, no less than all the previous examples
and the whole context, tenor, and sense of the entire passage,
do express in masterly fashion the downright stupendousness,
the wellnigh daemonic and wholly incomprehensible character
of the eternal creative power; how, incalculable and 'wholly
other', it mocks at all conceiving but can yet stir the mind
to its depths, fascinate and overbrim the heart. What is

meant is the mysterium not as mysterious simply, but at the same time also as 'fascinating' and 'august'; and here, too, these latter meanings live, not in any explicit concepts, but in the tone, the enthusiasm, in the very rhythm of the entire exposition.   And here is indeed the point of the whole passage, comprising alike the theodicy and the appeasement and calming of Job's soul.   The mysterium, simply as such, would merely (as discussed above) be a part of the 'absolute inconceivability' of the numen, and that, though it might strike Job utterly dumb, could not convict him inwardly.   That of which we are conscious is rather an *intrinsic value* in the incomprehensible—a value inexpressible, positive, and 'fascinating'.   This is incommensurable with thoughts of rational human teleology and is not assimilated to them : it remains in all its mystery.   But it is as it becomes felt in consciousness that Elohim is justified and at the same time Job's soul brought to peace.

*   *   *

A very real parallel to this experience of Job is to be found in the work of a writer of our own day, which is not the less deeply impressive because it is found in the fictitious context of a novel.   Max Eyth recounts in his story *Berufs-Tragik* (in the collection *Hinter Pflug und Schraubstock*) the building of the mighty bridge over the estuary of the Ennobucht. The most profound and thorough labour of the intellect, the most assiduous and devoted professional toil, had gone to the construction of the great edifice, making it in all its significance and purposefulness a marvel of human achievement.   In spite of endless difficulties and gigantic obstacles, the bridge is at length finished, and stands defying wind and waves. Then there comes a raging cyclone, and building and builder are swept into the deep.   Utter meaninglessness seems to triumph over richest significance, blind 'destiny' seems to stride on its way over prostrate virtue and merit.   The narrator tells how he visits the scene of the tragedy and returns again.

'When we got to the end of the bridge, there was hardly

G 2

a breath of wind; high above, the sky showed blue-green, and with an eerie brightness. Behind us, like a great open grave, lay the Ennobucht. The Lord of life and death hovered over the waters in silent majesty. We felt His presence, as one feels one's own hand. And the old man and I knelt down before the open grave and before Him.'

Why did they kneel? Why did they feel constrained to do so? One does not kneel before a cyclone or the blind forces of nature, nor even before Omnipotence merely as such. But one does kneel before the wholly uncomprehended Mystery, revealed yet unrevealed, and one's soul is stilled by feeling the way of its working, and therein its justification.

It would be possible to cite many other traces of numinous feeling in the Old Testament. But they have already been admirably put together by one who wrote sixteen hundred years ago in the same sense as we 'upon the non-rational'. This was Chrysostom. We shall be considering him later on and will not anticipate farther in this place.[1]

---

[1] See Appendix I.

CHAPTER XI

THE NUMINOUS IN THE NEW TESTAMENT

In the Gospel of Jesus we see the consummation of that process tending to rationalize, moralize, and humanize the idea of God, which began with the earliest period of the old Hebrew tradition and became specially prominent as a living factor in the Prophets and the Psalms, continually bringing the apprehension of the numinous to a richer fulfilment by recognizing in it attributes of clear and profound value for the reason. The result was the faith in 'the fatherhood of God' in that unsurpassable form in which it is peculiar to Christianity.

But in this case, too, it would be a mistake to think that such a rationalization means that 'the numinous' is excluded or superseded. That is a misunderstanding into which we are led by the all too plausible delineations of 'Jesus's faith in God as Father' now prevalent, but it certainly misrepresents the attitude of the first Christian congregations. The error is only possible if we disregard in the message of Christ that which it really purports to be, first, last, and all the time, viz. the Gospel *of the Kingdom*. As against all rationalizing attempts to tone it down into something less startling, the most recent research shows quite decisively that the 'kingdom' is just greatness and marvel absolute, the 'wholly other' 'heavenly' thing, set in contrast to the world of here and now, 'the mysterious' itself in its dual character as awe-compelling yet all-attracting, glimmering in an atmosphere of genuine 'religious awe'. As such, it sheds a colour, a mood, a tone, upon whatever stands in relation to it, upon the men

who proclaim it or prepare for it, upon the life and practice
that are its precondition, upon the tidings of it, upon the
congregation of those who await it and attain to it. All is
made into a 'mystery'—all, that is, becomes 'numinous'.
This is shown most strikingly in the name by which the
company of the disciples call themselves collectively and each
other individually, the numinous 'technical term' οἱ ἅγιοι,
the holy ones or 'the Saints'. It is manifest at once that
this does not mean 'the morally perfect' people : it means
the people who participate in the mystery of the final Day.
Their title is the clear and unambiguous antithesis to the
term 'the profane', which we have already met with. For
this reason the early Christians are able later to call themselves also actually a 'priestly'— or sacerdotal—'people', that
is, a group of 'consecrated' persons. But the precondition
of all this was given with the Gospel itself and its claim to be
the preaching of the coming Kingdom.

What of the lord of this kingdom, the 'heavenly Father'?
As its lord He is not less, but far more 'holy', 'numinous',
mysterious, 'qādôsh', ἅγιος, 'sacer', and 'sanctus' than His
kingdom. He is all these in an absolute degree, and in this
aspect of His nature He represents the sublimation and the
consummation of all that the old Covenant had grasped by way
of 'creature-consciousness', 'holy awe', and the like. Not to
realize this is to turn the Gospel of Jesus into a mere idyll.
That these moments do not occur severally in Jesus's message
in the form of special 'doctrines' is due to the circumstances
already mentioned more than once. But apart from the
inherent impossibility of *teaching* them, how could He have
had need of 'teaching' what was simply the primary, self-
evident fact to every Jew, and especially to every believer in
'the Kingdom', namely, that God was 'the Holy One in Israel'?
Christ had rather to teach and to proclaim what was *not*
self-evident to the Jews, but His own original discovery and
revelation, that this very 'Holy One' is a 'heavenly Father'.
This point of view necessarily occupied the whole of His
'teaching', and all the more so because it was the point of
view thrust sharply into the foreground by the two opposed

influences of His time, against both of which the Gospel came
historically as a reaction. On the one hand was Pharisaism,
with its servitude to Law; on the other, John the Baptist,
with his harsh, ascetic interpretation of God; and, in contrast to both, the Gospel of the Sonhood of man and the
Fatherhood of God came as the easy yoke, the light burden.
But though it is necessarily this new message that the parables
and discourses and pronouncements of Jesus complete and fill
out, it is in such a way that it always remains an overwhelming and daring paradox, claiming our utmost homage,
that He who is 'in heaven' is yet 'our Father'. That that
'heavenly' Being of marvel and mystery and awe is Himself
the eternal, benignant, gracious, will: this is the resolved
contrast that first brings out the deep-felt harmony in true
Christian experience; and the harmony cannot be heard
aright by the man whose ear does not detect always sounding
in it this sublimated 'seventh'.

It is significant, and yet again so natural, that the first
petition in the prayer of the Christian fellowship is: 'Hallowed
be Thy name.' What I have already said should make the
meaning of this clear in its connexion with the Biblical meaning of the word. And we can sometimes detect, even in the
teaching of Jesus, notes still vibrating which seem to suggest
a trace of that weird awe and shuddering dread before the
mysteries of the transcendent of which we have already
spoken. Such a passage is Matthew x. 28: 'But fear him
which is able to *destroy both soul and body in hell.*'

The dark and awful ring of this saying cannot be missed, and
it is a rationalization of it merely to refer it to the Judge and
His judgement on the Last Day. The same note rings out again
clearly in the saying in Hebrews x. 31: 'It is a fearful thing
to fall into the hands of the living God'; and in Hebrews xii.
29: 'Our God is a consuming fire.' (Here the adaptation of
Deuteronomy iv. 24: 'The Lord is a consuming fire' into 'Our
God is a consuming fire' gives a contrast whose effect enhances
the horror of the saying.) And when occasion demands it
the Old Testament God of 'vengeance' recurs even in the
teaching of Jesus Himself, unveiled and in His own authentic

character; as, for instance, in Matthew xxi. 41: 'He will miserably destroy those wicked men.'

Finally, it is in the light of, and with the background of, this numinous experience, with its mystery and its awe — its *mysterium tremendum*—that Christ's Agony in the night of Gethsemane must be viewed, if we are to comprehend or realize at all in our own experience what the import of that agony was.   What is the cause of this 'sore amazement' and 'heaviness', this soul shaken to its depths, 'exceeding sorrowful even unto death', and this sweat that falls to the ground like great drops of blood?   Can it be ordinary fear of death in the case of one who had had death before his eyes for weeks past and who had just celebrated with clear intent his death-feast with his disciples?   No, there is more here than the fear of death; there is the awe of the creature before the 'mysterium tremendum', before the shuddering secret of the numen.   And the old tales come back into our mind as strangely parallel and, as it were, prophetically significant, the tales of Yahweh who waylaid Moses by night, and of Jacob who wrestles with God 'until the breaking of the day'.   'He had power with God . . . and prevailed', with the God of 'Wrath' and 'Fury', with the *numen*, which yet is itself '*My Father*'.   In truth even those who cannot recognize 'the Holy One of Israel' elsewhere in the God of the Gospel must at least discover Him here, if they have eyes to see at all.

I have no need to dwell upon the numinous atmosphere pervading the writings of St. Paul.   'God dwelleth in a light that none may come nigh.'   The 'over-aboundingness' of the idea of God and the feeling of God leads with Paul to the special terminology and experiences of Mysticism.[1]   But it is

---

[1] As a provisional definition of Mysticism I would suggest that, while sharing the nature of religion, it shows a preponderance of its non-rational elements and an over-stressing of them in respect to the 'overabounding' aspect of the 'numen'.   A type of religious experience acquires 'mystical colouring' if it shows an inclination to Mysticism.   In this sense Christianity since St. Paul and St John is not Mysticism, but religion with a mystical colouring.   And this is justified.

not confined to these: it can be seen alive through all his utterances in the feelings of exalted enthusiasm and his spiritual terminology of the 'pneuma', which are alike far removed from the merely rational side of Christian piety. His dualistic depreciation of 'the Flesh', as of all that pertains to creaturehood, is that numinous self-disvaluation spoken of on pp. 52 ff. carried to its extreme.   These catastrophes and sudden reversals that befall the religious conscious-ness, the tragedy of sin and guilt, or again the glow of· beatific joy, are only possible and intelligible on the basis of numinous experience.   And just as the ὀργὴ Θεοῦ with St. Paul is more than the mere reaction of righteous retri-bution, just as it is permeated by the 'awefulness' of the numinous, so on the other side is the 'fascination' of the experienced love of God, that bears the spirit beyond its boundaries into the third heaven, more than the mere con-summation of the natural human feeling of a child for its parent.   The ὀργὴ Θεοῦ is potently and vividly present in the grand passage in Romans i. 18 ff., where we recognize directly the jealous, passionate Yahweh of the Old Testament, here grown to a God of the Universe of fearful power, who pours out the blazing vials of His wrath over the whole world. In this passage there is an intuition, genuinely non-rational in char-acter, the sublimity of which has an almost horrible quality: that the commission of sin is the angry God's punishment for sin. St. Paul reiterates this thought — so intolerable, if con-sidered 'rationally'— in three separate verses.   'Wherefore God also gave them up to uncleanness through the lusts of their own hearts, to dishonour their own bodies between themselves ' (Romans i. 24); ' For this cause God gave them up unto vile affections' (i. 26) ; ' God gave them over to a repro-bate mind, . . . being filled with all unrighteousness', &c. (i. 28, 29).

To feel the full weight and force of this intuition it is necessary to escape as far as possible from the mental atmosphere of our dogmatic interpretations and judiciously toned-down catechisms, and to try to recapture the awe that could be felt by the Jew toward the fury of Yahweh, by the

Hellenistic Greek toward the horror of Heimarmenē or Destiny, and by primitive man in general toward the ' ira deorum ' or anger of the gods.

There is one other point in the teaching of Paul that demands notice in this connexion—his doctrine of predestination. It is perhaps precisely the ' rationalist ' who feels most directly that with the idea of predestination we are standing on downright non-rational ground. Nothing remains so alien to the rationalist as this doctrine. And from his point of view he is quite right; from the standpoint of the rational this notion of predestination is a sheer absurdity, an absolute offence. Let him acquiesce in all the paradoxes of the Trinity and Christology, predestination will yet remain perpetually to confront him as a stumbling-block.

Not, as need hardly be said, in the form in which it has been put forward since the time of Schleiermacher, following the tradition of Leibniz and Spinoza. That is simply a capitulation to Natural Law and ' causae secundae ', a surrender to the claim of modern Psychology that all human resolves and actions are subject to the compelling force of motives, so that a man is unfree and predetermined thereby. And so, this predetermination by *nature*, having been identified with the all-embracing efficacy of God, in the end the outcome of the profound and purely religious intuition of divine predetermination—which has no concern at all with ' laws of nature '—is the comparatively trivial ' scientific ' notion of universal causal connexion. There can be no more spurious product of theological speculation, no more fundamental falsification of religious conceptions than this ; and it is certainly not against this that the Rationalist feels an antagonism, for it is itself a piece of solid rationalism, but at the same time a complete abandonment of the real religious idea of ' predestination '.

This false ' scientific ' interpretation of ' predestination ' having been put aside, it may be shown that as a religious idea it springs from two sources and has two quite distinct aspects, which should be distinguished by separate names. The one is ' election ', the other—striking an essentially different note —' predestination ' proper.

The idea of 'election'—i. e. of having been chosen out and pre-ordained by God *unto salvation*—is an immediate and pure expression of the actual religious experience of grace. The recipient of divine grace feels and knows ever more and more surely, as he looks back on his past, that he has not grown into his present self through any achievement or effort of his own, and that, apart from his own will or power, grace was imparted to him, grasped him, impelled, and led him. And even the resolves and decisions that were most his own and most free become to him, without losing the element of freedom, something that he *experienced* rather than *did*. Before every deed of his own he sees love the deliverer in action, seeking and selecting, and acknowledges that an eternal gracious purpose is watching over his life. But this 'providence' is purely a providence unto salvation and has in itself nothing to do with the 'praedestinatio ambigua', the predetermination of all men *either* to be saved *or* to be damned. The rational and logical conclusion of course would be that, if he is elected of God but others are not, God, in appointing the elect to bliss, determines also the rejected for damnation. But this conclusion is not, and must not be, drawn, for what we are concerned with is a religious intuition which, as such, stands alone and is only warrant for itself, and which indeed is outraged by any attempt to weave it into a system or make it yield a series of inferences. In this respect Schleiermacher is quite right when he says in his *Discourses upon Religion*[1]: 'Every (*sc.* religious) intuition is a self-subsistent work . . . knowing nothing of derivation and point of connexion.'

So much for 'election'. From it must be distinguished 'predestination' proper, as it appears in St. Paul, e. g. Romans ix. 18: 'Therefore hath He mercy on whom He will, and whom He will He hardeneth.'

It is true that the thought of 'election', prominent in St. Paul, can be detected here as well. But the reflection in v. 20 is obviously the utterance of quite a different frame of mind: 'Nay, but, O man, who art thou that repliest against

[1] Schleiermacher, *Reden über die Religion*, ed. R. Otto, 4th ed., pp. 37-8.

God ?   Shall the thing formed say to him that formed it, Why
hast thou made me thus ? '   That is a line of thought wholly
out of keeping with the set of ideas centring about 'election'.
And yet even less can it be derived from any abstractly
theoretic 'doctrine' of the all-causing nature of God.   Such
a doctrine we find in Zwingli, and with him it does indeed
give rise to a 'doctrine of predestination', but one that is
rather the artificial product of philosophical speculation than
the result of immediate religious experience.   The true 'predestination', springing directly from religious intuition, has
its origin beyond question in St. Paul.   But in him it is easily
recognized as the numinous feeling in face of the 'mysterium
tremendum'; and that unique phase of it that we met with above
(pp. 9 ff.) in the narrative of Abraham recurs here in a signally
intensified form.   For the religious conception in the notion of
predestination is nothing but that 'creature-consciousness',
that self-abasement and the annulment of personal strength
and claims and achievements in the presence of the transcendent, as such.   The numen, overpoweringly experienced,
becomes the all in all.   The creature, with his being and doing,
his coming and going, his schemes and resolves, becomes
nothing.   The conceptual expression to indicate such a felt
abasement and annihilation over against the numen is then—
here impotence and there omnipotence; here the futility of
one's own choice, there the will that ordains all and determines all.

It is next to be noted that 'predestination' in this sense,
as identical with the absolute supremacy of the numen, has
nothing whatever to do with the 'unfree will' of 'Determinism'.
Rather, it finds very frequently precisely in the ' free will' of
the creature the contrast which makes it stand out so prominently.   'Will what thou wilt and how thou canst; plan
and choose; yet must all come about as it shall and as is
determined': that is the earliest and most genuine expression
of the matter.   In face of the eternal power man is reduced to
nought, *together with* his free choice and action.   And the
eternal power waxes immeasurable just because it fulfils its
decrees *despite* the freedom of human will.   This is the aspect

of the matter designedly thrust into the foreground in many typical Mohammedan narratives which profess to display the inflexibility of the decrees of Allah. In these, men are *able* to devise and decide and reject; but, however they choose or act, Allah's eternal will is accomplished to the very day and hour that was ordained. The purport of this is precisely, *not* that God and God alone is an active cause, but rather that the activity of the creature, be it never so vigorous and free, is overborne and determined absolutely by the eternal operative purpose.[1] The thought of the deity as the absolutely sole and all-embracing active cause first occurs where the creature-feeling is intensified still further, and is at the same time combined with theoretic considerations. It then leads to Mysticism; and it is only again a further consequence if the speculations about Being, peculiar to and characteristic of Mysticism, become then attached to the thought of God as sole cause. To the creature then is denied, not merely *efficacy* as a cause, but true *reality* and complete being, and all existence and fullness of being is ascribed to the absolute entity, who alone really *is*, while all 'being' of creatures is either a function of this absolute Being—which brings them into existence—or mere illusion. This sequence of ideas is found in particularly explicit form in the Mysticism of Geulincx and the Occasionalists. 'Ubi nihil vales, ibi nihil velis.' Sometimes we hear the same mystical chord in St. Paul also, as in his mysterious saying about the final issue of all things, where

---

[1] The story told by Beidhavi, an expositor of the Koran, illustrates this: Once when Asrael, the angel of Death, came before Solomon he directed his gaze upon one of the king's companions. 'Who is that?' asked the man. 'The angel of Death,' replied Solomon. 'He seems to be looking at me,' continued the other, 'so command the wind that it bear me hence and set me down in India.' Solomon did so. Then said the Angel, 'I gazed upon him for so long out of astonishment, seeing it had been commanded me to fetch his soul out of India, while he was yet with thee in Canaan.' This is a predestination which presupposes free will just as its foil. However freely man makes his plans, Allah has always set this countermine.

[This story is told in verse by Leigh Hunt in his poem 'The Inevitable'; cf. Oxford ed. (1922), pp. 95-6. (*Trans.*)]

'God shall be all in all'.   But the passage in Romans is different.   It goes no farther than the thought of predestination
itself; and predestination we have found to be nothing but
the intensified 'creature-feeling' in conceptual expression, and
to be altogether rooted in the numinous consciousness.

A further consideration may make it plainer that this must
be so.   If it be really true that the consciousness of the
numinous, as 'creature-feeling', is the root of the predestination idea, then we should expect that the form of religious
faith marked by an undue and exaggerated insistence on the
non-rational elements in the idea of God would also lean most
markedly to predestination.   And such is obviously the case.
No religion has such a leaning to predestination as Islam; and
the special quality of Islam is just that in it, from its commencement onwards, the rational and specifically moral aspect of the
idea of God was unable to acquire the firm and clear impress
that it won, e. g., in Christianity or Judaism.   In Allah the
numinous is absolutely preponderant over everything else.   So
that, when Islam is criticized for giving a merely 'fortuitous'
character to the claim of morality, as though the moral law
were only valid through the chance caprice of the deity, the
criticism is well justified, only 'chance' and fortuitousness have
nothing to do with the matter.   The explanation is rather that
the numinous in Allah, nay, even his uncanny and daemonic
character, outweighs what is rational in him.   And this will
account for what is commonly called the 'fanatical' character
of this religion.   Strongly excited feeling of the numen, that
runs to frenzy, untempered by the more rational elements of
religious experience—that is everywhere the very essence of
Fanaticism.

The above interpretation of the notion of predestination
gives at the same time our estimate of it.   It is an attempted
statement, in conceptual terms and by *analogy*, of something
that at bottom is incapable of explication by concepts.   Fully
justified in this sense as an analogical expression, it is wholly
unjustified ('summum jus' becoming 'summa injuria') if its
character as analogy is missed, so that it is taken as an adequate
formulation of theological theory.   In that case it is disastrous

and intolerable to a rational religion like Christianity, in spite
of the attempts that are made to render it innocuous by all the
arts of evasion and mitigation.

There is another element in the thought of Paul besides
his notion of predestination that is rooted in the numinous :
I refer to his utter depreciation of 'the Flesh'. 'The Flesh'
with Paul is simply the condition of the creature in general.
And this is utterly disparaged and depreciated by the numinous
consciousness (as we saw on pp. 9 ff., 52 ff.) in contrast to the
transcendent, both in regard to its existence and its value ; in
respect to the first as 'Dust and ashes', 'nothingness', insufficient, weak, transient, and perishing, and in respect to the
second as the 'profane', the impure, which is unable to assume
the worth of holiness or to come into its presence. We find
these two same sorts of depreciation among the ideas of Paul,
and the specifically Pauline feature in them is only the vigour
and completeness with which he expresses them. It is a quite
separate question whence Paul derives this intensity in his
denunciation and depreciation of 'the Flesh', whether it is
original to him or stimulated by the 'dualistic' environment
of thought in which he moved. As has been already said, one
can determine nothing about the essential nature or the value
of a thing by tracing its genesis and continuous historic
derivation from other sources. And at least we may maintain that Paul might well be stimulated to this emphatic
expression by many genuine cases of the numinous experience
recorded in the Old Testament. There too Bāsār, the flesh,
is both the principle of being 'dust and ashes' and the
principle of the 'pollution' of the creature in the presence of
holiness.

In St. John, no less than in St. Paul, there is a strong strain
of the numinous. The element of 'awefulness', it is true, dies
away in him, as so commonly in mysticism, without ever
quite vanishing, for, pace Ritschl, even in John 'the wrath of
God abideth' (John iii. 36) ; but this only makes the elements
of 'mystery' and 'fascination' the stronger, even in their
mystical form. In John, Christianity absorbs φῶς and ζωή,
'light' and 'life', into itself from the religions at rivalry with

it;[1] and justly so, for only in Christianity do they win home. But what is this 'light' and this 'life'? Not to *feel* what they are is to be made of wood, but none can express it. They are a sheer abounding overplus of the non-rational element in religion.

And the same is true even of that saying of St. John to which the 'Rationalists' are so specially fond of referring : 'God is a Spirit' (John iv. 24). This was the text on account of which Hegel held Christianity to be the highest because the most truly spiritual (*geistig*) religion. But Hegel meant by 'spirit' the 'absolute reason'. St. John when he speaks of πνεῦμα is not thinking of 'absolute reason' but of that which is in absolute contrast to everything of 'the world' and 'the flesh', the utterly mysterious and miraculous heavenly Being who surpasses all the understanding and reason of the 'natural' man. He is thinking of that 'Spirit' which 'bloweth where it listeth, and thou hearest the sound thereof, but canst not tell whence it cometh and whither it goeth'—the Spirit which just on that account is not confined to Zion or Gerizim, and whose worship is only for those who are themselves 'in spirit and in truth'. So that this saying, apparently wholly 'rational' in import, is itself the strongest and clearest indication of the non-rational element in the Biblical idea of God.

---

[1] And thereby drains these religions of their life-blood, according to 'the right of the stronger'. And henceforth these elements belong to Christianity indissolubly as its very own. For

> Wenn starke Geisteskraft
> Die Elemente
> An sich hereingerafft :
> Kein Engel trennte
> Geeinte Zwienatur
> Der innigen Beiden—

and still less can the criticism of scholars! ['When the vigour of the spirit has gathered the elements into itself, then may no angel sunder the double nature now made single of the united twain.']

CHAPTER XII

THE NUMINOUS IN LUTHER

IN Catholicism the feeling of the numinous is to be found as a living factor of singular power. It is seen in Catholic forms of worship and sacramental symbolism, in the less authentic forms assumed by legend and miracle, in the paradoxes and mysteries of Catholic dogma, in the Platonic and neo-Platonic strands woven into the fabric of its religious conceptions, in the solemnity of churches and ceremonies, and especially in the intimate *rapport* of Catholic piety with Mysticism. For reasons already suggested, the mysterious is much less in evidence in the official systems of doctrine, whether Catholic or Protestant. Particularly since the time when the great mediaeval scholastics (the 'theologi moderni', so called) replaced Plato by Aristotle and welded the latter and his method on to the doctrines of the Church, Catholic orthodoxy has been subjected to a strong rationalizing influence, to which, however, actual living religious practice and feeling never conformed or corresponded. The battle here joined between so-called 'Platonism' and 'Aristotelianism', and in general the long persistent protest against the scholastics, is itself in large part nothing but the struggle between the rational and the non-rational elements in the Christian religion. And the same antithesis is clearly operative as a factor in Luther's protest against Aristotle and the 'theologi moderni'.

At that time Plato himself was known (very imperfectly) chiefly through the interpretations — and misinterpretations — of him by Augustine, Plotinus, and Dionysius the Areopagite. Yet it was a true feeling that led the contrasted attitudes of

H

mind to choose the names of Plato and Aristotle as their battle-cries. Plato did indeed make a powerful contribution towards the rationalization of his religion, for according to his *philosophy* the deity had to become identical with the ' Idea of the Good ', and consequently something wholly rational and conceivable. But the most remarkable characteristic of Plato's thought is just that he himself finds science and philosophy too narrow to comprise the whole of man's mental life. He has indeed properly no Philosophy of Religion; he grasps the object of religion by quite different means than those of conceptual thinking, viz. by the ' ideograms ' of myth, by ' enthusiasm ' or inspiration, ' eros ' or love, ' mania ' or the divine frenzy. He abandons the attempt to bring the object of religion into one system of knowledge with the objects of ' science ' (ἐπιστήμη), i.e. reason, and it becomes something not less but greater thereby; while at the same time it is just this that allows the sheer non-rational aspect of it to be so vividly felt in Plato, and indeed vividly expressed as well as felt. No one has enunciated more definitively than this master-thinker that God transcends all reason, in the sense that He is beyond the powers of our conceiving, not merely beyond our powers of comprehension.

' Therefore is it an *impossible* task both to discover the Creator and Father of this Whole Universe and to publish the discovery of him in words for all to understand.'[1]

Aristotle's thought is much more theological than Plato's, but his temper is far less religious; and at the same time his theology is absolutely rationalistic. And this contrast between the two is repeated among those who profess themselves ' Platonists ' or ' Aristotelians '.

---

[1] *Timaeus*, 28 c τὸν μὲν οὖν ποιητὴν καὶ πατέρα τοῦδε τοῦ παντὸς εὑρεῖν τε ἔργον καὶ εὑρόντα εἰς πάντας ἀδύνατον λέγειν. For the non-rational and supra-rational strain in Plato the reader is referred to von Wilamowitz-Möllendorff, *Plato*, i. 418: and especially to the splendid passage from Plato's seventh letter: 341 c: ' Concerning these things (*sc.* ultimate truth) there is not, nor will there be, any treatise written by me. For they do not at all admit of being expounded in writing, as do objects of other (scientific) studies. . . . Only after long, arduous conversance with the matter itself... a light suddenly breaks upon the soul as from a kindled

Another influence which orthodox doctrine underwent, from the earliest patristic period onwards, and which tended to weaken the non-rational element in religion, came from the acceptance of the ancient theory of the divine ἀπάθεια or immunity from passion. The God of Greek, and especially of Stoic, theology was constructed after the ideal of the 'Wise man', who achieves this 'apathy' by the overcoming of his 'passions' and 'affections'; and the attempt was now made to assimilate this God to the 'living God' of Scripture. And, as intimated above, an effective if unconscious factor in this contest was the antithesis between the non-rational and the rational aspects of the deity. Lactantius, in his treatise *De Ira Dei*, illustrates particularly strikingly this fight against the God of the philosophers. He uses the same wholly rational terms, taken from man's emotional life, as do his opponents, but raises them to a higher power, so that he makes God, as it were, a gigantic mind, quick with an immense vitality. But whoever in this way contends for the 'living God' is at the same time contending unwittingly for the divine in God, that which cannot be reduced to Idea, world-order, moral order, principle of Being, or purposive will. And many of Lactantius's own expressions point of themselves to something beyond. Thus, quoting Plato, he says: 'Quid omnino sit Deus, non esse quaerendum: quia nec inveniri possit nec enarrari.'[1] He is in general fond of emphasizing the 'incomprehensibilitas' of God: 'Quem nec aestimare sensu valeat humana mens nec eloqui lingua mortalis. Sublimior enim ac maior est, quam ut possit aut cogitatione hominis aut sermone comprehendi.'[2] He is fond of the expression 'maiestas Dei', and blames the philosophers for

flame, and once born keeps alive of itself. . . . Only to a few men is the exposition of these things of any profit, and they only need a slight indication of them for their discovery.'

[1] Ed. Fritsche, p. 227: 'We ought not to ask what God is altogether; for it can neither be discovered by any nor stated in words.'

[2] Ibid., p. 116: '(God) whom the human mind has no power to appraise, nor tongue of mortals to utter. For he is too sublime and too great to be grasped in the thought or the speech of man.'

misjudging the 'unique majesty' of God. And he feels the
'tremendum' in the 'maiestas' when he asserts that God
'is wroth', and demands 'awe' as a fundamental characteristic
of religion when he says: 'Ita fit, ut religio et maiestas
et honor *metu* constet. Metus autem non est, ubi nullus
irascitur.'[1] He says that a God who cannot be angry cannot
love either: and a God that knows neither love nor anger
would be 'immobilis' and not the 'Deus *vivus*', the *living*
God of Scripture.

This ancient battle of Lactantius against the 'deus philo-
sophorum' comes to life again in the Middle Ages in Duns
Scotus's battle for the God of 'Willing', as opposed to the God
of 'Being', and for the validity of volition as an essential
in religion, as opposed to 'cognition'. And the non-rational
elements which are still latent in Duns Scotus break out
openly in Luther in a whole series of some of his most
characteristic thoughts.

This aspect of Luther's religion was later tacitly expunged,
and is to-day readily dismissed as 'not the authentic Luther',
or as 'a residuum of the scholastic speculations of the nomi-
nalists'. But, if that is so, it is strange that this 'residuum
of Scholasticism' exercised such a power in Luther's own
mental life as it palpably did. In point of fact this is not
a 'residuum' at all, but beyond all question the mysterious
background of his religious life, obscure and 'uncanny', and
to estimate it in all its power and profundity we need to
abstract the lucid bliss and joyfulness of Luther's faith in the
divine grace, and to see this faith in relation to the background of that mysterious experience on which it rests. It
matters not from what source, whether 'nominalism' or the
traditional teaching of his Order, his consciousness was first
stirred; we have in any case in Luther the numinous consciousness at first hand, stirred and agitated through its
typical 'moments', as we have come to know them. It is
a corroboration that these 'moments' appear in Luther in

[1] ' Thus it comes that religion and majesty and honour depend upon
fear. But there is no fear where none is angry.'

their completed series, and so point back to the common basis that unites them all.

(1) We are not here concerned with the many strands, strong at the outset, weaker later, but never altogether disappearing, that connect him with Mysticism. Nor are we concerned with the surviving effects of the 'numinous' element of the Catholic worship in his doctrine of the Eucharist, which cannot be wholly derived either from his doctrine of the forgiveness of sins or from his deference to the written word of scripture. Let us rather consider Luther's 'mirae speculationes' upon the 'unrevealed' in God in contrast to the 'facies Dei revelata' (revealed face of God), upon the 'divina maiestas' and the 'omnipotentia Dei' in contrast to his 'gratia', as he treats of them in his work *De Servo Arbitrio*. The investigation as to how far Luther took over 'doctrines' from Scotus does not amount to much; they stand in most intimate connexion with his own innermost religious life, of which they are a genuine first-hand utterance, and should be examined as such. Luther himself guarantees expressly that he does not teach such things merely as subjects of dispute in the schools or as philosophical deductions and corollaries, but because they are a central part of the religious experience of the Christian, who must know them in order to have faith and to have life. He rejects the cautious foresight of Erasmus's view, that such things should at least be withheld from the common people, preaching them himself in public sermons (e.g. upon Exodus, in reference to the hardening of Pharaoh's heart) and writing them in his letter to the men of Antwerp. And again, just before his death, speaking of his book *De Servo Arbitrio*, in which these ideas stand clearly expressed, Luther acknowledges that nothing he wrote was so truly his own.

Is this borne out in his general teaching? His words in the *Great Catechism*, 'To have a God is nothing else than to trust Him from the heart', might seem to imply the negative. And certainly to Luther God is He who 'overbrims with pure goodness'. Yet this same Luther knows depths and abysses in the Godhead that make his heart despond, from which he flees for refuge to the 'Word', like a 'hare to his cleft in the rocks', flees, it may be, to the Sacrament or to absolution, or to the comforting official pronouncements of Dr. Pommeranus, but in general no less to every word of comfort or promise in the Psalms and the Prophets. But that before which his soul quails again and again in awe is not merely the stern Judge, demanding righteousness—for He is wholly a 'God of revelation'—but rather at the same time God in His 'unrevealedness', in the aweful majesty of His very Godhead; He before whom trembles not simply the transgressor of the law, but the creature, as such, in his 'uncovered' creaturehood. Luther even ventures to designate this awe-inspiring, non-rational character of deity as 'Deus ipse, ut est in sua natura et maiestate'[1] (an assumption which would be in fact a dangerous and erroneous one; for no distinction of the non-rational and the rational aspects of God should imply that the latter is less essential than the former).

The passages relevant in this connexion from Luther's *De Servo Arbitrio* are cited often enough: but to understand the wellnigh daemonic character of this numinous feeling the reader should particularly note the effect of the following passage from Luther's sermon on Exodus xx. The preacher leaves no means untried to bring out effectively the element of numinous horror in his text:

'Yea, for the world it seemeth as though God were a mere silly yawner, with mouth ever agape, or a cuckold, who lets another lie with his wife and feigneth that he sees it not.'

But 'He assaileth a man, and *hath such a delight* therein that He is of His Jealousy and Wrath impelled to *consume* the wicked'.

'Then shall we learn how that God is a consuming fire, . . .' 'That is then the consuming, devouring fire.' 'Wilt thou sin? Then will He *devour thee up*.' 'For God is a fire, that consumeth, devoureth, rageth; verily He is your undoing, as fire consumeth a house and maketh it dust and ashes.'

---

[1] 'God Himself, as He is in his own very nature and majesty.'

And in another place :

'Yea, He is more terrible and frightful than the Devil. For He dealeth with us and bringeth us to ruin with power, smiteth and hammereth us and payeth no heed to us.' 'In His majesty He is a consuming fire.' 'For therefrom can no man refrain: if he thinketh on God aright, his heart in his body is struck with terror . . . Yea, as soon as he heareth God named, he is filled with trepidation and fear.'[1]

It is the absolute 'numen', felt here partially in its aspect of 'maiestas' and 'tremendum'. And the reason I introduced these terms above to denote the one side of the numinous experience was in fact just because I recalled Luther's own expressions, and borrowed them from his 'divina maiestas' and 'metuenda voluntas', which have rung in my ears from the time of my earliest study of Luther. Indeed I grew to understand the numinous and its difference from the rational in Luther's *De Servo Arbitrio* long before I identified it in the 'qādosh' of the Old Testament and in the elements of 'religious awe' in the history of religion in general.

One must have beheld these gulfs and abysses in Luther to understand aright how significant it is that it is the same man who on the other hand endeavours to put the whole of Christianity into a confiding faith. The same contrast noted above in the religion of the Gospel and in the paradoxes of the 'faith in God the Father' recurs in the religious experience of Luther, but in unexampled intensity. That it is the *unapproachable* which becomes approachable, the *Holy One* who is pure goodness, that it is '*Majesty*' which makes itself familiar and intimate—there is the inwardness of the matter, and this finds only very dubious expression in the subsequent one-sided doctrine of the schools, where the mystical character of the 'Wrath',—which is of the essence of 'holiness' infused with that of 'goodness',—is referred simply to the righteousness of God, and taken thus as righteous anger or indignation.

---

[1] *Vide* the Erlangen edition of Luther's works, xxxvi, pp. 210 ff., 222, 231, 237 ; xxxv, p. 167 ; xlvii, p. 145 ; l, p. 200.

(2) Once the numinous consciousness has been aroused, it
is to be expected, seeing that it is a unity, that one of its
moments will be found to be bound up with the rest. In
the case of Luther we find next after this element of ' Wrath '
the numinous manifesting itself in the set of ideas which we
may fairly call those of Job. The Book of Job, as was seen
above, is not so much concerned with the *awefulness* of the
majesty of the numen as with its *mysteriousness*; it is concerned with the non-rational in the sense of the irrational,
with sheer paradox baffling comprehension, with that which
challenges the 'reasonable' and what might be reasonably
expected, which goes directly against the grain of reason.
To this place belong Luther's violent onslaughts upon the
' whore Reason', which must seem grotesque to any one who
has not rightly grasped the problem of the non-rational
element in the idea of God. But certain set phrases, constantly recurring in Luther and very typical of him, are
specially significant in this connexion, as showing the strong
feeling he had for the non-rational aspect of the divine nature
in general. The most interesting passages are not those in
which he gives this feeling currency in the small change of
popular edification, that soothes itself with the thought that
God's ways are too high for us men ; but those in which he
lays hold of some startling paradox. He can indeed tell in
quite a homely and popular way ' how strange a lord our God
is ', and refer this to the fact that God does not esteem or
count as the world counts, and that He disciplines us by
the strange ways of His guidance. Such expressions are of
general currency ; but others—and these the more characteristic—strike a loftier note. God is altogether ' mysteriis suis
et iudiciis impervestigabilis ' ('beyond tracking out in His
mysteries and His judgements'), displays—as in Job—His
' vera maiestas ' ' in metuendis mirabilibus et iudiciis suis incom-
prehensibilibus ' (' in His fearful marvels and incomprehensible
judgements'), is in His essence hidden away from all reason,
knows no measure, law, or aim, and is verified in the paradox :
' ut ergo fidei locus sit, opus est, ut omnia, quae creduntur,
abscondantur ' (' in order, therefore, that there may be a place

for faith, all the things that are believed must be hidden away'). And his concern is not simply to note this as an inconceivable paradox, to acknowledge it and bow before it, but to recognize that such a paradox is essential to the nature of God and even its distinguishing characteristic.

'Si enim talis esset eius iustitia, quae humano captu posset iudicari esse iusta, *plane non esset divina* et nihilo differret ab humana iustitia. At cum sit Deus verus et unus, deinde totus incomprehensibilis et inaccessibilis humana ratione, par est, immo necessarium est, ut et iustitia sua sit incomprehensibilis.'[1]

Theology gives expression to its perplexed endeavour to find a name for the elements of the non-rational and the mysterious in the repulsive doctrine that God is 'exlex' (outside the law), that good is good because God wills it, instead of that God wills it because it is good, a doctrine that results in attributing to God an absolutely fortuitous will, which would in fact turn Him into a 'capricious despot'. These doctrines are specially prominent in the theology of Islam, and this can be immediately understood if the two positions we maintain are sound, viz. that such doctrines are really perplexed expressions of the non-rational, numinous side of the divine nature, and that this is altogether the preponderant aspect in Islam. And we find them also in Luther in the same connexion. In this very fact, however, lies the excuse for doctrines in themselves so blasphemous and horrible: they are caricatures prompted by a deficient psychology and a mistaken choice of expressions, and not by any disregard of the absoluteness of moral values.

(3) From the point of view already considered in detail it will be seen that, with such feelings as a basis, it was inevitable that the doctrine of predestination would in due course make its appearance in Luther's religion. And in his

---

[1] 'For were His justice such as could be adjudged as just by the human understanding it were manifestly not divine, and would differ in nothing from human justice. But since God is true and single, yea in His entirety incomprehensible and inaccessible to human reason, it is right, nay it follows necessarily, that His justice also is incomprehensible.'

case we do not need, as we did in the case of Paul, to *postulate* the close inner connexion between this doctrine and the numinous temper, for in the *De Servo Arbitrio* it is palpably evident. The one explicitly depends upon the other, and the inward bond of union between the two is so unmistakable that this treatise of Luther's becomes a sort of psychological key to related phases of religious experience.

It is only occasionally that these purely numinous elements in Luther's religious consciousness are displayed so strongly and forcibly as in the treatise *De Servo Arbitrio*. But in his battles with 'desperatio' and with Satan, in his constantly recurring religious catastrophes and fits of melancholy, in his wrestlings for grace, perpetually renewed, which bring him to the verge of mental disorder, in all these there are more than merely rational elements at work in his soul. Moreover, even when he is speaking solely in rational terms of Judgement, Punishment, and the Wrath of God, we must, if we are to recapture the real Luther in these expressions, hear sounding in them the profoundly non-rational strain of 'religious awe'. For this Wrath of God also has often, perhaps has always, something in it of that Fury of Yahweh, that ὀργή of the numen.

(4) This circumstance suggests a further point. The expressions 'unrevealed God' and 'tremenda maiestas' manifestly repeated only those 'moments' of the numinous which we found first in our analysis of it (p. 13), especially the 'tremendum', the *daunting* aspect of the numinous. What of that of 'fascination' in Luther? Is it missing altogether, to be replaced merely by the rational attributes of trustworthiness and love and the corresponding element in the mind of the worshipper, viz. faith and trustfulness? No, beyond all question it is not. Only, the element of fascination is in Luther wholly interwoven with these rational elements and comes to utterance with them and in them. This can be felt forcibly in the boisterous, almost Dionysiac, blissfulness of his experience of God.

'Christians are a blissful people, who can rejoice at heart

and sing praises, stamp and dance and leap for joy. That is well pleasing to God and doth our heart good, when we trust in God and find in Him our pride and our joyfulness. Such a gift should only kindle a fire and a light in our heart, so that we should never cease dancing and leaping for joy.

Who will extol this enough or utter it forth? It is neither to be expressed nor conceived.

If thou feelest it truly in the heart, it will be such a great thing to thee that thou wilt rather be silent than speak aught of it.' [1]

Here should be borne in mind what was remarked earlier (p. 48) respecting the interweaving of the non-rational with the rational and the consequently deepened import of rational expressions. As the awe-inspiring character of the Transcendent is comprised in the God of sternness and punishment and justice, so is its bliss-giving character included in the God who 'overbrims with pure goodness'. Indeed it is involved in the 'overabounding' and mystical tone of Luther's actual creed. Here, as elsewhere, there is no mistaking his connexion with Mysticism.[2] Though for Luther faith begins more and more to take the place of 'knowledge' and 'Love of God' (Gottes-Minne)—which means a marked qualitative alteration of the whole religious temper, as compared with that of Mysticism—yet, despite the change, it remains obvious that there are definite features in 'Faith', as the term is used by Luther, which justify us in classing it with the mystical ways of response to which it is in apparent contrast, and clearly distinguish it from the 'fides' taught by the Lutheran school with its determinate, well-ordered, unmystical temper. 'Faith' for Luther plays the same essential part, mutatis mutandis, as 'knowledge' and 'love' for the earlier mystics: it is the unique power of the soul, the 'adhaesio Dei', which unites man with God: and 'unity' is the very signature of the mystical. So that when Luther says that Faith makes man 'one cake' (ein Kuche) with God, or holds him 'as a ring holds a jewel' (sicut annulus gemmam), he is not speaking any more figuratively than when Tauler says the same of Love. 'Faith' for Luther, as 'Love' for Tauler and the

_____
[1] Erlangen ed., xi. 194,   [2] See Appendix VI.

mystics generally, is a something that cannot be exhaustively
comprised in rational concepts, and to designate which 'figures'
and 'images' are a necessity. To him 'Faith' is the centre of
the Soul—the *fundus animae* or 'basis of the soul' of the
mystics—in which the union of man with God fulfils itself.
It is at the same time an independent faculty of knowledge,
a mystical *a priori* element in the spirit of man, by which
he receives and recognizes supra-sensible truth, and in this
respect identical with the 'Holy Spirit in the heart' (*Spiritus
Sanctus in corde*). 'Faith' is further the 'mighty creative
thing' in us and the strongest of *affects*, most closely akin to the
Greek 'enthusiasm' (ἐνθουσιάζεσθαι). It even takes over all
the functions which all 'enthusiasts' from Paul onwards have
ascribed to 'the Spirit'; for it is 'faith' that 'transforms us
inwardly and brings us forth anew'. In this regard, different
as it is in its inner attitude, 'Faith' is very similar to the
'amor mysticus'. And in the bliss of the 'assurance of
salvation' (*certitudo salutis*) that it arouses, and the intensity
of Luther's 'childlike faith', we have in a subdued form
a recurrence of the 'childhood' feelings of Paul, which go
beyond mere comfort of the soul, appeasement of conscience,
or feeling of protectedness. All subsequent mystics from
Johann Arndt to Spener and Arnold[1] have always felt
these aspects of Luther's inner life to be congenial and akin
to their own, and have carefully collected the relevant passages
from his writings as a defence against the attacks of the
rationalized doctrine of the Lutheran school.

For in opposition to the 'rationalizations' of the schools
the non-rational elements are maintained and fostered in the
western Mysticism that came to its later flower both on
Catholic and Protestant soil. In this, as in Christian Mysticism as a whole from its first stirrings, the elements of
the non-rational already detailed are easily recognizable,
most prominently of all those of 'mystery', 'fascination',
and 'majesty'. The element of 'awe', on the other hand,

---

[1] [Johann Arndt, 1555–1621; Gottfried Arnold, 1666–1697; Philipp
Jacob Spener, 1635–1705: the last-named was one of the founders of
'Pietism' in Germany. (*Trans.*)]

recedes and is subdued; there has never been in the West a Mysticism of Horror, such as we find in certain kinds of Indian Mysticism, both Buddhist and Hindu—in Bhagavad-Ghita, ch. 11 [1]—in some forms of the Shiva and Durgā worship, and in the horrible form of Tantrism. Yet, though the *tremendum* element in Christian mysticism is subdued, it is not entirely lacking. It remains a living factor in the *Caligo* and the *altum Silentium*, in the 'Abyss', the 'Night', the 'Deserts' of the divine nature, into which the soul must descend, in the 'agony', 'abandonment', 'barrenness', *taedium*, in which it must tarry, in the shuddering and shrinking from the loss and deprivation of self-hood and the 'annihilation' of personal identity. Thus Suso writes:

'In this inconceivable mountain of the supra-divine Where (the 'height of the divine Majesty transcending substance') there is a precipitousness of which all pure spirits are sensible. Here the Soul enters a secret namelessness, a marvellous alienation. It is the bottomless abyss no creature can sound— ... the spirit perishes there, to become all-living in the wonders of the Godhead.' [2]

And he can pray:

'Ah, woe is me, Thy wrathful countenance is so full of fury. Thy turning away in anger is so unendurable. Woe is me! And the words of Thy enmity are so fiery, they cleave through heart and soul.' [3]

This note is familiar also to the later mystics. Thus St. John of the Cross says:

'As this clear sight of the divine comes like a violent assault upon the soul to subdue it, the soul feels such anguish in its weakness that all power and breath leave it together, while sense and spirit as though they stood burdened beneath a dark unmeasured load suffer such agony and are oppressed by such deadly fear that the soul would choose death as a mitigation and refreshment.' [4]

And again:

'The fourth kind of anguish is brought into being in the soul ... from the Majesty and Glory of God.' [5]

---

[1] See Appendix II.
[2] Suso, German writings, ed. Denifle, pp. 289 ff.   [3] Ibid., p. 353.
[4] St. John of the Cross, *The Ascent of Mount Carmel.*   [5] Ibid.

Once more:

'Therefore He destroys, crushes and overwhelms (the soul) in such a deep darkness, that it feels as though melted and in its misery destroyed by a cruel death of the spirit. Even as though it were to feel it had been swallowed by some savage beast and buried in the darkness of his belly.' [1]

But in our Western Mysticism the writer in whom the non-rationally 'dreadful' and even the 'daemonic' phase of the numinous remains a most living element is Jakob Böhme. For all his adoption of its motives, Böhme is in his speculation and 'theosophy' sharply distinguished from the earlier Mysticism. He is at one with this (as represented, for instance, by Eckhart) in aiming at a 'construction' and an understanding of God, and from Him of the world: and, like Eckhart, he finds as a starting point for his speculation the 'primal bottom', the supra-comprehensible and inexpressible. But this stands to him, not for Being and Above-being, but for Stress and Will; it is not good and above-good, but a supra-rational identification of good and evil in an Indifferent, in which is to be found the potentiality for evil as well as for good, and therewith the possibility of the dual nature of deity itself as at once goodness and love on the one hand and fury and wrath on the other.[2] If the

---

[1] St. John of the Cross, *The Ascent of Mount Carmel.*

[2] The 'ferocity' is the origin of Lucifer, in whom the mere potentiality of evil is actualized. It might be said that Lucifer is 'fury', the ὀργή, hypostatized, the 'mysterium tremendum' cut loose from the other elements and intensified to *mysterium horrendum.* The roots at least of this may be found in the Bible and the early Church. The ideas of propitiation and ransom are not without reference to Satan as well as to the divine Wrath. The rationalism of the myth of the 'fallen angel' does not render satisfactorily the horror of Satan and of the 'depths of Satan' (Rev. ii. 24) and the 'mystery of iniquity' (2 Thess. ii. 7). It is a horror that is in some sort numinous, and we might designate the object of it as the negatively numinous. This also holds good of other religions than that of the Bible. In all religions 'the devilish' plays its part and has its place as that which, opposed to the divine, has yet something in common with it. As such it should be the subject of a special inquiry, which must be an analysis of fundamental feelings, and something very different from a mere record of the 'evolution of the idea of the devil'.

inventions and comparisons, with whose aid Böhme com-
poses a sort of chemico-physical romance of God, strike us
as extremely queer and bizarre, the strange intuitions of the
religious feeling underlying them are yet highly significant.
They are intuitions of the numinous, and are akin to those
of Luther. With Böhme, as with Luther, the non-rational
energy and majesty of God and his 'awefulness' appear con-
ceptualized and symbolized as 'Will'. And with Böhme, as
with Luther, this is conceived as fundamentally independent
of *moral* elevation or righteousness, and as indifferent toward
good or evil action. It is rather a 'ferocity', a 'fiery wrath'
about something unknown; or, better still, not about anything
at all, but Wrath on its own account and without reference
to any object; an aspect of character which would be quite
meaningless if taken literally in the sense of a real conceivable and apprehensible anger. Who is not directly conscious that it is simply the non-rational element of 'awefulness',
the *tremendum*, for which 'Wrath', 'Fire', 'Fury', are excellent
ideograms?[1] If such an ideogram is taken as an adequate
concept, the result is anthropomorphism, such as mythology
illustrates, and the writings of Lactantius (v. p. 99). And if
speculation follows, based upon such concepts, the result is
the pseudo-science of theosophy. For the characteristic mark
of all theosophy is just this: having confounded analogical
and figurative ways of expressing feeling with rational concepts, it then systematizes them, and out of them spins, like
a monstrous web, a 'Science of God', which is and remains
something monstrous, whether it employs the doctrinal terms
of scholasticism, as Eckhart did, or the alchemical substances
and mixtures of Paracelsus, as Böhme did, or the categories of an animistic logic, as Hegel did, or the elaborate

---

[1] Böhme's disciple, Johann Pordage, has some feeling of this when
he writes:—' So hope I then, that you will not be angered with me, if
you find that I impute to God acerbity and bitterness, dread, wrath,
fire, . . . and the like.   For even Jakob Böhme found no other words in
which to express his exalted *sensation* (*Empfindung*) of God. You must
then take all those forms of speech in a high divine sense, far removed
from all imperfection' (*Divine and True Metaphysic*, i. 166).

diction of Indian religion, as Mrs. Besant does.[1] For the
history of religion it is not on account of his theosophy
that Böhme is interesting, but because in him behind the
theosophy the consciousness of the numinous was astir and
alive as an element of genuine value: so that herein Böhme
was an heir of Luther, preserving what in Luther's own school
came to be overlooked and disregarded.

For the Lutheran school has itself not done justice to the
numinous side of the Christian idea of God. By the exclusively
moral interpretation it gave to the terms, it distorted the
meaning of ' holiness ' and the ' wrath of God ', and already
from the time of Johann Gerhardt and onwards Lutheranism
was returning to the doctrine of divine ἀπάθεια or passion-
lessness. More and more it deprived the forms of worship
of the genuinely contemplative and specifically ' devotional '
elements in them. The conceptual and doctrinal—the ideal
of orthodoxy—began to preponderate over the inexpressible,
whose only life is in the conscious mental attitude of the
devout soul. The Church became a school, and her communi-
cations, in truth, found a more and more contracted access to
the mind, as Tyrrell has put it somewhere, ' through the
narrow clefts (?) of the understanding '.

Schleiermacher was the first to attempt to overcome this
rationalism, most boldly and uncompromisingly in the rhapsody
of his *Discourses*, with less heat and more subdued tone in
his *Glaubenslehre* and his theory of the ' feeling of absolute
dependence ', which in point of fact give a representation—as
has been pointed out already—of the first stirring of the
feeling of the numinous. It will be a task for contemporary
Christian teaching to follow in his traces and again to deepen
the rational meaning of the Christian conception of God by
permeating it with its non-rational elements.

[1] The ' fluid concepts ' of Bergson are also properly ideograms of
aesthetic and religious feelings and intuitions. In so far as he confounds
them with scientific conceptions, in his case too we have the same mixing
up of ' idea ' and ' experience ' for which Schiller found fault with Goethe.
Cf. my *Goethe und Darwin*, Göttingen, 1906.

CHAPTER XIII

THE TWO PROCESSES OF DEVELOPMENT

THIS permeation of the rational with the non-rational is to lead, then, to the 'deepening' of our rational conception of God; it must not be the means of blurring or diminishing it. For if (as suggested at the close of the last chapter) the disregard of the numinous elements tends to impoverish religion, it is no less true that 'holiness', 'sanctity', as Christianity intends the words, cannot dispense with the rational, and especially the clear ethical elements of meaning which Protestantism more particularly emphasizes in the idea of God. To get the full meaning of the word 'holy' as we find it used in the New Testament (and religious usage has established it in the New Testament sense to the exclusion of others), we must no longer understand by 'the holy' or 'sacred' the merely numinous in general, nor even the numinous at its own highest development; we must always understand by it the numinous completely permeated and saturated with elements signifying rationality, purpose, personality, morality. It is in this combined meaning that we retain and apply the term 'holy' in our subsequent chapters. But that the course of the historical development may be clearly understood, we venture first to recapitulate our view upon this matter as explicitly as possible.

That which the primitive religious consciousness first apprehends in the form of 'daemonic dread', and which, as it further unfolds, becomes more elevated and ennobled, is in origin not something rational or moral, but something distinct, non-rational, an object to which the mind responds in a unique way with the special feeling-reflexes that have been described. And this element or 'moment' passes in itself through a process of development of its own, quite apart

I

from the other process—which begins at an early stage—
by which it is ' rationalized ' and ' moralized ', i. e. filled with
rational and ethical meaning.   Taking this non-rational process of development first, we have seen how the ' daemonic
dread ', after itself passing through various gradations, rises to
the level of ' fear of the gods ', and thence to ' fear of God '.
The δαιμόνιον or daemonic power becomes the θεῖον or divine
power : ' dread ' becomes worship ; out of a confusion of inchoate
emotions and bewildered palpitations of feeling grows ' religio ',
and out of ' shudder ' a holy awe.   The feelings of dependence
upon and beatitude in the numen, from being relative, become
absolute.   The false analogies and fortuitous associations are
gradually dispelled or frankly rejected.   The numen becomes
God and Deity.   It is then to God and Deity, as ' numen '
rendered absolute, that the attribute denoted by the terms
qādôsh, sanctus, ἅγιος, holy, pertains, in the first and directest
sense of the words.   It is the culmination of a development
which works itself out purely in the sphere of the non-
rational.   This development constitutes the first central fact of
religious study, and it is the task of religious history and
psychology to trace its course.

Next, secondary and subsidiary to this, is the task of tracing
the course of the process of rationalization and moralization
on the basis of the numinous consciousness.   It nearly, if not
quite, synchronizes and keeps pace with the stages of the
purely numinous development, and, like that, it can be traced
in its different gradations in the most widely different regions
of religious history.   Almost everywhere we find the numinous
attracting and appropriating meanings derived from social
and individual ideals of obligation, justice, and goodness.
These become the ' will ' of the numen, and the numen their
guardian, ordainer, and author.   More and more these ideas
come to enter into the very essence of the numen and charge the
term with ethical content.   ' Holy ' becomes ' good ', and ' good '
from that very fact in turn becomes ' holy ', ' sacrosanct ' ; until
there results a thenceforth indissoluble synthesis of the two
elements, and the final outcome is thus the fuller, more complex sense of ' holy ', in which it is at once *good and sacrosanct*.

The greatest distinction of the religion of ancient Israel, at least from Amos onwards, is precisely the intimate coalescence of both elements. No God is like the God of Israel : for He is the absolutely Holy One (= perfectly good). And, on the other hand, no law is like Yahweh's Law, for it is not merely good, but also at the same time 'holy' (= sacrosanct).

And this process of rationalization and moralization of the numinous, as it grows ever more clear and more potent, is in fact the most essential part of what we call 'Sacred History' and prize as the ever-growing self-revelation of the divine. But at the same time it should be clear to us that this process of the 'moralization of the idea of God', often enough represented to us as a principal problem, setting the main line for inquiry into the history of religion, is in no wise a suppression of the numinous or its supersession by something else—which would result not in a God, but a God substitute—but rather the completion and charging of it with a new content. That is to say, the 'moralization' process assumes the numinous and is only completed upon this as basis.

CHAPTER XIV

THE HOLY AS AN *A PRIORI* CATEGORY

PART I

IT follows from what has been said that the 'holy' in the fullest sense of the word is a combined, complex category, the combining elements being its rational and non-rational components. But in *both*—and the assertion must be strictly maintained against all Sensationalism and Naturalism—it is a *purely a priori* category.

The rational ideas of Absoluteness, Completion, Necessity, and Substantiality, and no less so those of the good as an objective value, objectively binding and valid, are not to be 'evolved' from any sort of sense-perception. And the notions of ' epigenesis ', ' heterogony ', or whatever other expression we may choose to denote our compromise and perplexity, only serve to conceal the problem, the tendency to take refuge in a Greek terminology being here, as so often, nothing but an avowal of one's own insufficiency. Rather, seeking to account for the ideas in question, we are referred away from all sense-experience back to an original and underivable capacity of the mind implanted in the ' pure reason ' independently of all perception.

But in the case of the non-rational elements of our category of the Holy we are referred back to something still deeper than the ' pure reason ', at least as this is usually understood, namely to that which Mysticism has rightly named the 'fundus animae', the ' bottom' or 'ground of the soul' (*Seelengrund*). The ideas of the numinous and the feelings that correspond to them are, quite as much as the rational ideas and feelings, absolutely ' pure ', and the criteria which Kant suggests for the ' pure ' concept and the ' pure ' feeling of respect are most precisely applicable to them. In the famous opening words of the ' *Critique of Pure Reason* ' he says:—

' That all our knowledge begins with experience there can be no doubt. For how is it possible that the faculty of cognition should be awakened into exercise otherwise than by means

of objects which affect our senses ? ... But, though all our knowledge begins *with* experience, it by no means follows that all
arises *out of* experience.'

And, referring to empirical knowledge, he distinguishes that
part which we receive through impressions and that which our
own faculty of cognition supplies from itself, *sense-impressions
giving merely the occasion*.

The numinous is of the latter kind. It issues from the
deepest foundation of cognitive apprehension that the soul
possesses, and, though it of course comes into being in and
amid the sensory data and empirical material of the natural
world and cannot anticipate or dispense with those, yet it does
not arise *out of* them, but only *by their means*. They are the
incitement, the stimulus, and the ' occasion ' for the numinous
experience to become astir, and, in so doing, to begin—at first
with a naïve immediacy of reaction—to be interfused and
interwoven with the present world of sensuous experience,
until, becoming gradually purer, it disengages itself from this
and takes its stand in absolute contrast to it. The proof that
in the numinous we have to deal with purely *a priori* cognitive elements is to be reached by introspection and a critical
examination of reason such as Kant instituted. We find, that
is, involved in the numinous experience, beliefs and feelings
qualitatively different from anything that ' natural ' sense-
perception is capable of giving us. They are themselves not
perceptions at all, but peculiar interpretations and valuations,
at first of perceptual data, and then—at a higher level—of
posited objects and entities, which themselves no longer belong
to the perceptual world, but are thought of as supplementing
and transcending it. And as they are not themselves sense-
perceptions, so neither are they any sort of ' transmutation ' of
sense-perceptions. The only ' transmutation ' possible in respect
to sense-perception is the transformation of the intuitively
given concrete percept, of whatever sort, into the corresponding
concept ; there is never any question of the transformation of
one class of percepts into a class of entities qualitatively *other*.
The facts of the numinous consciousness point therefore—as
likewise do also the ' pure concepts of the understanding ' of

Kant and the ideas and value-judgements of ethics or aesthetics
—-to a hidden substantive source, from which the religious ideas
and feelings are formed, which lies in the mind independently
of sense-experience ; a ' pure reason ' in the profoundest sense,
which, because of the surpassingness of its content, must be
distinguished from both the pure theoretical and the pure
practical reason of Kant, as something yet higher or deeper
than they.

The justification of the ' evolutionist ' theory of to-day stands
or falls with its claim to ' explain ' the phenomenon of religion.
That is in truth the real task of the psychology of religion.
But in order to explain we must have the data from which an
explanation may be forthcoming ; out of nothing nothing can be
explained.   Nature can only be explained by an investigation
into the ultimate fundamental forces of nature and their laws :
it is meaningless to propose to go further and explain these
laws themselves, for in terms of what are they to be explained ?
But in the domain of spirit the corresponding principle from
which an explanation is derived is just the spirit itself, the
reasonable spirit of man, with its predispositions, capacities,
and its own inherent laws.   This has to be presupposed : it cannot itself be explained.   None can say how mind or spirit ' is
made '—though this is in effect just what the theory of Epigenesis is fain to attempt. The history of humanity begins
with man, and we have to presuppose man, to take him for
granted as he is, in order that from him we may understand
his history.   That is, we must presuppose man as a being
analogous to ourselves in natural propensities and capacities.
It is a hopeless business to seek to lower ourselves into the
mental life of a *pithecanthropus erectus* ; and, even if it
were not, we should still need to start from man as he is, since
we can only interpret the psychical and emotional life of animals
regressively by clumsy analogies drawn from the developed
human mind.   To try, on the other hand, to understand and
deduce the human from the sub-human or brute mind is
to try to fit the lock to the key instead of vice versa ; it is to
seek to illuminate light by darkness.   In the first appearance
of conscious life on dead unconscious matter we have a simple,

irreducible, inexplicable datum.   But that which here appears
is already a manifold of qualities, and we can only interpret
it as a seed of potentiality, out of which issue continually
maturer powers and capacities, as the organization of the body
increases in stability and complexity.   And the only way we
can throw any light upon the whole region of sub-human
psychical life is by interpreting it once again as a sort of 'predisposition' (*Anlage*) at a second remove, i. e. a predisposition
to form the predispositions or faculties of the actual developed
mind, and standing in relation to this as an embryo to the
full-grown organism.   But we are not completely in the dark
as to the meaning of this word 'predisposition'.   For in
our own awakening and growth to mental and spiritual
maturity we trace in ourselves in some sort the evolution
by which the seed develops into the tree—the very opposite of
'transformation' and 'epigenesis' by successive addition.[1]

We call the source of growth a hidden 'predisposition' of
the human spirit, which awakens when aroused by divers
excitations.   That there are 'predispositions' of this sort
in individuals no one can deny who has given serious study
to the history of religion.   They are seen as propensities,
'predestining' the individual to religion, and they may grow
spontaneously to quasi-instinctive presentiments, uneasy seeking and groping, yearning and longing, and become a religious
impulsion, that only finds peace when it has become clear to
itself and attained its goal.   From them arise the states of

---

[1] The physical analogue to these spiritual or mental relationships is
the relation of potential to kinetic energy. The assumption of such a relation in the world of mind (i. e. a relation between potential and kinetic
mind) is, of course, only to be expected from one who is prepared to accept
as the final cause of all mind in the world as a whole the absolute mind
as 'pure actuality' whose *ellampatio* or effulgence (in Leibniz's phrase)
all other mind is.   For all that is potential presupposes an *actual* as the
ground of its possibility, as Aristotle long ago showed.   But indeed how
can we afford to reject such a 'pure actuality'?   It is an inconsequent
proceeding to postulate actuality, as is done, for a starting point for the
physical world, as a system of stored-up energy, whose transference to
kinetic energy constitutes the 'rush of worlds and wheel of systems', and
yet to reject the analogous assumption in the world of mind and spirit.

mind of 'prevenient grace', described in masterly fashion by
Suso:—

'Loving, tender Lord! My mind has from the days of my
childhood sought something with an earnest thirst of longing,
Lord, and what that is have I not yet perfectly apprehended.
Lord, I have now for many a year been in hot pursuit of it,
and never yet have I been able to succeed, for I know not
aright what it is. And yet it is something that draws my
heart and my soul after it, and without which I can never
attain to full repose. Lord, I was fain in the earliest days of
my childhood to seek it among created things, as I saw others
before me do. And the more I sought, the less I found it; and
the nearer I went, the further I wandered from it.... Now my
heart rages for it, for fain would I possess it. . . . Woe is me!
. . . What is this, or how is it fashioned, that plays within me
in such hidden wise ? '[1]

These are manifestations of a *predisposition* becoming a
search and a driving *impulsion*. But here, if nowhere else,
the 'fundamental biogenetic law' really does hold good, which
uses the stages and phases in the growth of the individual
to throw light upon the corresponding stages in the growth of
his species. The *predisposition* which the human reason
brought with it when the species Man entered history became
long ago, not merely for individuals but for the species as
a whole, a *religious impulsion*, to which incitements from
without and pressure from within the mind both contributed.
It begins in undirected, groping emotion, a seeking and shaping
of representations, and goes on, by a continual onward striving,
to generate ideas, till its nature is self-illumined and made
clear by an explication of the obscure *a priori* foundation
of thought itself, out of which it originated.[2] And this emotion,
this searching, this generation and explication of ideas, gives
the warp of the fabric of religious evolution, whose woof
we are to discuss later.[3]

[1] *Works*, ed. Denifle, p. 311.

[2] The reader may compare what Kant says in his Lectures on Psychology
(Leipsic ed., 1889, p. 11) of 'the treasure buried in the field of obscure
ideas, constituting the deep abyss of human knowledge, which we cannot
sound.' This 'deep abyss' is just the 'fundus animae' that is aroused
in Suso.   [3] Cf. pp. 180, 181.

CHAPTER XV

ITS EARLIEST MANIFESTATIONS

ONLY upon the basis of the foregoing assumptions is it possible to understand the historical origin and further development of religion. It must be admitted that when religious evolution first begins sundry curious phenomena confront us, preliminary to religion proper and deeply affecting its subsequent course. Such are the notions of ' clean ' and ' unclean ', belief in and worship of the dead, belief in and worship of ' souls ' or ' spirits ', magic, fairy tale, and myth, homage to natural objects, whether frightful or extraordinary, noxious or advantageous, the strange idea of ' power ' (*orenda* or *mana*), fetishism and totemism, worship of animal and plant, daemonism and polydaemonism. Different as these things are, they are all haunted by a common—and that a numinous—element, which is easily identifiable. They did not, perhaps, take their origin out of this common numinous element directly ; they may have all exhibited a preliminary stage at which they were merely ' natural ' products of the naïve, rudimentary fancies of primitive times. But these things acquire a strand of a quite special kind, which alone gives them their character as forming the vestibule of religion, brings them first to clear and explicit form, and furnishes them with the prodigious power over the minds of men which history universally proves them to possess. Let us attempt to grasp this peculiar strand, common to all these modes of thought and practice which stand upon the threshold of religion.

1. We will begin with *magic*. There has been at all times, and there still is to-day, a ' natural ' magic, that is to say, modes of behaviour exhibiting some simple analogy and carried out quite unreflectively and without any basis in theory, whose

object is to influence and regulate an event in accordance with
the wishes of the agent. It may be noticed on any skittle-
alley or bowling-green. A bowler aims and plays his bowl,
wishing it to roll straight and hit the jack. He watches eagerly
as it rolls, nodding his head, his body bent sideways, stands
balancing on one leg, jerks over violently to the other side as
the critical point is reached, makes as though to push the ball
on with hand or foot, gives a last jerk—and the end is reached.
Its hazards past, the ball rolls safely into position. What was
the man doing in this case ? He was not simply imitating the
course of the ball; he meant to prescribe and determine it, but
this obviously without any reflection on his queer behaviour,
without the belief of primitive man in ' universal animism ', i. e.
in the animatedness of everything, in this instance of the ball,
and without a belief in some sympathetic *rapport* between his
own ' soul ' power and the ' soul ' of the ball. His action was
merely naïvely analogical, for the attainment of a definite
wish. The proceedings of ' rain-makers ' were often, perhaps
at first were always, just the same sort of thing; and so were
the naïve charms purporting to influence the course of sun and
moon, clouds and winds. But clearly, so long as they are not
more than this, these are not by any means *magic* in the proper
sense. There must be in addition a new ingredient, unique
in quality, the element that is usually called ' supernatural
efficacy '. But this expression is a misnomer: ' supernatural '
has nothing to do with the case; it is much too imposing an
expression, and ascribes far too much to the naïve mind. The
conception of Nature as a single connected system of events
united by laws is the final and most difficult outcome of
abstraction; and this conception of nature, or at least some
hint of it, must have been arrived at before there could be any
place for its negation, the ' supernatural '. Again, nothing is
explained, as Wundt would have it, by ' spirit-power ' or ' soul-
power '. For, first, it is to-day universally recognized that
magic is independent of a belief in spirits or souls, and probably
existed before it. And, second, the point at issue is not by
means of what *class* of powers the magical effect was produced
—whether ' soul-powers ' or others—but by means of what

quality or *character* in the powers. And this quality can be indicated solely through the 'daemonic', a character ascribed to certain definite operations of force, be they strong or weak, extraordinary or quite trivial. The quality can be only suggested through that unique element of feeling, the feeling of 'uncanniness', of which we have already spoken, whose positive content cannot be defined conceptually, and can only be indicated by that mental response to it which we called 'shuddering'.

2. The same is true of the *worship of the dead*. It does not arise out of any theory of animism, according to which the primitive man thinks of inanimate objects, and so also of the dead, as animate and operative. Even in itself this entire theory of an ostensible attribution of 'soul' or the principle of animation to everything is a mere fabrication of the study. How much more when it is clumsily spatchcocked and welded together with 'belief in spirits or souls', which is something quite different! The dead man, in point of fact, exercises a spell upon the mind only when, and only because, he is felt as a thing of horror and 'shudder'. But alike to the naïve mind of the savage and to the blasé mind of modern civilized man this feeling comes about with such an immediate compelling force that we usually accept it as something immediately self-evident, failing altogether to remark that even the estimating something as 'horrible' or 'grisly' shows the emergence of a qualitatively separate content of feeling which the mere fact of death does not explain. Feeling-reactions to the dead, if prompted 'naturally', are pretty obviously only of two kinds: on the one hand, the experient feels *disgust* at the corpse's putrefaction, stench, revoltingness: on the other, he feels his own will to life disturbed and checked, the fear of death and the startled fright that directly follows on the sight of a corpse, especially if it be that of a member of one's own species. Both these sorts of feeling-response, viz. disgust and startled fright, are already found manifested among animals. I observed this in a very pronounced degree on one occasion, when, upon a lonely ride, we suddenly came upon the body of a dead horse, and Diana, my excellent mount, on recog-

nizing her dead fellow, gave every indication of the most natural fright and disgust. But these two 'moments' of feeling do not by any means afford in themselves the materials for the 'art of making shudder' (in the words of the old folk-tale). It is something new and demands to be 'learnt' as the folk-tale rightly declares : that is, this is a feeling that is not simply present with the other 'natural' and normal mental functions, disgust, or fright, and cannot be got from these by analysis. It is a 'dread' (or awe), qualitatively *sui generis* ; and even with regard to this rudimentary stage represented by the primitive 'worship of the dead' we cannot admit that we have to do merely with a universal feeling, that has simply to be presupposed at the outset as a regular factor of folk psychology, a collectively engendered feeling that explains itself. On the contrary, it cannot be disputed that here too there have been persons endowed with special propensities in this direction, who possessed such feelings actually, and then, by giving expression to them, aroused them in others. Even the 'awe of the dead' and from it the 'worship of the dead' have been, as it were, 'instituted' and have had 'founders'.

3. We consider next ideas of '*souls*' and '*spirits*'. It would be possible to show, did not the subject lead us too far afield, that these were not conceived by the fanciful processes of which the animists tell us, but had a far simpler origin. But again the important point is not the origin of 'spirits' in their ideational aspect, but the qualitative element of feeling relative to them. And this does not consist in the fact that 'spirits' or 'souls' are thinner or less easily visible than the body, or quite invisible, or fashioned like air : often all this is true of them; no less often none of it is; most frequently of all it is both true and false. The essence of the 'soul' lies *not* in the imaginative or conceptual expression of it, but first and foremost in the fact that it is a *spectre*; that it arouses 'dread' or 'awe', as described above. But again, a 'spectre' is not to be explained from 'natural' feelings, and these are equally unable to explain the further development by which these 'somethings' (and this is the only core of conceptual meaning that can really be given them), at first

always very eagerly shunned, later on become beings honoured in a positive way and loved, capable of rising into heroes, *pitris*, daemons, holy or sacred ones, and gods.

4. We turn to the idea of '*power*', the *mana* of the Pacific Islands and the *orenda* of the North American Indians. It can have its antecedents in very 'natural' phenomena. To notice power in plants, stones, and natural objects in general and to appropriate it by gaining possession of them; to eat the heart or liver of an animal or a man in order to make his power and strength one's own—this is not religion but science. Our science of medicine follows a similar prescription. If the 'power' of a calf's glands is good for goitre and imbecility, we do not know what virtue we may not hope to find in frogs' brains or Jews' livers. All depends here upon observation, and our science of medicine in this respect only differs from that of the medicine-man in being more exact and in possessing experimental methods. 'Power' does not take its place in the ante-chamber of religion, is not appropriated by religion in 'communion rites' and 'sacraments' (as we call them), until it too has come to include the idea of 'spell' and 'magic'.

5. Volcanoes, mountain peaks, moon, sun, and clouds are regarded by primitive man as being *alive* or *animate*, not in consequence of a naïve theory of the omnipresence of 'spirit' or 'soul'—'Panthelism', so called—but as a result of precisely the same criterion that we ourselves apply when we recognize anything to be alive or animate, apart from the one live thing we can observe directly, our self; that is to say, both we and the primitive credit an object with life if, and in so far as, we think we remark in it living efficacy and agency; and whether we do so rightly or wrongly is again simply a matter of more or less exact observation. But while from this criterion the natural objects mentioned above, and of course others, may be invested with life by the naïve observer, this does *not* in itself lead to myth or religion. Purely as *animate* or living beings, these entities are far from being yet 'divine' or 'gods'; nay, they do not even become so when the man turns to them with desire and petition; for petition is something less than prayer

and trust need not have a religious character. The objects in question only become 'divine'—objects of *worship*—when the category of the numinous is applied to them, and that does not come about until, first, an attempt is made to *influence* them by numinous means, viz. by magic; and, second, their special efficacy or way of working is at the same time accepted as something numinous, viz. something magical.

6. As regards *fairy-stories*, these presuppose the 'natural' impulse to fantasy, narrative, and entertainment, and its products. But the fairy-story proper only comes into being with the element of the 'wonderful', with miracle and miraculous events and consequences, i. e. by means of an infusion of the numinous. And the same holds good in an increased degree of *myth*.

7. All the factors and elements named so far in this chapter are but, as it were, the vestibule at the threshold of the real religious feeling, an earliest stirring of the numinous consciousness, which comes upon the scene blended with associated feelings in conformity to principles of analogy which it would be easy to specify for each several case. Only with the rise of the '*daemon*' do we have a really separate beginning. The most authentic form of the 'daemon' may be seen in those strange deities of ancient Arabia, which are properly nothing but wandering demonstrative pronouns, neither 'given shape and feature by means of myth', for there is in the main no mythology attached to them at all, nor 'evolved out of nature-deities,' nor grown out of 'souls' or 'spirits', but none the less felt as deities of mighty efficacy, who are the objects of very living veneration. They are pure products of the religious consciousness itself. And in their case it is very evident that they do not arise as a collective product of crowd-imagination, and that they do not therefore have their origin in 'group-' or 'folk-' psychology, but were the intuitions of persons of innate prophetic powers. For there is always the Kāhin (the primitive form of the 'prophet') belonging to these 'numina', and he alone experiences a 'numen' or divine-daemonic power at first hand. Only where and when it has been 'revealed' through such a one do the forms of worship and a common

cult arise.   To each numen is assigned a Seer and there is none
without one.

8. The notions 'clean' and 'unclean', 'pure' and 'impure',
are already found in a purely natural sense, prior to their
religious application. The unclean is the loathsome, that which
stirs strong feelings of natural disgust.   And it is just during
the more primitive stages of human development that the
emotion of disgust exercises such special power. Probably these
emotional reactions are a part of our natural self-protective
endowment, instinctive safeguards for many important vital
functions. The effect of civilization is to refine these emotions
of disgust and loathing by diverting them to different objects,
so that things which were loathsome to the savage cease to be
so and things which were not become so.   This refinement
spells at the same time a weakening in the intensity of the
emotion ; we do not now *loathe* and feel disgust with the
unbridled violence and strength of the savage.   In this respect
we can notice even to-day a plain distinction between our more
primitive rural and our more 'refined' urban population : we
townsmen feel disgust at much that is harmless to the country-
man, but where the latter does feel it he is affected by the
emotion more radically than we are ; it is a profounder reaction
in him.

We have so far been concerned with the ordinary feeling of
disgust.   Between this and the feeling of the 'horrible' there
is a very close analogy ; and from this it becomes apparent,
in accordance with the law of reciprocal attraction between
analogous feelings and emotions, how the 'natural' unclean or
impure is bound to pass over into, and develop in, the sphere
of the numinous.   Once, in fact, we have in our hand the key
of the problem—the analogy and the law just mentioned—we
can reconstruct *a priori* the actual genetic process involved,
by which the one emotion prompts the other.   We indeed have
ourselves a direct experience of the same thing to-day in our
emotional reaction to the sight of flowing blood, in which it
would be hard to say whether the element of 'disgust' or
'horror' is the stronger.

Later, then, when the more maturely developed elements of

'awe' came upon the scene and went to shape the more elevated ideas of the daemonic and the divine, *sacer* and *sanctus*, things could become 'unclean' or 'impure' in the numinous sense without any substratum of 'natural' impurity to serve as point of departure.   And we can learn something of the relation of feeling-analogy involved from the fact that in the reverse direction the feeling of the *numinously* impure calls up easily by association the 'natural' emotion of disgust (i. e. the feeling of the 'naturally' impure), so that things become disgustful or loathsome which intrinsically were not objects of disgust at all, but of numinous horror.   In fact such secondary and derived feelings of disgust can maintain themselves independently long after the original numinous awe which they once evoked has died away.   Certain *social* feelings of loathing, such as those of caste, can be explained in this way: they had once a purely daemonic root, but long after that has died out they still survive in their secondary, acquired character as feelings of disgust.

9. If the examples numbered 1 to 8 may be termed 'pre-religion', this is not in the sense that religion and the possibility of religion are explicable by their means: rather, they are themselves only made possible and can only be explained from a religious basic element, viz. the feeling of the numinous. This is a primal element of our psychical nature that needs to be grasped purely in its uniqueness and cannot itself be explained from anything else.   Like all other primal psychical elements, it *emerges* in due course in the developing life of human mind and spirit and is thenceforward simply present. Of course it can only emerge if and when certain conditions are fulfilled, conditions involving a proper development of the bodily organs and the other powers of mental and emotional life in general, a due growth in suggestibility and spontaneity and responsiveness to external impressions and internal experiences.   But such conditions are no more than conditions; they are not its causes or constituent elements.   To recognize this is not to relegate the whole matter to the domain of mystery and supernaturalism, but simply to maintain that the same thing holds good of this which holds good of all other primal ele-

ments of our mental or spiritual life. Pleasure or pain, love or hate, all faculties of sense-perception, such as susceptibility to light and sound, consciousness of space and time, and subsequently all higher capacities of the mind, all duly emerge, sooner or later, in the course of development. That they do so in conformity to laws and under definite conditions is indisputable, but not the less is each a new, original, underivable fact, and they are only to be 'explained' on the assumption of a rich potentiality of spirit or mind, which underlies the course of their development and realizes itself more and more abundantly in them in proportion as the conditions of organic and cerebral evolution are more fully realized. And what is true of all these other elements of our mental life is also true of the feeling of the numinous.

10. The purest case, however, of the spontaneous stirring of numinous emotion would seem to be that mentioned in No. 7 (the feeling of daemons), which is of quite special significance for the evolution of religion. This is because here the 'religious' emotion does not from the first get diverted (following the 'stimulation' of emotional associations) to earthly things, wrongly taken as numinous: but either it remains a pure feeling, as in 'panic' terror (in the literal sense of the word), or itself invents, or, better, discovers, the numinous object by rendering explicit the obscure germinal ideas latent in itself. Even this latter case is not altogether beyond the reach of introspective analysis, which, moreover, can throw some light upon the transition from mere feeling to its 'explication' and to the positing of the numinous object. At least there is none of us who has any living capacity for emotion but must have known at some time or at some place what it is to feel really 'uncanny', to have a feeling of 'eerieness'. And more exact psychological analysis will notice the following points in such a state of mind. First, there is the point of which we have already spoken, its separate and underivable, irreducible, qualitative character. Second, there is the very curious circumstance that the external features occasioning this state of mind are often quite slight, indeed so scanty that hardly any account can be given of them, so disproportionate are they to

K

the strength of the emotional impression itself. Indeed the
clutching force and violence of the emotion so far exceeds any
impressiveness contributed by the circumstances of time and
place that one can often scarcely speak of an 'impression' at
all, but at most of an encounter, serving as cue or occasion for
the felt experience. This experience of eerie shuddering and
awe breaks out rather from depths of the soul which the circum-
stantial, external impression cannot sound, and the force with
which it breaks out is so disproportionate to the mere external
stimulation that the eruption may be termed, if not entirely,
at least very nearly, spontaneous. And with this we are
brought to the third point which psychological analysis of the
'uncanny' experience brings to view; meanings are aroused
and awakened in it of a unique and special content, though
altogether obscure, latent, and germinal, which are the real
ground for the emotion of awe. For, if such meanings are not
there at the start in some form or other, the mental and
emotional disturbance could never take place. In the fourth
place, the mental state we are discussing may, on the one hand,
remain pure 'feeling', pursue its course and pass away without its obscure thought-content being rendered explicit. If in
this implicit form it is summed up in a phrase, this will be
merely some such exclamation as: 'How uncanny!' or 'How
eerie this place is!' On the other hand, the implicit meaning
may be rendered explicit. It is already a beginning of this
explicative process—though still in merely negative terms—
when a man says: '*It* is not quite right here;' '*It* is
uncanny.' The English 'This place is haunted' shows a
transition to a positive form of expression. Here we have the
obscure basis of meaning and idea rising into greater clarity
and beginning to make itself explicit as the notion, however
vague and fleeting, of a transcendent Something, a real operative entity of a numinous kind, which later, as the development
proceeds, assumes concrete form as a 'numen loci', a daemon,
an 'El', a Baal, or the like.

In Genesis xxviii. 17 Jacob says: 'How dreadful is this
place! This is none other than the house of Elohim.' This
verse is very instructive for the psychology of religion; it

exemplifies the point that has just been made. The first sentence gives plainly the mental impression itself in all its immediacy, before reflection has permeated it, and before the meaning-content of the feeling itself has become clear or explicit. It connotes solely the *primal numinous awe*, which has been undoubtedly sufficient in itself in many cases to mark out ' holy ' or ' sacred ' places, and make of them spots of aweful veneration, centres of a cult admitting a certain development. There is no need, that is, for the experient to pass on to resolve his mere impression of the eerie and aweful into the idea of a ' numen ', a divine power, dwelling in the ' aweful ' place, still less need the *numen* become a *nomen*, a named power, or the ' nomen ' become something more than a mere pronoun. Worship is possible without this farther explicative process. But Jacob's second statement gives this process of explication and interpretation ; it is no longer simply an expression of the actual experience.

The German expression *Es spukt hier* (literally, it haunts here) is also instructive. It has properly no true subject, or at least it makes no assertion as to what the *es*, the ' it ', is which ' haunts '; in itself it contains no suggestion of the concrete representations of ' ghost ', ' phantom ', ' spectre ', or ' spirit ' common to our popular mythology. Rather is the statement simply the pure expression of the emotion of ' eerieness ' or ' uncanniness ' itself, when just on the point of detaching and disengaging from itself a first vaguely intimated idea of a numinous something, an entity from beyond the borders of ' natural ' experience. It is to be regretted that the German language possesses no general word less vulgar than ' spuken ', no word which, instead of pointing us aside, as this word does, to the domain of superstition and the impure offshoots of the numinous consciousness, should retain its fundamental meaning in an unperverted form.[1] But even so we can feel by an effort of

[1] The expression *es geistet hier* may serve, but it has an artificial sound. The English ' to haunt ' is a nobler expression than the German ' spuken '. We might legitimately translate Habakkuk ii. 20 : ' Yahweh haunts His holy Temple.' Such a ' haunting ' is frequently the meaning of the Hebrew *shākan*. And we get a fuller and truer rendering of

K 2

imaginative introjection how akin the debased feeling of haunting, given by this word, is to those primary numinous experiences by which long ago seers had experience of 'aweful', 'holy',
numen-possessed places, discovering thereby the starting-points
for local cults and the birth-places of the 'El' worshipped
there.   The echo of such primaeval experiences lingers in
Genesis xxviii. 17 (Jacob at Bethel) and Exodus iii (the burning bush).   The places here set apart by Moses and Jacob are
genuine 'haunted places', at which '*es spukt*', places about which
'there is something eerie'.   Only, the feeling of being haunted
has in these cases not the impoverished and debased sense of
our modern eerie feeling of being haunted by ghosts and
spectres; it comprises all the rich potentialities and possibilities
of development inherent in the true primal numinous emotion.
Nor can we doubt that even to-day the finer awe that may
steal over us in the stillness and half-gloom of our own present-
day sanctuaries has ultimate kinship not only with that of
which Schiller writes in his verses:

> Und in Poseidons Fichtenhain
> Tritt er mit frommen Schauder ein,[1]

but also with genuine 'ghostly' emotions.   The faint shiver
that may accompany such states of mind is not unrelated to
the feeling of 'creeping flesh', whose numinous character we
have already considered (p. 16).   In its efforts to derive
'daemon' and 'god' forcibly from 'souls' and 'spirits', animism
is looking the wrong way.   It would be, at any rate, on the
right path if it maintained that they are haunting apparitions.

This is partially proved by certain ancient, still extant
terms, which long ago had reference to the original awe of the
haunting spirit (in the good sense), and later grew to become
designations both of the lowest and the highest forms of 'awe'.
Such a term is the enigmatical word '*asura*' in Sanskrit.

Ps. xxvi. 8: 'the place where Thine honour dwelleth' by translating it:
'the places haunted by Thy majesty'.   The *Shekinah* is properly the
haunting presence of Yahweh in the Temple at Jerusalem.

[1] Schiller, *Die Kraniche des Ibykus* (The Cranes of Ibykus):

> 'And to Poseidon's grove of pine
> With awe devout he enters in.'

Asura is the ' aweful' or ' dreadful' in the sense in which Jacob used the word, the eerie or uncanny.   Later, in Indian religion, it is used as the technical expression for the lower forms of the spectral, ghostly, and daemonic.   But at the same time it is from primaeval times a title of the sublimest of all the gods of the Rig-Veda, the weirdly exalted *Varuna*.   And in the Persian expression *Ahura-mazda* it becomes the name of the one and only eternal godhead itself.   The same thing is true of the term ' *adbhuta* '.   You experience an *adbhuta* when you are ' in an empty house ', says an old definition.[1] It is the experience of our ' shuddering '.   But, on the other hand, *adbhuta* is also the name for the supreme transcendent marvel and its attractive spell, the element of ' fascination ', even for the eternal Brahman himself and his salvation, the *Adbhutam* that passes beyond the reach of speech.[2]

11. Finally, it is only upon our assumption of an *a priori* basis of ideas and feelings that an explanation is forthcoming for the interesting phenomena to which Andrew Lang [3] rightly drew attention.   These do not, of course, support the hypothesis of a ' primitive monotheism ', that offspring of missionary apologetic, which, eager to save the second chapter of Genesis, yet feels the shame of a modern at the walking of Yahweh ' in the garden in the cool of the day '.   But they do point to facts which remain downright riddles, if we start from any naturalistic foundation of religion—whether animism, panthelism, or another—and must in that case be got out of the way by the most violent hypotheses.   The essence of the matter is this,

---

[1] *A-dbhuta* means literally the inapprehensible, inexpressible.   But in the first instance it is exactly our *mysterium stupendum*, whereas ' *asura* ' is the *tremendum*.

[2] *Adbhuta* (and *āscarya*) would be an accurate rendering in Sanskrit for our ' numinous ', were it not that the word, like the German ' wunderbar' and the English 'awful ', has long ago become trite and shallow from the ' profane '–non-religious—uses to which it has been so perpetually put.

[3] *Myth, Ritual, and Religion*, 1899.   *The Making of Religion*, 1902. *Magic and Religion*, 1901.   Cf. also P. W. Schmidt, *Grundlinien einer Vergleichung der Religionen und Mythologien der austronesischen Völker*, Vienna, 1910.

that elements and strands are to be found in numerous mythologies and the stories of savage tribes, which reach altogether beyond the point they have otherwise attained in religious rites and usages.   Notions of 'high gods' are adumbrated, with whom the savage has often hardly any relations in practice, if any at all, and in whom he yet acknowledges, almost in spite of himself, a value superior to that of all other mythological images, a value which may well accord with the divine in the highest sense.

Sometimes, but by no means always, we can discern that these anticipations of a higher religious experience are the outcome of a past growth of myth.   What is characteristic and at the same time so puzzling is the elevation with which they stand out from the surrounding more primitive religious life amid which they are found.   Indeed, in cases where missions have introduced the preaching of Christian theism, these apprehended, exalted divinities are readily and frequently identified with God and reinforce the preaching of the missionary.   And converts often come to admit that, though they had not honoured God, they had had knowledge of Him.   It is, of course, true that this sort of fact can sometimes be explained as due to traditional influences, protracted from an earlier time, when the tribe in question was in contact with a higher theistic religion : the very names given to these higher beings sometimes prove as much.   But even in this form the phenomenon is a very singular one.   Why should 'savages', set in other respects in an utterly alien milieu of barbaric superstition, accept and, what is more, retain these notions, unless their own savage minds were so predisposed to them that, so far from being able to let them go, they were obliged to take at least an interest in them as a tradition and very frequently to acknowledge their authority by the felt witness of their own consciences ?   But, though the theory of a surviving tradition is sometimes applicable, there are many of these cases in which it is impossible to apply it without doing violence to the facts.   In these we have clearly to do with anticipations and presentiments rather than survivals.   Assuming the continual pressure and operation of an inward reasonable disposition to form certain ideas, these anticipations are not only no matter for surprise; they are as naturally to be expected as are the achievements of gipsy musicians, who, set otherwise in a milieu of the most primitive culture, yet respond to the pressure of a strong, innate, musical disposition. Without such an assumption, the facts would remain as an insoluble puzzle.

Naturalistic psychologists, in this as in other cases, ignore a fact which might be thought at least to have a psychological interest, and which they could notice in themselves by careful introspection, namely, the *self-attestation* of religious ideas in one's own mind. This is, to be sure, more certain in the case of the naïve than in that of the more blasé mind; but many people would identify it in their own consciousness if they would only recall deliberately and impartially their hours of preparation for the ceremony of 'confirmation'. But what the mind 'attests' it can also under favourable circumstances evince and elicit from itself in premonitory stirring and felt surmise. The upholders of the theory of 'Primitive Monotheism', on the other hand, show no less serious disregard of this central fact than the naturalistic psychologists. For if the phenomena we have been considering were based simply and solely on historical traditions and dim memories of a 'prehistoric revelation', as on such a theory they must be, this self-attestation from within would be just as much excluded as before.

CHAPTER XVI

THE 'CRUDER' PHASES

IT is not only the more developed forms of religious experience that must be counted underivable and *a priori*. The same holds good throughout and is no less true of the primitive, 'crude', and rudimentary emotions of 'daemonic dread' which, as we have seen, stand at the threshold of religious evolution. *Religion is itself present at its commencement:* religion, nothing else, is at work in these early stages of mythic and daemonic experience. Let us consider the circumstances in which alone the primitive and crude character of these consists.

(a) First, it is due to the merely gradual emergence and successive awakening of the several moments of the numinous. The numinous only unfolds its full content by slow degrees, as one by one the series of requisite stimuli or incitements becomes operative. But where any whole is as yet incompletely presented its earlier and partial constituent moments or elements, aroused in isolation, have naturally something bizarre, unintelligible, and even grotesque about them. This is especially true of that religious moment which would appear to have been in every case the first to be aroused in the human mind, viz. daemonic dread. Considered alone and *per se*, it necessarily and naturally looks more like the opposite of religion than religion itself. If it is singled out from the elements which form its context, it appears rather to resemble a dreadful form of auto-suggestion, a sort of psychological nightmare of the tribal mind, than to have anything to do with religion; and the supernatural beings with whom men at this early stage profess relations appear as phantoms, projected by a morbid, undeveloped imagination afflicted by a sort of persecution-phobia. One can understand how it is that not a few inquirers could seriously imagine that 'religion' began with devil-worship, and that at bottom the devil is more ancient than God.

To this serial and gradual awakening of the different aspects and moments of the numinous is also to be ascribed the difficulty of classifying religions by genus and species. Every one who undertakes the task produces a different classification. For the facts to be classified are for the most part not at all related as the distinct species of one and the same genus; they are not alternative, determinate forms into which the whole—'religion'—may be analysed, but constituent elements, out of which it is to be 'synthesized' or built up. It is as though a whale should begin to show itself above the water part by part, and as though people should then attempt to classify the arched back, the end of the tail, and the head spouting water, by genus and species, instead of seeking for such a real understanding of these phenomena as would recognize each of them in its place and proper connexion with the rest as a part and member of *one* whole body, which must itself have been grasped in its entirety before its parts could be properly apprehended.

(b) In the second place, the 'primitiveness' of the cruder phases is due to the abrupt, capricious, and desultory character which marks the earliest form of numinous emotion ; and, in consequence, to its indistinctness, which causes it to be merged and confounded with 'natural' feelings.

(c) It is due, next, to the fact that the valuation prompted by the moment of numinous consciousness (e. g. the 'daemonic dread' phase) is attached in the first place, and very naturally, to objects, occurrences, and entities falling within the workaday world of primitive experience, which prompt or give occasion to the stirring of numinous emotion by analogy and then divert it to themselves. This circumstance is more than anything else the root of what has been called nature-worship and the deification of natural objects. Only gradually, under pressure from the numinous feeling itself, are such connexions subsequently 'spiritualized' or ultimately altogether rejected, and not till then does the obscure content of the feeling, with its reference to absolute transcendent reality, come to light in all its integrity and self-subsistence.

(d) A fourth factor contributing to the crudity of primitive

'religion' is the uncontrolled, enthusiastic form, making for
wild fanaticism, in which the numinous feeling storms the
savage mind, appearing as religious mania, possession by
the numen, intoxication, and frenzy.

(e) Again, a quite essential factor is the wrong schematiza-
tions it undergoes, when interpreted in terms of some experience analogous, perhaps, but not really appertaining to it.
Examples of this have already been given (e.g. p. 127).

(f) Finally, and most important, there is the deficient
rationalization and moralization of the experience, for it is
only gradually that the numinous feeling becomes charged
with progressively rational, moral, and cultural significance.

These considerations account for the primitive and savage
character of the numinous consciousness at its outset.   But it
must be repeated that in its content even the first stirring of
'daemonic dread' is a purely *a priori* element.   In this respect
it may be compared from first to last with the aesthetic judgement and the category of the beautiful.   Utterly different as
my mental experiences are when I recognize an object as
'beautiful' or as 'horrible', yet both cases agree in this, that
I ascribe to the object an attribute that professes to interpret
it, which I do not and cannot get from sense-experience, but
which I rather ascribe to it by a spontaneous judgement of my
own.   Intuitively I apprehend in the object only its sensuous
qualities and its spatial form, nothing more.   That the *meaning* I call 'beautiful' fits the object, i. e. that these sense-data
mean 'beautiful', or even that there *is* any such meaning
at all—these are facts which sensory elements can in no wise
supply or tell me.   I must have an obscure conception of 'the
beautiful itself', and, in addition, a principle of subsumption,
by which I attribute it to the object, else even the simplest
experience of a beautiful thing is rendered impossible.   And
this analogy may be pursued further.   Joy in the beautiful,
however analogous to mere pleasure in the agreeable, is yet
distinguishable from it by a plain difference in quality, and
cannot be derived from anything other than itself; and just
such is the relation of the specific religious awe to mere natural
fear.

The 'crude' stage is transcended as the numen reveals 'itself' (i. e. becomes manifest to mind and feeling) ever more strongly and fully. An essential factor in this is the process by which it is filled out and charged with rational elements, whereby it passes at the same time into the region of the conceivable and comprehensible. Yet all the time all the elements of non-rational 'inconceivability' are retained on the side of the numinous and intensified as the revelation proceeds. 'Revelation' does not mean a *mere* passing over into the intelligible and comprehensible. Something may be profoundly and intimately known in feeling for the bliss it brings or the agitation it produces, and yet the understanding may find no concept for it. To *know* and to *understand conceptually* are two different things, are often even mutually exclusive and contrasted. The mysterious obscurity of the numen is by no means tantamount to unknowableness. Assuredly the '*deus absconditus et incomprehensibilis*' was for Luther no '*deus ignotus*'. And so, too, St. Paul 'knows' the Peace, which yet 'passeth understanding'.

CHAPTER XVII

THE HOLY AS AN *A PRIORI* CATEGORY

PART II

WE conclude, then, that not only the rational but also the non-rational elements of the complex category of 'holiness' are *a priori* elements and each in the same degree. Religion is not in vassalage either to morality or teleology, '*ethos*' or '*telos*', and does not draw its life from postulates; and its non-rational content has, no less than its rational, its own independent roots in the hidden depths of the spirit itself.

But the same *a priori* character belongs, in the third place, to the *connexion* of the rational and the non-rational elements in religion, their inward and necessary union. The histories of religion recount indeed, as though it were something axiomatic, the gradual interpretation of the two, the process by which 'the divine' is charged and filled out with ethical meaning. And this process is, in fact, *felt* as something axiomatic, something whose inner necessity we feel to be self-evident. But then this inward self-evidence is a problem in itself; we are forced to assume an obscure, *a priori* knowledge of the necessity of this synthesis, combining rational and non-rational. For it is not by any means a *logical* necessity. How should it be logically inferred from the still 'crude', half-daemonic character of a moon-god or a sun-god or a numen attached to some locality, that he is a guardian and guarantor of the oath and of honourable dealing, of hospitality, of the sanctity of marriage, and of duties to tribe and clan? How should it be inferred that he is a god who decrees happiness and misery, participates in the concerns of the tribe, provides for its well-being, and directs the course of destiny and history? Whence comes this most surprising of all the facts in the history of religion, that beings, obviously born originally of horror and terror, become *gods*—beings to whom men pray, to whom they confide their sorrow or their happiness, in whom they behold the origin and the sanction of morality, law, and the whole canon of justice ? And how does all this come about in such a way that, when once such ideas have been aroused, it is understood at once as the plainest and most evident of axioms, that so it must be ?

Socrates, in Plato's *Republic*, ii. 382 E, says: 'God then is single and true in deed and word, and neither changes himself nor deceives others . . .' And Adeimantos answers him: 'So too is it apparent to me, now that you say it.' The most interesting point in this passage is not the elevation and purity of the conception of God, nor yet the lofty rationalization and moralization of it here enunciated, but, on the side of Socrates, the apparently 'dogmatic' tone of his pronouncement—for he does not spend the least pains in demonstrating it—and, on the side of Adeimantos, the ingenuous surprise and, at the same time, the confident assurance with which he admits a truth novel to him. And his assent is such as implies convincement ; he does not simply believe Socrates ; he sees clearly for himself the truth of his words. Now this is the criterion of all *a priori* knowledge, namely, that, so soon as an assertion has been clearly expressed and understood, knowledge of its truth comes into the mind with the certitude of first-hand insight. And what passed here between Socrates and Adeimantos has been repeated a thousand times in the history of religions. Amos, also, says something new when he proclaims Yahweh as the God of inflexible, universal, and absolute righteousness, and yet this is a novelty that he neither proves nor justifies by an appeal to authorities. He appeals to *a priori* judgements, viz. to the religious conscience itself, and this in truth bears witness to his message.

Luther, again, recognizes and maintains such an *a priori* knowledge of the divine nature. His rage against the 'whore Reason ' leads him, to be sure, usually to utterances in the opposite sense, such as the following:

' It is a knowledge *a posteriori*, in that we look at God from without, at His works and His government, as one looketh at a castle or house from without and thereby feeleth (*spüret*) the lord or householder thereof. But *a priori* from within hath no wisdom of men yet availed to discover what and of what manner of being is God as He is in Himself or in His inmost essence, nor can any man know nor say aught thereof, but they to whom it has been revealed by the Holy Ghost.'

Here Luther overlooks the fact that a man must 'feel' or detect the 'householder' *a priori* or not at all. But in other passages he himself allows the general human reason to possess many true cognitions of what 'God is in Himself or in His inmost essence'. Compare the following:

'Atque ipsamet ratio naturalis cogitur eam concedere *proprio suo iudicio convicta*, etiamsi nulla esset scriptura. Omnes enim homines inveniunt hanc sententiam in cordibus suis scriptam et *agnoscunt* eam ac probatam, licet inviti, cum *audiant* eam tractari: primo, Deum esse omnipotentem ... deinde, ipsum omnia nosse et praescire, neque errare neque falli posse ... Istis duobus corde et sensu concessis ...' [1]

The interesting words of this statement are: *proprio suo iudicio convicta*, for they make the distinction between *cognitions* and mere 'innate ideas' or supernaturally instilled notions, both of which latter may produce 'thoughts', but not convictions '*ex proprio iudicio*'. Note also the words: 'cum *audiant* eam tractari', which exactly correspond to the experience of Plato's Adeimantos, already quoted.[2]

---

[1] Luther, Weimar ed., xviii. 719: 'And the natural reason itself is forced, even were there no holy scripture, to grant it (*sc.* this assertion), *convinced by its own judgement*. For all men, *as soon as they hear it treated of*, find this belief written in their hearts, and acknowledge it as proved, even unwillingly: first, that God is omnipotent, . . . then, that He has knowledge and foreknowledge of all things and can neither err nor be deceived . . . Since these two things are admitted by heart and feeling . . .'

[2] The most interesting features in Luther in this connexion, however, are the passages upon 'Faith', in which Faith is described as a unique cognitive faculty for the apprehension of divine truth, and as such is contrasted with the 'natural' capacities of the Understanding, as elsewhere the 'Spirit' is contrasted. 'Faith' is here like the 'Synteresis' in the theory of knowledge of the mystics, the 'inward teacher' (*magister internus*) of Augustine, and the 'inward light' of the Quakers, which are all of them of course 'above reason', but yet an *a priori* element in ourselves.

It is the same experience which missionaries have so often undergone. Once enunciated and understood, the ideas of the unity and goodness of the divine nature often take a surprisingly short time to become firmly fixed in the hearer's mind, if he show any susceptibility for religious feeling. Frequently, thereupon, the hearer adapts the religious tradition that has hitherto been his to the new meaning he has learned. Or,

A particularly striking passage is the following from Luther's *Table-Talk* (Wei. v. 5820) :

'Omnium hominum mentibus impressa est divinitus notitia Dei. Quod sit Deus, omnes homines sine ulla artium et disciplinarum cognitione sola . natura duce sciunt, et omnium hominum mentibus hoc divinitus impressum est. Nulla umquam fuit tam fera gens et immanis, quae non crediderit, esse divinitatem quandam, quae omnia creavit. Itaque Paulus inquit : Invisibilia Dei a creatura mundi per ea, quae facta sunt, intellecta conspiciuntur, sempiterna eius virtus et divinitas. Quare omnes ethnici sciverunt esse Deum, quantumvis fuerunt Epicurei, quantumvis contenderunt, non esse Deum. Non in eo, quod negant esse Deum, simul confessi sunt esse Deum ? Nemo enim negare id potest, quod nescit. Quare, etsi quidam per omnem vitam in maximis versati sunt flagitiis et sceleribus et non aliter omnino vixerunt, ac si nullus esset Deus, tamen nunquam conscientiam animis potuerunt eicere testantem et affirmantem, quod sit Deus. Et quamvis illa conscientia pravis et perversis opinionibus ad tempus oppressa fuit, redit tamen et convincit eos in extremae vitae spiritu.'

'The knowledge of God is impressed upon the mind of every man by God. Under the sole guidance of nature all men know that God is— without any acquaintance with the arts or sciences ; and this is divinely imprinted upon all men's minds. There has never been a people so wild and savage that it did not believe that there is some divine power that created all things. And thus it is that Paul says : "the invisible things of God from the creation of the world are clearly seen, being understood by the things that are made, even His eternal power and Godhead." Wherefore all the Gentiles knew that there is a God, however much they were Epicureans, however much they maintained that there is no God. Did they not confess God's being in that very denial of Him ? For no one can deny that of which he has no knowledge. Wherefore, although men have all their lives long been occupied in the greatest sins and crimes and have lived just as though there were no God, yet they have never been able to cast forth from their minds the conscience that testifies and affirms that God is. And although that conscience has been overborne for a time by evil and perverse opinions, yet it comes back to convict them in their life's final breath.'

where resistance is offered to the new teaching, it is yet often
noticeably in the face of pressure the other way from the
man's own conscience. Such experiences have been made
known to me by missionaries among the Tibetans and among
African negroes, and it would be interesting to make a collection
of them, both in regard to the general question of the *a priori*
factors in religion, and especially as throwing light upon the
a priori knowledge of the essential interdependence of the
rational and the non-rational elements in the idea of God.
For this the history of religion is itself an almost unanimous
witness. Incomplete and defective as the process of moralizing
the ' numina ' may often have been throughout the wide regions
of primitive religious life, everywhere there are traces of it to
be found. And wherever religion, escaping from its first
crudity of manifestation, has risen to a higher type, this
process of synthesis has in all cases set in and continued
more and more positively. And this is all the more remarkable when one considers at what widely different dates the
imaginative creation of the figures of gods had its rise in
different cases, and under what diverse conditions of race,
natural endowment, and social and political structure its
evolution proceeded. All this points to the existence of
a priori factors universally and necessarily latent in the
human spirit : those, in fact, which we can find directly in
our own religious consciousness, when we, too, like Adeimantos,
naïvely and spontaneously concur with Socrates' saying, as
with an axiom whose truth we have seen for ourselves : ' God
is single, and true in deed and word.'

As the rational elements, following *a priori* principles, come
together in the historical evolution of religions with the non-
rational, they serve to 'schematize' these. This is true, not
only in general of the relation of the rational aspect of ' the
holy', taken as a whole, to its non-rational, taken as a whole,
but also in detail of the several constituent elements of the
two aspects. The *tremendum*, the daunting and repelling
moment of the numinous, is schematized by means of the
rational ideas of justice, moral will, and the exclusion of what
is opposed to morality ; and schematized thus, it becomes the

holy ' Wrath of God ', which Scripture and Christian preaching alike proclaim. The *fascinans*, the attracting and alluring moment of the numinous, is schematized by means of the ideas of goodness, mercy, love, and, so schematized, becomes all that we mean by Grace, that term so rich in import, which unites with the holy Wrath in a single ' harmony of contrasts ', and like it is, from the numinous strain in it, tinged with Mysticism. The moment *mysteriosum* is schematized by the *absoluteness* of all rational attributes applied to the Deity. Probably the correspondence here implied—between ' the mysterious ' and the *absoluteness* of all rational attributes—will not appear at first sight so immediately evident as in the two foregoing cases, Wrath and Grace. None the less it is a very exact correspondence. God's rational attributes can be distinguished from like attributes applied to the created spirit by being not relative, as those are, but absolute. Human love is relative, admitting of degrees, and it is the same with human knowledge and human goodness. God's love and knowledge and goodness, on the other hand, and all else that can be asserted of Him in conceptual terms, are formally absolute. The *content* of the attributes is the same ; it is an *element of form* which marks them apart as attributes of God. But such an element of form is also the ' mysterious ' as such : it is, as we saw on p. 31, the formal aspect of the ' wholly other '. But to this plain correspondence of the two things, ' the mysterious ' and the absoluteness of rational attributes, a further one must be added. Our understanding can only compass the relative. That which is in contrast absolute, though it may in a sense be *thought*, cannot be *thought home, thought out* ; it is within the reach of our conceiving, but it is beyond the grasp of our comprehension. Now, though this does not make what is ' absolute ' itself genuinely ' mysterious ', as this term was expounded on p. 28, it does make it a genuine *schema* of ' the mysterious '. The absolute exceeds our power to comprehend ; the mysterious wholly eludes it. The absolute is that which surpasses the limits of our understanding, not through its actual qualitative character, for that is familiar to us, but through its formal character. The mysterious, on the other

L

hand, is that which lies altogether outside what can be thought, and is, alike in form, quality, and essence, the utterly and ' wholly other '. We see, then, that in the case of the moment of ' mystery ', as well as those of ' awefulness ' and ' fascination ', there is an exact correspondence between the non-rational element and its rational *schema*, and one that admits of development.

By the continual living activity of its non-rational elements a religion is guarded from passing into ' rationalism '. By being steeped in and saturated with rational elements it is guarded from sinking into fanaticism or mere mysticality, or at least from persisting in these, and is qualified to become a religion for all civilized humanity. The degree in which both rational and non-rational elements are jointly present, united in healthy and lovely harmony, affords a criterion to measure the relative rank of religions—and one, too, that is specifically religious. Applying this criterion, we find that Christianity, in this as in other respects, stands out in complete superiority over all its sister religions. The lucid edifice of its clear and pure conceptions, feelings, and experiences is built up on a foundation that goes far deeper than the rational. Yet the non-rational is only the basis, the setting, the woof in the fabric, ever preserving for Christianity its mystical depth, giving religion thereby the deep undertones and heavy shadows of Mysticism, without letting it develop into a mere rank growth of mysticality. And thus Christianity, in the healthily proportioned union of its elements, assumes an absolutely classical form and dignity, which is only the more vividly attested in consciousness as we proceed honestly and without prejudice to set it in its place in the comparative study of religions. Then we shall recognize that in Christianity an element of man's spiritual life, which yet has its analogies in other fields, has for the first time come to maturity in a supreme and unparalleled way.

CHAPTER XVIII

THE MANIFESTATIONS OF THE 'HOLY' AND THE FACULTY OF 'DIVINATION'.

It is one thing merely to believe in a reality beyond the senses and another to have experience of it also; it is one thing to have ideas of 'the holy' and another to become consciously aware of it as an operative reality, intervening actively in the phenomenal world. Now it is a fundamental conviction of all religions, of religion as such, we may say, that this latter is possible as well as the former. Religion is convinced not only that the holy and sacred reality is attested by the inward voice of conscience and the religious consciousness, the 'still, small voice' of the Spirit in the heart, by feeling, presentiment, and longing, but also that it may be directly encountered in particular occurrences and events, self-revealed in persons and displayed in actions, in a word, that beside the inner revelation from the Spirit there is an outward revelation of the divine nature. Religious language gives the name of 'sign' to such demonstrative actions and manifestations, in which holiness stands palpably self-revealed. From the time of the most primitive religions everything has counted as a sign that was able to arouse in man the sense of the holy, to excite the feeling of apprehended sanctity, and stimulate it into open activity. Of this kind were those factors and circumstances of which we have already spoken—the thing terrible, sublime, overpowering, or astounding, and in an especial degree the uncomprehended, mysterious thing, which became the 'portent' and 'miracle'. But, as we saw, all these were not 'signs' in the true sense, but opportunities, circumstances, prompting the religious feeling to awake of itself; and the factor promoting this result was found to lie in an element common to them all, but merely analogous with 'the holy'. The interpretation of them as actual appearances of the holy itself in its own nature meant, we saw, a confounding of the category of holiness with something only outwardly resembling it : it was not a genuine '*anamnesis*', a genuine recognition of the holy in its own authentic nature, made manifest in appearance.   And therefore we find that such false recognitions of the holy are later rejected and wholly or partly extruded as inadequate or simply unworthy, so soon as a higher level of development and a purer religious judgement have been reached. There is a precisely parallel process in another department of judgement, that of aesthetic taste.   While the taste is still crude, a feeling or fore-feeling of the beautiful begins to stir, which must come from an obscure *a priori* conception of beauty already present, else it could not occur at all.   The man of crude taste, not being capable of a clear 'recognition' of authentic beauty, falls into confusion and *misapplies* this obscure, dim conception of the beautiful, judging things to be beautiful which are in fact not beautiful at all.   Here, as in the case of the judgement of holiness, the principle underlying the erroneous judgement of beauty is one of faint analogy. Certain elements in the thing wrongly judged to be beautiful have a closer or remoter analogy to real beauty.   And later here, too, when his taste has been educated, the man rejects with strong aversion the quasi-beautiful but not really beautiful thing and becomes qualified to see and to judge rightly, i. e. to recognize as beautiful the outward object in which the 'beauty' of which he has an inward notion and standard really 'appears'.

Let us call the faculty, of whatever sort it may be, of *genuinely* cognizing and recognizing the holy in its appearances, the faculty of *divination*.   Does such a faculty exist, and, if so, what is its nature ?

To the 'supernaturalistic' theory the matter is simple enough.   Divination consists in the fact that a man encounters an occurrence that is not 'natural', in the sense of being inexplicable by the laws of nature.   Since it has actually occurred, it must have had a cause; and, since it has no 'natural' cause, it must (so it is said) have a supernatural one. This theory of divination is a genuine, solidly rationalist theory, put together with rigid concepts in a strict demonstrative form and intended as such. And it claims that the capacity or faculty of divination is the *understanding*, the faculty of reflection in concept and demonstration. The transcendent is here proved as strictly as anything can be proved, logically from given premisses.

It would be almost superfluous to adduce in detail in opposition to this view the argument that we have no possibility of establishing that an event did not arise from natural causes or was in conflict with the laws of nature. The religious consciousness itself rises against this desiccation and materialization of what in all religion is surely the most tender and living moment, the actual discovery of and encounter with very deity. Here, if anywhere, coercion by proof and demonstration and the mistaken application of logical and juridical processes should be excluded; here, if anywhere, should be liberty, the unconstrained recognition and inward acknowledgement that comes from deep within the soul, stirred spontaneously, apart from all conceptual theory. If not 'natural science' or 'metaphysics', at least the matured religious consciousness itself spurns such ponderously solid intellectualistic explanations. They are born of rationalism and engender it again; and, as for genuine 'divination', they not only impede it, but despise it as extravagant emotionalism, mysticality, and false romanticism. Genuine divination, in short, has nothing whatever to do with natural law and the relation or lack of relation to it of something experienced. It is not concerned at all with the way in which a phenomenon—be it event, person, or thing—came into existence, but with what it *means*, that is, with its significance as a 'sign' of the holy.

The faculty or capacity of divination appears in the language of dogma hidden beneath the fine name '*testimonium Spiritus Sancti internum*', the inner witness of the Holy Spirit —limited, in the case of dogma, to the recognition of *Scripture* as 'Holy'. And this name is the only right one, and right in a more than figurative sense, when the capacity of divination is itself grasped and appraised by divination. This is not our task here. We therefore employ a psychological rather than a religious expression as being more appropriate to the nature of our discussion.

In this sense, then, 'divination' is no new theological discovery. Schleiermacher, in his *Discourses upon Religion* (1799), Jacob Friedrich Fries, in his doctrine of '*Ahndung*' ('inkling', surmise, presage), and Schleiermacher's colleague and Fries's pupil, De Wette, have all in effect made use of it and given it a footing in theology, the last-named with special reference to the divination of the divine in history, under the name 'Surmise of the divine government of the world'. I have discussed Schleiermacher's discovery at greater length in my edition of his *Discourses*,[1] and in my volume, *Kantisch-Fries'sche Religionsphilosophie und ihre Anwendung auf die Theologie*, I have given a more precise statement of the 'Ahndung' theory, as it is found in Fries and De Wette. To these two works the reader is referred for a more detailed exposition of the matter, and I shall here note only very briefly the more salient features of this doctrine.

What Schleiermacher is feeling after is really the faculty or capacity of deeply absorbed *contemplation*, when confronted by the vast, living totality and reality of things as it is in nature and history. Wherever a mind is exposed in a spirit of absorbed submission to impressions of 'the universe', it becomes capable—so he lays it down—of experiencing 'intuitions' and 'feelings' (*Anschauungen* and *Gefühle*) of something that is, as it were, a sheer overplus, in addition to empirical reality. This overplus, while it cannot be apprehended by mere theoretic cognition of the world and the cosmic system in the form it assumes for science, can nevertheless be really and truly grasped and experienced in *intuition*, and is given form in single 'intuitions'. And these, in turn, assume shape in definite statements and propositions, capable of a certain groping formulation, which are not without analogy

[1] Schleiermacher's *Über die Religion*.   Vandenhoeck & Ruprecht, Göttingen, pp. 17 ff.

with theoretic propositions, but are to be clearly distinguished from them by their free and merely felt, not reasoned, character. In themselves they are groping intimations of meanings figuratively apprehended. They cannot be employed as 'statements of doctrine' in the strict sense, and can neither be built into a system nor used as premisses for theoretical conclusions. But, though these intuitions are limited and inadequate, they are none the less indisputably *true*, i. e. true as far as they go ; and for all Schleiermacher's aversion to the word in this connexion they must certainly be termed *cognitions*, modes of *knowing*, though, of course, not the product of reflection, but the intuitive outcome of feeling. Their import is the glimpse of an Eternal, in and beyond the temporal and penetrating it, the apprehension of a ground and meaning of things in and beyond the empirical and transcending it. They are *surmises* of a Reality fraught with mystery and momentousness. And it is to be noted that Schleiermacher himself sometimes avails himself of the term '*ahnden*' (divining, surmise) instead of his principal ones, ' intuition ' and ' feeling', and expressly connects together the divination of prophecy and the knowledge of 'miracle' in the religious sense of a 'sign'.

When Schleiermacher, in expounding the nature of the experience, tries to elucidate its object by giving examples, he is for the most part led to adduce impressions of a higher τέλος, an ultimate, mysterious, cosmic purposiveness, of which we have a prescient intimation. Here he is quite in agreement with the exposition of Fries, who defines the faculty of ' *Ahndung* ' as being just a faculty of divining the ' objective teleology ' of the world. And De Wette says the same thing even more unreservedly. But in Schleiermacher this rational element is none the less grounded in eternal mystery, that basis of the cosmos that goes beyond reason. This is shown in the groping, hesitant, tentative manner in which the meaning of the experience always reveals itself. And it is emphasized especially forcibly when Schleiermacher shows where in his own case this experience is to be found in the world he confronts; that it is not so much in its universal conformity to law—a rational quality, interpretable by the intellect in terms of purpose—but rather by means of what appears to us as a baffling 'exception' to law, thereby hinting at a meaning that eludes our understanding.[1]

No intellectual, dialectical dissection or justification of such intuition is possible, nor indeed should any be attempted, for the essence most peculiar to it would only be destroyed thereby.   Rather it is once again to aesthetic judgements we must look for the plainest analogy to it.   And the faculty of judging (*Urteilsvermögen*),here presupposed by Schleiermacher, certainly belongs to that 'Judgement' (*Urteilskraft*), which Kant analyses in his Third Critique, and which he himself sets as 'aesthetic judgement' in antithesis to logical judgement. Only, we may not infer from this that the particular several judgements passed in this way need be judgements of 'taste' in their *content*.   Kant's distinction between the 'aesthetic' and logical judgement did not mean to imply that the faculty of 'aesthetic' judgement was a judgement upon 'aesthetic' objects in the special narrow sense of the term 'aesthetic', as being concerned with the beautiful.   His primary intention is simply and in general terms to separate the faculty of judgement based upon feeling of whatever sort from that of the understanding, from discursive, conceptual thought and inference; and his term 'aesthetic' is simply meant to mark as the peculiarity of the former that, in contrast to logical judgement, it is not worked out in accordance with a clear intellectual scheme, but in conformity to obscure, dim principles which must be felt and cannot be *stated* explicitly as premisses.   Kant employs sometimes another expression also to denote such obscure, dim principles of judgement, based on pure feeling, viz. the phrase 'not-unfolded' or 'unexplicated concepts' ('*unausgewickelte Begriffe*'); and his meaning is here exactly that of the poet, when he says:

> Und wecket der dunklen Gefühle Gewalt,
> Die im Herzen wunderbar schliefen.[2]

[1] Op. cit., p. 53.

[2] 'It waketh the power of feelings obscure
That in the heart wondrously slumbered.'
(SCHILLER: *Der Graf von Habsburg.*)

Or again:

> Was von Menschen nicht gewusst
> Oder nicht bedacht,
> Durch das Labyrinth der Brust
> Wandelt bei der Nacht.[1]

On the other hand, those judgements that spring from pure contemplative feeling also resemble judgements of aesthetic taste in claiming, like them, objective validity, universality, and necessity. The apparently subjective and personal character of the judgement of taste, expressed in the maxim : ' De gustibus non disputandum ', simply amounts to this, that tastes of different degrees of culture and maturity are first compared, then so opposed one to the other that agreement is impossible. But unanimity, even in judgements of taste, grows and strengthens in the measure in which the taste matures with exercise; so that even here, despite the proverb, there is the possibility of taste being expounded and taught, the possibility of a continually improving appreciation, of convincement and conviction. And if this is true of the judgement arising from aesthetic feeling in the narrower sense, it is at least equally true of the judgement arising from ' contemplation '. Where, on the basis of a real talent in this direction, 'contemplation ' grows by careful exercise in depth and inwardness, there what one man feels *can* be ' expounded ' and ' brought to consciousness ' in another : one man can both educate himself to a genuine and true manner of feeling and be the means of bringing others to the same point ; and that is what corresponds in the domain of ' contemplation ' to the part played by argument and persuasion in that of logical conviction.

Schleiermacher's exposition of his great discovery suffers from two defects. We will consider one of them here, leaving the other to the next chapter. Schleiermacher, then, naïvely and unreflectingly assumes this faculty or capacity of ' divination ' to be a universal one. In point of fact it is not

---

[1] 'What beyond our conscious knowing
Or our thought's extremest span
Threads by night the labyrinthine
Pathways of the breast of man.'

(GOETHE : *An den Mond.*)

universal if this means that it could be presupposed necessarily in every man of religious conviction as an actual fact, though of course Schleiermacher is quite right in counting it among the general capacities of mind and spirit, and regarding it indeed as the deepest and most peculiar element in mind, and in that sense—man being defined by his intelligent mind—calling it a 'universal human' element.   But what is a universal potentiality of man as such is by no means to be found in *actuality* the universal possession of every single man; very frequently it is only disclosed as a special endowment and equipment of particular gifted individuals.   And Schleiermacher gives an excellent indication of how the matter rightly lies in his very interesting exposition of the nature and function of the '*Mittler*' (mediator) in his first 'Discourse'. Not Man in general (as rationalism holds), but only special 'divinatory' natures possess the faculty of divination in actuality; and it is these that receive impressions of the transcendent, not the undifferentiated aggregate of homogeneous individuals in mutual interplay, as held by modern social psychology.[1]

It is questionable whether Schleiermacher himself, in spite of his (re-)discovery of 'divination', was a really 'divinatory' nature, although in his first 'Discourse' he maintains that he is.   One of his contemporaries, to wit, Goethe, was at any rate decidedly his superior in this respect.   In Goethe's life the power of divination, not latent but finding vital exercise, plays an important part, and it finds singular expression in the meaning he gives to the term 'daemonic', put with such emphasis in *Dichtung und Wahrheit*, Book 20, and in his *Talks* with Eckermann.[2]   Let us briefly examine these.   The most characteristic feature in his notion of the 'daemonic' is

[1] And this is undoubtedly true as far back as the lowest levels of development, when the 'religious dread' first begins to stir in primitive form and to manifest itself in ideas.   To derive these from an original group- and mass-fantasy collectively operating is itself sheer fantasy, and the results this theory helps to produce are about as queer and grotesque as any of the ideas of which it treats.

[2] Cf. Goethe's *Sämtliche Werke*, ed. Cotta, vol. xxv, pp. 124 ff.; Eckermann, *Gespräche mit Goethe*, ed. A. v. d. Linden, Part II, pp. 140 ff.

that it goes beyond all ' conceiving ', surpasses ' understanding' and ' reason ', and consequently is ' inapprehensible ' and cannot properly be put into a statement :

'The Daemonic is that which cannot be accounted for by understanding and reason. It chooses for itself obscure times of darkness. . . . In a plain, prosaic town like Berlin it would hardly find an opportunity to manifest itself. . . . In Poetry there is from first to last something daemonic, and especially in its unconscious appeal, for which all intellect and reason is insufficient, and which, therefore, has an efficacy beyond all concepts. Such is the effect in Music in the highest degree, for Music stands too high for any understanding to reach, and an all-mastering efficacy goes forth from it, of which however no man is able to give an account. Religious worship cannot therefore do without music. It is one of the foremost means to work upon men with an effect of *marvel.*'

'Does not the daemonic (asks Eckermann) also appear in *events* ? ' ' Pre-eminently so,' said Goethe, ' and assuredly in all which we cannot explain by intellect or reason. And in general it is manifested throughout nature, visible and invisible, in the most diverse ways. Many creatures in the animal kingdom are of a wholly daemonic kind, and in many we see some aspect of the daemonic operative.'

We notice here how the elements of the numinous we discovered plainly recur : the wholly non-rational, incomprehensible by concepts, the elements of mystery, fascination, awefulness, and energy. The note of the ' daemonic ' in the animal kingdom reminds us of Job and the ' leviathan '. But in another respect Goethe's intuition falls far short of Job's intuition of the ' mysterium '. By his ignoring of the warning of the book of Job and by applying to the ' mysterium ' the standards of the rational understanding and reason and conceptions of human purpose, the non-rational comes to involve for Goethe a contradiction between meaning and meaninglessness, sense and nonsense, that which promotes and that which frustrates human ends. Sometimes, however, he approximates it to *wisdom*, as when he says :

'So there was something daemonic governing the circumstances of my acquaintance with Schiller all through. We might have met earlier or later. But that we should have met just at the time when I had my Italian tour behind me and Schiller had begun to weary of his philosophical speculations—that was a fact of great significance and fraught with success for both of us.'

It even comes near the divine:

'Such occurrences have often befallen me throughout my life. And one comes in such cases to believe in a higher influence (*Einwirkung*), something daemonic, to which one pays adoration, without presuming to try to explain it further.'

Invariably the 'daemonic' has an import of 'energy' and 'overpoweringness', and sets its stamp upon men of vehement and overpowering personality.

'Napoleon', said I, 'seems to have been a daemonic sort of man.'

'He was so absolutely and to such a degree', said Goethe, 'that hardly any other man can be compared with him in this respect. The late Grand Duke also was a daemonic nature, full of limitless, active force and restlessness.'

'Has not Mephistopheles also " daemonic " traits ? '

'No, he is much too negative a being. The daemonic manifests itself in a downright positive and active power.'

In *Dichtung und Wahrheit* (p. 126) he delineates still better the impressions such numinous persons make, and in this passage especially sets in the foreground our 'tremendum' as the element alike of 'dread' and 'overpoweringness'.

'This daemonic character appears in its most *dreadful* form when it stands out dominatingly in some *man*. Such are not always the most remarkable men, either in spiritual quality or natural talents, and they seldom have any goodness of heart to recommend them.[1] But an incredible force goes forth from them and they exercise an incredible power over all creatures, nay, perhaps even over the elements. And who can say how far such an influence may not extend ? '

But the efficacy and influence of such a 'daemonic' man, even when it is beneficent, moves to amazement rather than to admiration; it is more a tumultuous urgency than ordinary agency, and is at any rate absolutely non-rational. This is

---

[1] i. e. they are merely '*numinous*', not '*holy*' men.

what Goethe tries to describe in the series of antitheses in *Dichtung und Wahrheit* (p. 124):

'... Something that only manifested itself in contradictions and therefore could not be comprehended under any concept, still less under any one word. It was not divine, for it seemed unreasonable; not human, for it lacked understanding; not devilish, for it was beneficent; not angelic, for it often displayed malicious joy. It was like chance, for it pointed to no consequence; it resembled providence, for it indicated connexion and unity. All that hems us in seemed penetrable to it; it seemed to dispose at will of the inevitable elements of our being, contracting time and expanding space. Only in the impossible did it seem at home, and the possible it spurned from itself with contempt.

'Although this daemonic thing can be manifested in everything corporeal and incorporeal, finding indeed most notable expression among animals, still it is pre-eminently with men that it stands in closest and most wonderful connexion, and there fashions a power which, if not opposed to the moral world order, yet intersects it in such a way that the one might be taken for the warp and the other for the woof.'

There can be no clearer expression than this of the prodigiously strong impression which divination of the numinous may make upon the mind, and that obviously not on a single occasion but repeatedly, till it has become almost a matter of habit. But at the same time this 'divination' of Goethe is not one that apprehends the numinous as the prophet does. It does not rise to the elevation of the experience of Job, where the non-rational mystery is at the same time experienced and extolled as supra-rational, as of profoundest *value*, and as holiness in its own right. It is rather the fruit of a mind which, for all its depth, was not equal to such profundities as these, and to which, therefore, the non-rational counterpoint to the melody of life could only sound in confused consonance, not in its authentic harmony, indefinable but palpable. Therefore, though it is genuine divination, it is the divination of Goethe 'the pagan', as he sometimes used to call himself. Indeed, it is a divination that functions only at the level of the 'daemonic' which, as we saw, precedes religion proper, not at the level of the divine

and the holy in the truest sense ; and it shows very clearly how
that sort of merely ' daemonic ' experience of the numinous
may in a highly cultivated mind only stir emotional reactions
of bewilderment and bedazzlement, without giving real light
or warmth to the soul. Goethe did not understand how to
adjust this divination of the ' daemonic ' to his own higher
conception of the divine ; and, when Eckermann turned the
conversation to that, his answer was hesitating and evasive :

' The operative, efficacious force (said I tentatively), which
we call the " daemonic ", does not seem to fit in with the idea
of the divine.' ' Dear boy,' said Goethe, ' what do we know
of the idea of the divine, and what can our narrow conceptions
presume to tell of the Supreme Being ?   If I called him by a
hundred names, like a Turk, I should yet fall short and have
said nothing in comparison to the boundlessness of his attributes.'

But, if we leave out of account the comparatively low level
of Goethe's ' divination ', we have yet in it a most exact
example of what Schleiermacher had in mind.   These are
' intuitions and feelings ', if not of something divine, still of
something numinous in the natural world and in history, and
intuitions brought to the higher vitality by an individual with
an innate ' divinatory ' gift.   At the same time the principles
on which this divination works cannot even be suggested, for
all the examples Goethe may give.   What does the ' daemonic '
really consist in ?   How does he come to be conscious of it ?
How does he identify it as one and the same through all the
manifold and contradictory forms in which it manifests itself?
These are the questions to which Goethe can suggest no answer.
It is evident that in this experience he is being guided by
'mere feeling ', that is, by an *a priori* principle that is not
explicit and overt, but dim and obscure.

CHAPTER XIX

DIVINATION IN PRIMITIVE CHRISTIANITY

In the last chapter we spoke of two defects in Schleier-macher's doctrine of divination. The first of these — his misleading assumption that this is a universal human faculty —has already been considered, and we have now to turn to the second. This is that, though Schleiermacher's description of divination in relation to the world of nature and history has both warmth and insight, he gives no clear detailed account, but only the scantiest hints, of what is after all its worthiest object and the object most propitious to its develop-ment, namely, the history of *religion*, especially that of the Bible and its culmination in the person of Christ himself. His concluding 'discourse' makes emphatic and significant mention of Christianity and Christ, but Christ is here only introduced as the supreme divining *subject*, not as the *object* of divination *par excellence*. And it is the same in Schleiermacher's '*Glaubens-lehre*'. In this, too, the significance of Christ is, essentially, intended to be fully given in the fact that he 'admits us into the power and beatitude of his consciousness of God'. Now this is a thought of high value, but it does not attain to that supreme value which Christianity imputes to Christ, of being in his own person 'holiness made manifest', that is, a person in whose being, life, and mode of living we realize of ourselves by 'intuition and feeling' the self-revealing power and pre-sence of the Godhead. For to the Christian it is a momentous question whether or no a real divination—a direct, first-hand apprehension of holiness manifested, the 'intuition' and 'feel-ing' of it—can be got from the person and life of Christ; whether, in short, 'the holy' can be independently experienced in him, making him a real revelation of it.

In this matter we can obviously get no help from the painful and fundamentally impossible inquiries, so often started, into ' Jesus' consciousness of himself '. They are impossible, if for no other reason, because the evidence at our disposal is neither sufficient in quantity nor appropriate to such a purpose. Jesus puts as the content of his message and all his utterances, not himself, but the ' kingdom ', its beatitude and righteousness, and, in its first and most straightforward interpretation, the 'gospel' is the 'good tidings' of the kingdom of God. What statements about himself do occur are fragmentary and incidental. But even were this not the case, even if we could find in the gospels a detailed theory of Jesus as to his own nature, what would this prove ? Religious enthusiasts have not infrequently had recourse to the most exalted modes of self-proclamation, and often enough no doubt their statements about themselves have been completely bona fide and sincere. And it is just such self-revealing statements of the prophets of all ages that are more than any others dependent for their form upon their temporal or local context, the equipment of myth or dogma with which his environment supplies the speaker. The fact that the prophet or seer or inspired teacher applies all this material to state something about himself merely demonstrates the intensity of his self-consciousness, his sense of mission, his conviction, and his claim to belief and obedience—all of which are to be taken for granted where a man stands forward in response to an inner call. The immediate, intuitive ' divination ' of which we are speaking would indeed *not* come as a result of such statements by the prophet about himself, however complete ; they can arouse a belief in his authority, but cannot bring about the peculiar experience of spontaneous insight that here is something holy made manifest. ' We have heard him ourselves and know that this is indeed the Christ ' (St. John iv. 42).

It cannot now be doubted that such an avowal was made to him as a result of a spontaneous, original divination. This must at any rate be true of Christ's own first disciples. Otherwise it would be unintelligible how the Church could have come into existence at all. Mere proclamation, mere authoritative statement, cannot bring about these massive certainties and that impelling strength, that power to maintain and assert itself, which were necessary if the Christian community was to come into being and which can be recognized in it as its unmistakable characteristics.

Misapprehension of this is only possible if, attempting a one-sided approach to the phenomenon of the origin of the Christian Church, we try to reconstruct the facts solely by the methods of scholarship and out of the material afforded by the staled feelings and blunted sensibility of our present-day artificial civilization and complex mentality. It would be an advantage if, in addition to these methods, an attempt were made to frame a less abstract intuition of the genesis of original and genuine religious communities with the aid of living instances of the thing as it may still be found to-day. It would be necessary for this to seek places and moments at which even to-day religion shows itself alive as a naïve emotional force, with all its primal quality of impulse and instinct. This can still be studied in remote corners of the Mohammedan and Indian world. Even to-day one may come upon scenes in the streets of Mogador or Marrakesh, which have the strangest outward resemblance to those recorded by the Synoptic Gospels : ' holy men ' (and very queer specimens they generally are !) now and then make their appearance, each the centre of a group of disciples, and about them the people come and go, listening to their sayings, looking at their miracles, observing how they live and what they do. Bands of adherents gather round them, more loosely or more closely united as the case may be. ' Logia ', tales, and legends form and accumulate ; [1] new brotherhoods arise or, if already arisen, extend in widen-

---

[1] It is astonishing that the main problem of Gospel criticism, viz. how the collection of ' Logia ' arose, is not studied in this still living milieu. It is even more astonishing that the logia-series were not long ago elucidated from the closely corresponding milieu of the ' Sayings of the Fathers ' (ἀποφθέγματα τῶν πατέρων), from the Hadith of Muhammed, or from the Franciscan legends. And a particular striking case of the same thing is the collection of the Logia of Rāma-Krishna, which has grown to completion in our own day and under our very eyes.

M

ing circles. But the centre of it all is always the man himself,
a 'holy man' in his lifetime, and what sustains the movement
is always the peculiar power of his personality, the special
impression he makes on the bystander. Those who should know
assure us that ninety-eight per cent. of these 'holy men' are
impostors ; but, even so, we are left with two per cent. who are
not, a surprisingly high percentage in the case of a matter that
invites and facilitates imposture as much as this does.   The
consideration of this remaining two per cent. should continue to
throw much light on the actual fact of the genesis of a religious community.   The point is that the 'holy man' or the
'prophet' is from the outset, as regards the experience of the
circle of his devotees, something more than a 'mere man'
(ψιλὸς ἄνθρωπος). He is the being of wonder and mystery,
who somehow or other is felt to belong to the higher order of
things, to the side of the numen itself.   It is not that he
himself teaches that he is such, but that he is experienced as
such.   And it is only such experiences, which, while they may
be crude enough and result often enough in self-deception,
must at least be profoundly and strongly felt, that can give
rise to religious communities.

Such cases of contemporary religious movements afford
after all a very inadequate analogy, far removed from that
which occurred long ago in Palestine. Yet, if even these movements are only made possible by the fact that men actually
experience, or presume that they experience, veritable holiness
in the personalities of individuals, how far more true must
this not be of the early Christian community ! That this was
so is attested directly by the whole spirit and the universal
conviction of the early communities as a whole, so far as we
can discern it in their modest records. And certain of the
slighter touches in the Synoptic portrait of Jesus confirm the
fact expressly in particular cases. We may instance here the
narratives already referred to of Peter's haul of fishes (Luke
v. 8), and of the centurion of Capernaum (Matt. viii. 8 ; Luke
vii. 6), which point to spontaneous responses of feeling when the
holy is directly encountered in experience.   Especially apt in
this connexion is the passage in Mark x. 32 : καὶ ἦν προάγων

αὐτοὺς ὁ Ἰησοῦς· καὶ ἐθαμβοῦντο, οἱ δὲ ἀκολουθοῦντες ἐφο-
βοῦντο ('and Jesus went before them: and they were amazed;
and as they followed, they were afraid'). This passage
renders with supreme simplicity and force the immediate
impression of the numinous that issued from the man
Jesus, and no artistry of characterization could do it so
powerfully as these few masterly and pregnant words. The
later saying in John xx. 28 (the confession of Thomas, ' My
Lord and my God ') may perhaps appear to us by contrast
the utterance of a time too far-reaching in its formulations, and
very far removed from the simplicity of the original experience of the disciples. And this passage in Mark may appeal
to us all the more just because the living emotion here dis-
dains any precise formulation at all; none the less does it
contain the real roots of all later developments of Christology.

Such intimations of the numinous impression made by Jesus
upon those who knew him occur in the Gospel narrative only,
as it were, incidentally to the main purpose of the narrator,
who is scarcely interested in them, but absorbed rather in
miracle- or other records. In our eyes their interest is all the
greater, and we can fancy how numerous similar experiences
must have been of which no trace survives in the records, just
because there was no miracle to be told of in connexion with
them and they were simply taken for granted by the narrator
as a matter of course.

To this place belong further the belief in Jesus' supremacy
over the demonic world and the tendency to legend that began
to take effect from the start; the fact that his own relatives
take him for a man 'possessed', an involuntary acknowledgement of the 'numinous' impression he made upon them; and
in an especial degree the conviction that breaks spontaneously
upon the minds of his disciples as by a sudden impact, won not
from his teaching but from the very experience of him, that
he is the 'Messiah', the being who stood for the circle in
which he moved as the numinous being *par excellence*. The
experiential character of this belief in his Messiahship stands
out clearly in Peter's first confession and Jesus' answer to
it (Matt. xvi. 15–17), ' Flesh and blood have not revealed it

M 2

unto thee, but my Father, which is in heaven.' Jesus himself
is astonished at Peter's confession, which shows that this was
not learnt on authority, but found out by Peter himself, a
genuine *discovery*, arising from the impression Jesus made
upon him and the testimony borne to it in the depth of the
mind, where no teaching of flesh and blood, or even of 'the
word', can avail, but only 'my Father in heaven' himself and
without any intermediary.

For this factor—the mind's own witness to the impression—
is, it need hardly be said, an indispensable one. Without it
all 'impression' is without effect, or rather no impression
could occur at all.   Therefore, all doctrines of the 'impression
made by Christ' are inadequate if they do not pay regard to this
second element, which indeed is nothing but the mental predisposition necessary for the experience of holiness, to wit, the
category of the holy, potentially present in the spirit as a dim
or obscure *a priori* cognition. 'Impress' or 'impression',
that is, presupposes something capable of receiving impressions, and that is just what the mind is not, if in itself it is
only a 'tabula rasa'. In that richer sense in which we use the
word here, we do not in fact mean by 'impression' merely the
'impression' which, in the theory of the Sensationalist school,
is the psychical result of sense-perception and is left behind as
a psychical trace or vestige of the percept. To be 'impressed' by
some one, in the sense we use the term here, means rather to
cognize or recognize in him a peculiar significance and to
humble oneself before it. And we maintain that this is only
possible by an element of cognition, comprehension, and valuation in one's own inner consciousness, that goes out to meet
the outward presented fact, i. e. by the 'spirit within'. In
Schleiermacher's language the 'presentiment' goes out to meet
the 'revelation' to which it belongs. Music can only be understood by the musical person; none but he receives an 'impression' of it. And to every unique kind of real impression
corresponds in the same way a unique and special sort of 'con-
geniality', if the word may be used in this special sense of
a particular disposition or aptitude, akin to the object
arousing the impression. 'Nemo audit verbum, nisi spiritu

intus docente.' Once again let us recall the example of the beautiful. A beautiful thing can only make an impression as such, i. e. as signifying beauty, if and in so far as a man possesses in himself *a priori* the potentiality of framing a special standard of valuation, viz. aesthetic valuation. Such a disposition can only be understood as an original, obscure awareness and appreciation of the value of 'beauty' itself. Because a man has this in him, or better, because he is capable of realizing it by training, he is able to recognize beauty in the particular given beautiful object that he encounters, to feel the correspondence of this object with the hidden 'standard of value' within him. And so, and only so, will he get an 'impression'.

CHAPTER XX

DIVINATION IN CHRISTIANITY TO-DAY

THE question whether the primitive Church did or could experience holiness in the person of Christ, which we can but answer in the affirmative, is not so important to us as the question whether we too to-day can still do so. Has the portrayal of Christ's life, his actions and achievement, as preserved and handed down by the Christian Church, the value and power of a revelation for us to-day, or do we in this matter but live upon the inheritance bequeathed us by the first community of Christians and base our faith on the authority and testimony of others? There would be no hope of answering this question, were it not that in us too that inner divining power of apprehension and interpretation which has already been considered may find a place—that witness of the spirit, only possible on the basis of a mental predisposition to recognize 'the holy' and to respond to it. If without this no understanding and no 'impression' of Christ was possible even to the first disciples, of what avail should any tradition be that requires the mediation of generations of Christian men? But if we may make this assumption of a predisposing inner 'witness of the Spirit'—as we must —the matter is very different. In that case there is no harm even in the fact that the records of Christ's life are fragmentary, that they contain manifold uncertainties, that they are intermingled with legendary and overlaid with Hellenistic elements. For the Spirit knows and recognizes what is of the Spirit.

As evidence of the way in which this inward principle— this co-witnessing spirit within us—works, prompting, interpreting, and sending out intimation and surmise, I have found the information of a keenly observant missionary from a remote field very instructive. He told me that he had found it a constant matter for fresh astonishment to see how a presentment of the Word so inadequate—which could only hint at its meaning in a difficult foreign tongue and had to work with alien conceptions—could yet at times win so surprisingly deep and inward an acceptance.   And he said that here too the best results always were due to the responsive apprehension that came out of the hearer's heart half-way to meet the presented truth.   Certainly it is only in this fact that we have a clue to the understanding of the problem of St. Paul.   Persecutor of the Church as he was, the intimations he had of the being and meaning of Christ and his Gospel must have come to him piecemeal, in fragmentary hints and caricature.   But the spirit from within forced upon him the acknowledgement to which he succumbed on the way to Damascus.   It taught him that infinitely profound understanding of the Christ made manifest which has led a critic like Wellhausen to confess that, when all is said, no man has understood Christ himself so deeply and thoroughly as Paul.

If, now, the experience of holiness and 'the holy' in Christ is still to be possible and so afford support to our faith, one thing is evidently to be presupposed at the outset, namely, that his own most immediate and primary achievement and intention can be directly understood and appraised in our experience, so that out of this may grow the 'impression' of his holiness with a like directness.   And here a difficulty seems to confront us, which has to be removed if the entire problem is not to be barred from the start.   It is this : is that which we to-day think we find in the person of Christ and in Christianity at bottom at all the same as that which he really intended to achieve and that which the first community of his disciples found in him ?   In other words, has Christianity really a 'principle' of its own, which, however capable of historical evolution, yet remains unchanged in essence, so that the Christianity of to-day may be measured against the faith of the first disciples and awarded a rank essentially the same ?

Is Christianity at all and in a strict sense Jesus' religion ? That is, is the religion we know to-day as Christianity, with its peculiar and unique content of belief and feeling, standing in all its historic greatness and supremacy when measured against other religions, with all its power to-day over the hearts and consciences of men to elevate or to excite, to launch accusation or confer benediction, to attract or to repel—is this religion still in its essence and inner meaning the same thing as the simple, unpretentious religion and form of piety which Jesus himself had, which he himself aroused and 'founded' in the circle of those little, heart-stirred bands of men in that out-of-the-way corner of the world, Galilee ? It must be generally agreed that it has at least changed its form and its colour very significantly since those days, and that it has been exposed to violent alterations and metamorphoses. But is there any abiding essence, any enduring 'principle' at all behind all the sequence of its manifestations, susceptible of evolution and development, but remaining one and the same throughout ? Is it a case of development and evolution, or rather merely of continual transmutation, the influx of something quite different, which one man laments as a perversion, a second admires as a welcome substitution, and a third merely records as a simple historical fact ?

Christianity, as it stands before us to-day in present actuality as a great 'world religion', is indubitably, so far as its claim and promise go, in the first and truest sense a religion of Redemption. Its characteristic ideas to-day are Salvation—overabounding salvation, deliverance from and conquest of the 'world' and from existence in bondage to the world, and even from creaturehood as such, the overcoming of the remoteness of and enmity to God, redemption from servitude to sin and the guilt of sin, reconciliation and atonement, and, in consequence, grace and all the doctrine of grace, the Spirit and the bestowal of the Spirit, the new birth and the new creature. These conceptions are common to Christendom, despite the manifold cleavages that divide it into different confessions, churches, and sects, and they characterize it sharply and definitely as a 'religion of redemption' *par excellence*, setting it in this respect on a level with the great religions of the East, with their sharp, dualistic antithesis of the state of liberation and bondage, nay, justifying its claim not to fall short of these in regard to the necessity of redemption and the grant of salvation, but to surpass them, both in the importance it gives to these conceptions and in the richness of meaning it finds in them.   It cannot be doubted that here, in these elements, is to be found the inner 'principle' and essence of contemporary Christianity to-day, and what we have to ask is whether the wealth of mental and emotional content was in very truth the 'principle' of that plain 'religion of Jesus' long ago, whose establishment must be termed the first and most immediate achievement of Christ.

In answering this question in the affirmative, we would point to a parable which, intended to have reference to the kingdom of God, fits the principle of Christianity equally well: the parable of the grain of mustard seed and the tree that grew therefrom.   This parable hints at a change and altera-tion, for the grown tree is something different from the seed, but an alteration that is no transformation, no transmutation or 'epigenesis', but genuine 'evolution' or development, the transition from potentiality to actuality.

The 'religion of Jesus' does not change gradually into a religion of redemption; it is in its whole design and ten-dency a religion of redemption from its earliest commencement, and that in the most uncompromising sense.   Though it lacks the theological terms which the Church later possessed, its 'redemptive' character is manifest and unambiguous.   If we try to determine as simply and concisely as possible what really characterized the message of Jesus, ignoring what was historically inessential, we are left with two central elements : (1) First, there is the proclamation of *the kingdom of God,* as no mere accessory, but the foundation of the whole Gospel.   This is characteristic of His ministry from the beginning and throughout its course.   (2) Second, there is the reaction against Phariseeism, and, in connexion with this, Jesus' ideal of godli-ness as the attitude and mind of a child when its fault has been forgiven.   But both points comprise in principle every-thing which later became separately formulated in the specifi-cally 'redemptive' doctrines of Christianity: Grace, Election, the Holy Ghost, and Renewal by the Spirit.   These were possessed by and experienced by that first group of disciples as truly as by any later Christians, though in an implicit form. A closer consideration may make this more plain.

To speak of a 'religion of redemption' is, one may say, to be guilty of a redundancy, at any rate if we are considering the more highly developed forms of religion. For every such religion, when once it has won its autonomy and freed itself from dependent reference to an ideal of merely worldly 'welfare' (εὐδαιμονία), whether private or public, develops in itself unique and overabounding ideals of beatitude which may be designated by the general term 'salvation'. Such a 'salvation' is the goal to which the evolution of Indian religions has tended ever more markedly and consciously, from their beginning with the notion of deification of the Upanishad-Pantheism on to the bliss-state of the Buddhist Nirvāna, which, as we have seen (p. 39), is negative only in appearance. It is also the goal of the 'religions of redemption', specifically so called, which spread with such vigour over the civilized world from Egypt, Syria, and Asia Minor about the beginning of our era. Further, it is obvious to an examination sharpened by the comparative study of religions that the same tendency to 'salvation' is operative also in the vesture of eschatology that gives form to the religion of Persia. Islam, too, embodies the longing for and the experience of salvation. In this case 'salvation' is not simply in the 'hope' of the joys of Paradise : rather the most vital element in Islam is 'Islam' itself, i. e. that surrender to Allah which is not merely the dedication of the will to him, but also at the same time the entering upon the 'Allah' state of mind here and now, the object of longing and striving, a frame of mind which is already 'salvation', and which may possess and enrapture the man like an intoxication and can give rise to a mystic transport of bliss.

But if the idea of 'salvation' thus lies at the base of all higher religion everywhere, it is manifested quite unmistakably and in supreme fashion, both in intensity and intrinsic purity, in the 'Kingdom of Heaven' of Christianity, which is at once a tenet of faith, an object of desire, and a present experience.

It is quite immaterial whether this thought in ancient Israel issued from purely political considerations, only gradually rising above the ground of mere fact, till it finally was exalted to a transcendent meaning, or whether there were from the first authentic religious motives at work to shape and develop it.   All this is beside the point, inasmuch as the materials by which the religious impulse works are very frequently at first of an unspiritual, earthly nature.   It is just the unresting activity and continual urgency of this impulsion, enabling it to attain to freedom and press onward and upward to ever higher levels of development,—it is just this that manifests it most characteristically, and reveals best its inner essential being.   And this is nothing else than the pure *impulsion* to *redemption*, and the pre-intimation and anticipation of a boded 'good', transcendent and 'wholly other', a 'salvation' comparable to those 'salvations' striven after in other religions, but supreme above them in the measure in which the Lord of the Kingdom found and possessed in the Christian experience is supreme above Brahmā, Vishnu, Ormuzd, Allah, as also above the Absolute in the form of Nirvāna, Kaivalyam, Tao, or whatever other name it may be given.   So redemption is throughout the purport of the gospel even in its first and simplest form, a redemption which is both to be fulfilled by God hereafter and yet at the same time already experienced here and now.   In the former aspect it comes as the assured promise of the Kingdom of God; in the latter, by the present experience of His fatherhood, instilled by the Gospel into the soul of the disciple as his most intimate possession.   That the early Christians were conscious of this as something entirely novel and unheard of and exceeding all measure (a good *news*), is seen in the saying of Jesus that 'the Law and the Prophets were until John: since that time the gospel of the kingdom of God is preached' (Luke xvi. 16), in which John the Baptist, who also preached a 'Kingdom of God', is yet classed with 'the Law and the Prophets'.

But to describe this novelty most truly and concisely it would be necessary to *invent* the saying of Paul (Romans viii. 15), did it not already stand written :

'For ye have not received the spirit of bondage again to fear; but ye have received the spirit of adoption, whereby we cry, Abba, Father.'

Here Paul has penetrated to the heart of the matter, breaking definitely with the older religion and seizing unerringly upon the very principle and essence of the new. And this 'principle and essence' was the same for the first fishermen by the Lake of Galilee and has remained one and the same throughout the whole history of Christianity. With it is given the new attitude to Sin and Guilt, to Law and to Freedom, and, *in principle*, 'Justification', 'Second Birth', 'Renewal', the bestowal of the Spirit, new creation, and the blissful freedom of God's children. It was inevitable that these or similar expressions and doctrines and the profound speculation to which they would give rise should make their appearance when the Word called to the Spirit and the Spirit answered.[1]

And so Christ's first and direct work and achievement, as we can clearly understand it to-day, is the effectual bestowal of 'salvation' as future hope and present possession by arousing a faith in his God and in the Kingdom of God.

And now how can Divination, in respect to such work of Christ, awake in us also, in us who stand so remote in time from him? How can we, too, come to experience in him 'holiness made manifest'?

Obviously not through demonstration and proof, by applying some conceptual rule. We cannot suggest any conceptual criterion in the form: 'When the elements x and y are brought together, a revelation results.' It is just this impossibility which makes us speak of 'divination', 'intuitive apprehension'. The experience must come, not by demonstration, but by pure *contemplation*, through the mind submitting itself unreservedly to a pure 'impression' of the object. For this purpose all that was given and contained in the message and work of Jesus must be combined with the picture of his person and life and viewed as a whole and in its context with the

---

[1] We can even comprehend thereby the later influx of 'dualistic' or 'gnostic' currents, or at least see how they became possible.

long and wonderful advance in the religious history of Israel
and Judah that was the preparation for it, and with the interplay of diverse tributary lines of development which, even where
apparently divergent, ultimately converged upon this as their
single culmination.   Account must be taken of the elements
of 'fulfilment' which the Gospel contains, and due heed given
to the attraction and impelling force which it owed to its
contrast with its Judaic environment or to parallels which it
bore to this.   And all the while, for the full impression to be
received, regard is to be paid to the non-rational, the woof of
the web, the strange setting of the whole experience, which
can nowhere be felt so palpably as in the case of Jesus Christ;
—how his effect upon the men of his own day rises and ebbs,
revealing his spiritual content, on which the salvation of the
world depends, ever more and more manifestly, and revealing at
the same time that mysteriously growing opposition of powers
in which the problem of Job recurs a thousandfold more
urgently—where we have the suffering and the defeat not
merely of a righteous person, but of all that is most vitally
important for the highest interests of humanity.   In fine there
is that burden of non-rational, mystical significance, which
hangs like a cloud over Golgotha.   Whoever can thus immerse
himself in contemplation and open his whole mind resolutely to
a pure impression of all this combined will surely find growing
in him, obedient to an inward standard that defies expression,
the pure feeling of 'recognition of holiness', the 'intuition of
the eternal in the temporal'.   If something eternal, something
holy, ever results from the blending and interpenetration of
rational and non-rational, purposive and indefinable elements
in the way we tried to describe, in the person of Jesus this
stands as nowhere else potently and palpably apparent.

And in a very real sense we of the later day are not worse
but more fortunately placed for grasping it than Jesus' own
contemporaries.   Realization of him through 'surmise (*Ahndung*) of the divine government of the world' [1] depends essentially upon two factors.   On the one hand there is the general view of the marvellous spiritual history of Israel as a

---

[1] An expression of De Wette.   (v. p. 150.)

connected whole, with its prophetic and religious development, and with Christ appearing as its culmination. And on the other hand there is the complete life-work and achievement of Christ himself in its entirety. Now in both cases a general comprehensive view is more perfectly to be attained by us to-day than in the time of Christ; for, not only is our historical insight more keen, but we can also see the whole in better perspective at our greater distance. Whoever sinks in contemplation of that great connected development of the Judaic religion which we speak of as the 'old covenant up to Christ' must feel the stirrings of an intimation that something Eternal is there, directing and sustaining it and urging it to its consummation. The impression is simply irresistible. And whoever then goes on to consider how greatly the scene is set for the completion of the whole story and the mighty stature of the personality that is its fulfilment, his firm, unfaltering hold upon God, his unwavering, unfailing righteousness, his certitude of conviction and assurance in action so mysterious and profound, his spiritual fervour and beatitude, the struggles and trustfulness, self-surrender and suffering, and finally the conqueror's death that were his—whoever goes on to consider all this must inevitably conclude: 'That is god-like and divine; that is verily Holiness. If there is a God and if He chose to reveal himself, He could do it no otherwise than thus.'

Such a conclusion is not the result of logical compulsion; it does not follow from clearly conceived premisses; it is an immediate, underivable judgement of pure recognition, and it follows a premiss that defies exposition and springs directly from an irreducible feeling of the truth. But that, as we have seen, is just the manner in which genuine divination, in the sense of an intuition of religious significance, takes place.

Such an intuition, once granted, issues, for us no less than for the first disciples, necessarily and independently of exegesis or the authority of the early Church, in a series of further intuitions respecting the Person, the Work, and the Words of Christ, and it is the task of theology to render these explicit. Such are the intuitions gained of 'sacred history' in general, of its preparation in prophecy, and of its fulfilment in Jesus'

' Messiahship '—the Being in whom all the religious potentialities of prophet and psalmist and all the anticipatory movements and currents in the old covenant became actualized,
in whom all previous development found its culmination, and
the evolution of a people at once its real significance and its
goal, the completion of its course and the consummation of its
allotted historical task.   And there are further intuitions
which have the same origin : the intuition by which we recognize in Christ the portrayal and presentment of God, divining
in his agony and victory, his redemptive search and love, the
very stamp and signature of God ; the intuition of his ' Sonship ', by which we recognize Christ as the ' only Begotten ',
the called, the fully empowered with deity, as one whose
being, only made possible and intelligible of God, repeats and
reveals the divine nature in human fashion ; or the intuition
of the ' new covenant ', of adoption and reconciliation through
Christ, of his life-work and self-surrender to God as sacrifice
and as a warrant of divine grace.   And last, not least, the
intuition of the ' covering ' and ' propitiating ' Mediator.   For
the abyss between creature and Creator, ' profanum ' and
' sanctum ', sin and holiness, is not diminished but increased by
that deeper knowledge that comes from the Gospel of Christ :
and, as a result of the emotion spontaneously stirred in the
recognition of it, that in which ' the holy ' stands self-revealed
is taken here, as in other cases, both as the refuge from, and
the means by which to approach, Holiness.   And this impulsion of the mind to see in Christ mediator and propitiator may
be roused to seek expression spontaneously, even in cases
where it is not,—as in Hebrew and primitive religion,—prepared for and sustained by a traditional cult and mysticism of
' sacrifice '.   That is, it is a natural religious instinct, due to
the pressure of the numinous experience and to nothing else.

    We are not, then, to deplore the fact that intuitions of this
kind find a place in the doctrines of the Christian faith : they
do so of necessity.   What we must deplore is, that their free
character, as springing from ' divination ', is so generally mis-
interpreted ; that too commonly we dogmatize and theorize
about them, deducing them from ' necessary truths ' of exegesis

or dogma (which are in fact always dubious), and so failing
to recognize them for what they are, free-floating utterances
and trial flights at expression of the numinous feeling; and
that too often we give them an emphasis which puts them
unwarrantably at the centre of our religious interest, a place
which nothing but the experience itself of God ought to
occupy.

In this connexion we may draw attention to what are commonly called the 'miracles' of Christ, but which we may perhaps more aptly call, in the words of Mark xvi. 20, 'signs
following' (ἐπακολουθοῦντα σημεῖα). It is not upon them
primarily that the experience of 'holiness made manifest' is
based; but, where there has been real 'divination', there certain traits in the portrait of Christ come to acquire a fresh
significance, as confirmation of the divination rather than its
ground. I refer to the signs of exalted spiritual power over
nature to be detected in the portrait of Jesus. These have
their parallels elsewhere in the history of religion: in the
great prophets of Israel, for instance, they are shown in the
form of that visionary intuition and boding foreknowledge
with which the prophet was endowed for his calling. In the
life of Christ they recur unmistakably as 'gifts of the Spirit',
raised to a supreme power. These things are not 'miracles',
for they are powers of the spirit, and so are as 'natural' as our
will itself is, with its control over our body. But they clearly
only come upon the scene where the spirit is itself exalted
to its fullest stature and in its fullest vitality, and are most
of all to be expected where the spirit is in closest and most
intimate union with its eternal cause and foundation, and is
thereby set free to the highest it can itself achieve.[1]

It is, in the last place, clear that it is in the Passion and
death of Christ that the objects of the strongest religious intuition must be sought. If his Incarnation, his mission, and the
manner of his life come to be considered as a piece of self-
revelation, in which an eternal Will of Love is mirrored, before
all else is this Love and Faith seen accomplished in the Passion.
The Cross becomes in an absolute sense the 'mirror of the

[1] See further Appendix VII.

eternal Father' (*speculum aeterni Patris*); and not of the 'Father' alone—the highest rational interpretation of the holy—but of Holiness as such.   For what makes Christ in a special sense the summary and climax of the course of antecedent religious evolution is pre-eminently this—that in his life, suffering, and death is repeated in classic and absolute form that most mystical of all the problems of the Old Covenant, the problem of *the guiltless suffering of the righteous,* which re-echoes again and again so mysteriously from Jeremiah and deutero-Isaiah on through Job and the Psalms.   The 38th chapter of Job is a prophecy of Golgotha.   And on Golgotha the solution of the problem, already adumbrated in Job, is repeated and surpassed.   It lay, as we saw, entirely in the non-rational aspect of deity, and yet was none the less a solution.   In Job the suffering of the righteous found its significance as the classic and crucial case of the revelation, more immediately actual and in more palpable proximity than any other, of the transcendent mysteriousness and 'beyondness' of God.   The Cross of Christ, that monogram of the eternal mystery, is its completion.   Here rational are enfolded with non-rational elements, the revealed commingled with the unrevealed, the most exalted love with the most awe-inspiring 'wrath' of the numen, and therefore, in applying to the Cross of Christ the category 'holy', Christian religious feeling has given birth to a religious intuition profounder and more vital than any to be found in the whole history of religion.

This is what must be borne in mind in the comparison of religions, when we seek to decide which of them is the most perfect.   The criterion of the value of a religion as religion cannot ultimately be found in what it has done for culture, nor in its relation to the 'limits of the reason' or the 'limits of humanity' (which, forsooth, are presumed capable of being drawn in advance apart from reference to religion itself!), nor in any of its external features.   It can only be found in what is the innermost essence of religion, the idea of holiness as such, and in the degree of perfection with which any given religion realizes this.

There can naturally be no defence of the worth and validity

of such religious intuitions of pure feeling that will convince a person who is not prepared to take the religious consciousness itself for granted. Mere general argument, even moral demonstrations, are in this case useless, are indeed for obvious reasons impossible from the outset. On the other hand the criticisms and confutations attempted by such a person are unsound from the start. His weapons are far too short to touch his adversary, for the assailant is always standing right outside the arena! But if these intuitions, these separate responses to the impress upon the spirit of the Gospel story and the central Person of it—if these intuitions are immune from rational criticism, they are equally unaffected by the fluctuating results of biblical exegesis and the laboured justifications of historical apologetics. For they are possible without these, springing, as they do, from first-hand *personal divination*.

CHAPTER XXI

HISTORY AND THE *A PRIORI* IN RELIGION: SUMMARY AND CONCLUSION

WE have considered 'the holy' on the one hand as an *a priori* category of mind, and on the other as manifesting itself in outward appearance. The contrast here intended is exactly the same as the common contrast of inner and outer, general and special revelation. And if we take 'reason' (*ratio*) as an inclusive term for all cognition which arises in the mind from principles native to it, in contrast to those based upon facts of history, then we may say that the distinction between holiness as an *a priori* category and holiness as revealed in outward appearance is much the same as that between 'reason' (in this wide sense) and history.

Every religion which, so far from being a mere faith in traditional authority, springs from personal assurance and inward convincement (i. e. from an inward first-hand cognition of its truth)—as Christianity does in a unique degree—must presuppose principles in the mind enabling it to be independently recognized as true.[1] But these principles must be *a priori* ones, not to be derived from 'experience' or 'history'. It has little meaning, however edifying it may sound, to say that they are inscribed upon the heart by the pencil of the Holy Spirit 'in history'. For whence comes the assurance that it was the pencil of the 'Holy Spirit' that wrote, and not that of a deceiving spirit of imposture, or of the 'tribal fantasy' of anthropology? Such an assertion is itself a

---

[1] The attestation of such principles is the 'testimonium Spiritus Sancti internum' of which we have already spoken. And this must clearly be itself immediate and self-warranted, else there would be need of another 'witness of the Holy Spirit' to attest the truth of the first, and so on *ad infinitum.*

presumption that it is possible to distinguish the signature of
the Spirit from others, and thus that we have an *a priori*
notion of what is of the Spirit independently of history.

And there is a further consideration. There is something
presupposed by history as such—not only the history of mind
or spirit, with which we are here concerned—which alone
makes it history, and that is the existence of a *quale*, something with a potentiality of its own, capable of *becoming*, in
the special sense of coming to be that to which it was predisposed and predetermined. An oak-tree can *become*, and thus
have a sort of 'history'; whereas a heap of stones cannot.
The random addition and subtraction, displacement and
rearrangement, of elements in a mere aggregation can certainly
be followed in narrative form, but this is not in the deeper
sense a historical narrative.   We only have the history of a
people in proportion as it enters upon its course equipped with
an endowment of talents and tendencies ; it must already *be
something* if it is really to *become* anything.   And biography
is a lamentable and unreal business in the case of a man who
has no real unique potentiality of his own, no special idiosyn-
crasy, and is therefore a mere point of intersection for various
fortuitous causal series, acted upon, as it were, from without.
Biography is only a real narration of a real life where, by the
interplay of stimulus and experience on the one side and predisposition and natural endowment on the other, something
individual and unique comes into being, which is therefore
neither the result of a 'mere self-unfolding' nor yet the sum
of mere traces and impressions, written from without from
moment to moment upon a 'tabula rasa'.   In short, to propose a history of mind is to presuppose a mind or spirit
determinately qualified ; to profess to give a history of religion is to presuppose a spirit specifically qualified for religion.

There are, then, three factors in the process by which religion comes into being in history.   First, the interplay of predisposition and stimulus, which in the historical development
of man's mind actualizes the potentiality in the former, and at
the same time helps to determine its form.   Second, the recognition, by virtue of this very disposition, of specific portions

of history as the manifestation of 'the holy', with consequent modification of the religious experience already attained both in its quality and degree.   And third, on the basis of the other two, the achieved fellowship with 'the holy' in knowing, feeling, and willing.   Plainly, then, Religion is only the off-spring of history in so far as history on the one hand develops our disposition for knowing the holy, and on the other is itself repeatedly the manifestation of the holy.   'Natural' religion, in contrast to historical, does not exist, and still less does 'innate' religion.[1]

A priori cognitions are not such as every one does have —such would be innate cognitions—but such as every one is capable of having.   The loftier a priori cognitions are such as—while every one is indeed capable of having them —do not, as experience teaches us, occur spontaneously, but rather are 'awakened' through the instrumentality of other more highly endowed natures.   In relation to these the universal 'predisposition' is merely a faculty of receptivity and a principle of acknowledgement, not a capacity to pro-duce the cognitions in question for oneself independently. This latter capacity is confined to those specially 'endowed'. And this 'endowment' is the universal disposition on a higher level and at a higher power, differing from it in quality as well as in degree.   The same thing is very evident in the sphere of art: what appears in the multitude as mere recep-tiveness, the capacity of response and judgement by trained aesthetic taste, reappears at the level of the artist as invention, creation, composition, the original production of genius.   This difference of level and power, e. g. in musical composition, seen in the contrast between what is a mere capacity for musical experience and the actual production and revelation of music, is obviously something more than a difference of degree. It is very similar in the domain of the religious consciousness, reli-gious production and revelation.   Here, too, most men have only the 'predisposition', in the sense of a receptiveness and susceptibility to religion and a capacity for freely recognizing

[1] For the distinction between 'innate' and a priori, cf. R. Otto, Religionsphilosophie, p. 42.

and judging religious truth at first hand.   The 'Spirit' is only
'universal' in the form of the '*testimonium Spiritus internum*'
(and this again only '*ubi ipsi visum fuit*').   The higher stage,
not to be derived from the first stage of mere receptivity, is in
the sphere of religion *the prophet*.   The prophet corresponds in
the religious sphere to the creative artist in that of art : he is
the man in whom the Spirit shows itself alike as the power to
hear the 'voice within' and the power of divination, and in
each case appears as a creative force.   Yet the prophet does
not represent the highest stage.   We can think of a third, yet
higher, beyond him, a stage of revelation as underivable from
that of the prophet as was his from that of common men.   We
can look, beyond the prophet, to one in whom is found the
Spirit in all its plenitude, and who at the same time in his
person and in his performance is become most completely the
object of divination, in whom Holiness is recognized apparent.

Such a one is more than Prophet.   He is the Son.

APPENDIX I

CHRYSOSTOM ON THE INCONCEIVABLE IN GOD

'BUT that is an impertinence to say that He who is beyond the apprehension of even the higher Powers can be comprehended by us earthworms, or compassed and comprised by the weak forces of our understanding!'

This protest of Chrysostom occurs at the beginning of the third of his five discourses περὶ ἀκαταλήπτου (*De Incomprehensibili*), which were directed against the 'ἀνόμοιοι' who were perverting the Christian community of Antioch, and more especially against disciples of the Arian Aetios, with their doctrine θεὸν οἶδα ὡς αὐτὸς ὁ θεὸς ἑαυτὸν οἶδε ('I know God as He is known to Himself'). Our histories of Dogma do not generally say much, if anything, upon these sermons of Chrysostom, and their contribution to 'dogmatics' is not indeed very important. But their interest for the psychology of religion is all the greater ; and this would still remain, even if they had not contained the passages bearing upon 'Christology', which begin at the conclusion of the fourth sermon. For we have in them the primary promptings of genuine religious feeling in its specifically numinous character, excited to a passionate intensity and directed with all the charm and eloquence of the 'Golden-mouthed' against the theoretical 'Aristotelian' God of the schools. All that is non-rational in the feeling of God is here in conflict with what is rational and capable of rationalization and threatens to break loose from it altogether.

A strange spectacle ! For does not the distinguishing character of Christianity consist in just this—that God is near us, that we can possess and apprehend Him, and that man himself is His image and likeness ? And yet we find this Father of the Church battling passionately, as for something that concerned the very essence of Christianity, for the view that God is the Inconceivable, the Inexpressible, that which gives denial to every notion. And this he does *not* do on speculative grounds, with the aid of the terms and phrases of any 'school' of theology ; it is rather a

sort of instinct in him that guides him with astonishing assurance
and accuracy to track out and collect the most wonderful texts of
Scripture, so that their full weight becomes felt, as his profoundly
penetrating interpretation explains and applies them.

First and chiefly he takes his stand against ' Conceiving' and
'Comprehension' in general, against the idea of τὸ καταληπτόν, and
against the οἰκεῖοι λογισμοί (i. e. constructions of the understanding)
which seek to delimit and circumscribe God (περιγράφειν, περιλαμ-
βάνειν). For his opponents had maintained that a conceptual knowledge of God is possible, definitive and exhaustive, by means of
notions, in fact by a single notion (viz. of ἀγεννησία, unbegottenness),
in a word, that it is possible ' to know God exactly ' (μετ᾿ ἀκριβείας
εἰδέναι). ' But we,' says Chrysostom, ' in opposition to this view,
call Him τὸν ἀνέκφραστον, τὸν ἀπερινόητον θεόν, τὸν ἀόρατον, τὸν ἀκατάληπτον, τὸν νικῶντα γλώττης δύναμιν ἀνθρωπίνης, τὸν ὑπερβαίνοντα θνητῆς
διανοίας κατάληψιν, τὸν ἀνεξιχνίαστον ἀγγέλοις, τὸν ἀθέατον τοῖς Σεραφίμ,
τὸν ἀκατανόητον τοῖς Χερουβίμ, τὸν ἀόρατον ἀρχαῖς ἐξουσίαις δυνάμεσιν,
καὶ ἁπλῶς πασῇ τῇ κτίσει.᾿ [1] (Migne, p. 721.) ' He insults God who
seeks to apprehend His essential being ' (ὑβρίζει δὲ ὁ τὴν οὐσίαν
αὐτοῦ περιεργαζόμενος, 714 e), he says, and goes on to urge that God
is incomprehensible even in His works—how much more in His
own essential nature ;—even in His ' demeanings ' (συγκαταβάσεις)
—how much more in His own transcendent majesty ; even to the
Cherubim and Seraphim—how much more to mere 'humanity '
(ἀνθρωπίνη φύσις)!

The ἀκατάληπτον in this sense is for Chrysostom primarily the
' exceeding greatness' of God, which escapes our mental grasp and
compass because of the ἀσθένεια τῶν λογισμῶν, the over-short reach
of our faculty of conception. We call it 'incomprehensibility ',
and distinguish from it the ' inapprehensibility' which springs,
not from the 'exceeding greatness', but from the 'wholly otherness' of God (θάτερον τοῦ θείου), from what is alien and remote in
Him, from what we have called the ' mysterium stupendum '.
And it is instructive to see how for Chrysostom too this latter
sense of ἀκατάληπτον passes into the former, sometimes blending
with it, sometimes plainly distinguished as something beyond and

---

[1] ' We call Him the inexpressible, the unthinkable God, the invisible,
the inapprehensible ; who quells the power of human speech and transcends the grasp of mortal thought ; inaccessible to the angels, unbeheld
of the Seraphim, unimagined of the Cherubim, invisible to rules and
authorities and powers, and, in a word, to all creation.'

higher than it. We have said already that we have the experience of the 'wholly other', where we come upon something
which not merely overtops our every concept, but astounds us
by its absolute and utter difference from our whole nature.
Chrysostom similarly contrasts the ἀνθρωπίνη φύσις with the θεῖα
φύσις as being incommensurable with it, and therefore incapable
of understanding it, and his words refer not only to the narrow-
ness and meagreness of our understanding, but just to this sheer
difference in quality of the 'wholly other'.

This sort of apostrophe is common with him : Ἄνθρωπος ὢν θεὸν
πολυπραγμονεῖς ; Ἀρκεῖ γὰρ τὰ ὀνόματα ψιλὰ τῆς ἀνοίας δεῖξαι τὴν
ὑπερβολήν· ἄνθρωπος γῆ καὶ σποδὸς ὑπάρχων, σὰρξ καὶ αἷμα, χόρτος καὶ
ἄνθος χόρτου, σκιὰ καὶ καπνὸς καὶ ματαιότης (712).[1] And the same
note sounds even more clearly in an exposition of Romans ix. 20,
21 (715). As little as the clay can master or comprehend the
potter because of its essential difference from him, even so little
can man comprehend God. 'Or rather, far less, for man—the
potter—is in the end himself but clay. But the difference between
the being of God and the being of man is of such a kind that no
word can express it and no thought appraise it.' His position is
put more unmistakably still in the following passage :

'He dwells, says St. Paul, in an unapproachable light.[2] Observe
here the exactitude of St. Paul's expression. . . . For he says not
merely in an incomprehensible, but (what conveys far more) in an
altogether " unapproachable " light. We say "inconceivable " and
"incomprehensible " of something which, though it eludes conception, does not elude all inquiry and questioning. "Unapproachable ", on the other hand, means something which in
principle excludes the very possibility of inquiry, which is quite
inaccessible by conceptual investigation. A sea into which divers
may plunge, but which they cannot fathom, would represent the
merely " incomprehensible " (ἀκατάληπτον). It would only represent the " unapproachable " (ἀπρόσιτον) if it remained in principle
beyond search and beyond discovery.' (p. 721.) And so too in the
fourth discourse (upon Eph. iii. 8) (p. 729) : Τί ἐστιν ἀνεξιχνίαστον ;
μὴ δυνάμενον ζητηθῆναι, οὐ μόνον δὲ μὴ δυνάμενον εὑρεθῆναι, ἀλλ' οὐδὲ

---

[1] 'Dost thou, a man, presume to busy thyself with God ? Nay, the
bare names (of man) suffice to show the extent of this folly ; man that is
earth and *dust*, *flesh* and *blood*, *dung* and the *flower of dung*, *shadow* and
smoke and *vanity*.'

[2] 1 Tim. vi. 16 φῶς οἰκῶν ἀπρόσιτον. R.V. ' unapproachable '.

ἀνιχνευθῆναι. ('What is "unsearchable"? To be beyond searching, that is, to be such as excludes not discovery only but also tracing.')

And this line of thought draws him imperceptibly farther. The bounds of the 'incomprehensible' are extended, and the whole numinous consciousness is set astir in it, one element in the feeling prompting to the others. The *mysterium stupendum* passes directly over into *mysterium tremendum* and *maiestas*, so that we might entitle the Discourses, instead of 'De Incomprehensibili', 'De Numine ac Numinoso'.

Specially noticeable in this connexion is the passage in which Chrysostom brings clearly out the psychological distinction between numinous and merely rational *wonder*. He cites that truly significant text from Ps. cxxxix. 14, which runs in the Septuagint: 'I praise Thee: for that Thou madest Thyself fearfully wondrous',[1] and then gives a subtle analysis of the feelings there expressed.

'What does "fearfully" mean here? Many things move us to wonder in which there is nothing "fearful"—the beauty of a colonnade, for example; the beauty of pictures, or bodily loveliness. Again, we wonder at the greatness of the sea and its measureless expanse, but terror and "fear" only seize upon us when we gaze down into its *depths*. So, too, here the Psalmist. When he gazes down into the immeasurable, yawning (ἀχανές) Depth[2] of the divine Wisdom, dizziness comes upon him and he recoils in terrified wonder and cries: . . . "Thy knowledge is too wonderful for me; it is high, above my power (I am too weak for it: LXX)."' The 'dizziness' and the unique feeling of the uncanny, which we have called *stupor* and *tremor*, are here clearly noted by Chrysostom. And he rightly cites also the profoundly numinous exclamation of St. Paul (Rom. xi. 33): 'Dizzy before the unfathomable main and gazing down into its yawning depths, he recoils precipitately and cries aloud: "O the depth of the riches both of the wisdom and knowledge of God...."' (Migne, p. 705).

The passage on page 733 should be read in close connexion with this. Nowhere has the awe and even the eerie shuddering and amazement at the supernatural been more vividly and truly recaptured in feeling, and nowhere has it been portrayed with

---

[1] Ἐξομολογήσομαί σοι ὅτι φοβερῶς ἐθαυμαστώθης.

[2] Reading βάθος for the undoubtedly erroneous πέλαγος.

a more gripping and constraining power. *Expertus loquitur!* This is the voice not of the Platonist or Neo-Platonist; it is the voice of antiquity itself, typified in one who had found in Paganism and Judaism and Christianity alike those primal and elemental experiences out of which all religion has arisen and without which no religion is worthy of the name, and who had made them his very own in all the force of growth—sometimes rank and violent enough—which originally characterized them. Chrysostom describes thus the experience of Dan. x. 5–8, and the state of ecstasy into which Daniel falls in his encounter with the Unseen : ' For just as happens when the charioteer looses hold of the reins in terror, so that the horses bolt and the chariot overturns, . . . so it befell the Prophet. His affrighted soul could not bear the sight of the Angel made manifest, could not endure the supernatural light, and was overwhelmed. It strove to break free from the bonds of the flesh as from a harness . . . and he lay there in a swoon.' Very similar is the comment on the vision of Ezekiel. Chrysostom realizes that the awe in these experiences does not find its origin in any self-depreciation of an ethical or rational sort (e. g. from an uneasy conscience or the like), but that they are the natural reactions of the creature, of the ἀσθένεια φύσεως face to face with transcendent, unearthly reality, as such. ' I cite to you the case of the holy Daniel, the friend of God, who, because of his wisdom and righteousness, might well have been justly confident, just in order that no one may suppose, if I show even him to you weakening, collapsing, powerless, and overwhelmed before the presence of the Angel, that this befalls him because of his sins and his evil conscience, but that this example may throw a clear light on the impotence of our nature.'

Naturally the passage in Genesis xviii. 27 has not escaped him ; still less the scene in Isa. vi. ' But let us now leave St. Paul and the prophets and ascend into Heaven to see if haply any one there knows what God's essential being is. . . . What do we hear from the Angels ? Do they inquire and reason meticulously among themselves about God's nature ? By no means. What do they do ? They praise Him. They fall down and worship Him with a great trembling (μετὰ πολλῆς τῆς φρίκης, p. 707). They turn their eyes away, and can themselves not endure the vouchsafed revelation of God.' Again : 'Tell me, wherefore do they cover their faces and hide them with their wings ? Why, but

that they cannot endure the dazzling radiance and its rays that
pour from the Throne?' Nor does he ignore the *loci classici* of
the *tremenda maiestas*, viz. Ps. civ. 32 and Job ix. 6 sqq.: 'He
looketh on the earth and it trembleth: he toucheth the hills and
they smoke.' Ps. cxiv. 3: 'The sea saw and fled: Jordan was
driven back.' 'πᾶσα ἡ κτίσις σαλεύεται, δέδοικε, τρέμει.' And he
concludes his commentary upon all this with the remark: (I
will conclude, for) 'thought grows weary, not from the extent of
what I have spoken but from the trembling it brings. For the
soul that concerns itself in these contemplations trembles and is
appalled (ἔκαμεν ἡμῖν ἡ διάνοια, οὐ τῷ πλήθει ἀλλὰ τῇ φρίκῃ τῶν
εἰρημένων. τρέμει γὰρ καὶ ἐκπέπληκται ἡ ψυχὴ ἐπὶ πολὺ ταῖς ἄνω
ἐνδιατρίβουσα θεωρίαις)' (p. 725).

Chrysostom, then, is combating the arrogance and overweening
presumptuousness of the human understanding and of the creature
in general in imagining that any escape is possible from the
incomprehensible, supreme, transcendent, and 'wholly other'
nature of God. And it is because he wishes to shatter this human
complacency, to overawe and overwhelm, that he portrays these
aspects of the numinous. But he does not leave out the others or
fail to note the paradox, that this 'incomprehensible' is at the
same time a '*fascinans*' and an intimate and essential possession
of the human soul. Blank amazement is to him at the same time
enraptured adoration; speechlessness in the presence of the inapprehensible passes over—and only an understanding of the
'harmony of contrasts' can show how—into a humble gratitude
that it *is* so, that it is 'fearfully wonderful'. He cites again
Ps. cxxxix. 14, and interprets it thus: 'See here the nobility
of this servant of God (David). "I thank Thee" (εὐχαριστῶ σοι), he
says in effect, "for that I have a Lord who is beyond comprehension."' Tersteegen means the same when he uses the words
'A comprehended God is no God' to express praise; as does Goethe,
in the words of the archangels' hymn in *Faust*:

> Ihr Anblick gibt den Engeln Stärke,
> *Weil* keiner sie ergründen mag.[1]

And so with Chrysostom: this ἀκατάληπτον is ἐκείνη μακαρία οὐσία
—a favourite and recurring expression of his. And we feel that

---

[1] 'Its (*sc.* the Sun's) aspect gives the angels strength *because* none may
fathom it.' [The usual reading is *wenn*, 'though', for *weil*, 'because'.
Trans.]

this 'Being' is 'incomprehensible' *because* it is 'blessed', and 'blessed' *because* it is 'incomprehensible'. In the very passion with which he battles for the unimaginable God, who makes His worshipper weak and dizzy with awe, there yet glows—unuttered and unexpressed — an enthusiastic sense of the soul having been carried away in rapture and taken up into the being of God.

The ἀκατάληπτον involves a denial of conceptual designations, and hence come the negative attributes of deity, which Chrysostom frequently employs, singly or in series—a *negativa theologia* in little. But this 'negative theology' does not mean that faith and feeling are dissipated and reduced to nothing; on the contrary, it contains within it the loftiest spirit of devotion, and it is out of such 'negative' attributes that Chrysostom fashions the most solemn confessions and prayers. He thereby shows once more that feeling and experience reach far beyond conceiving, and that a conception negative in form may often become the symbol (what we have called an 'ideogram') for a content of meaning which, if absolutely unutterable, is none the less in the highest degree positive. And the example of Chrysostom at the same time shows that a 'negative theology' can and indeed must arise, not only from the 'infusion of Hellenistic speculation and nature mysticism', but from purely and genuinely religious roots, namely, the experience of the numinous.

The insistence upon the 'inconceivable and incomprehensible' in God did not cease to be a point of honour in Christian theology with Chrysostom. The forms this protest took did indeed vary: it appears as the assertion at one time that God stands above the reach of all possible predication whatever, and so is Nothingness and the 'Silent desert'; at another, that He is ἀνώνυμος, πανώνυμος, ὁμώνυμος; at another, that He can indeed be made the subject of predication, but only in so far as all attributes are mere '*nomina ex parte intellectus nostri*'; or again, the sternest form of all, it reproduces the line of thought of Job, as can be seen now and then in Luther in his notion of the *deus absconditus*—the thought, namely, that God Himself is not only *above* every human grasp, but in *antagonism* to it.[1]

---

[1] Compare also Luther's *Short Form of the Ten Commandments, the Creed, and the Lord's Prayer* (1520): 'I venture to put my trust in the one God alone, the invisible and *incomprehensible*, who hath created Heaven and Earth and is alone above all creatures.'

All these doctrines are preserving a heritage passionately won against the opposition of ancient errors. They do so, certainly, at the cost of a one-sided emphasis, for the meaning Christians attach to the word 'God' is indubitably also a profoundly rational one, the basis indeed of all reason. Yet this is bound up with a still profounder meaning, which, as we have seen, is beyond and above all conception.

With the discourse of Chrysostom we may compare Gregory of Nyssa, *Contra Eunomium* (Migne, *S. Gr.* 45). What stirs Chrysostom passionately as a matter of the first moment is indeed only of secondary importance in Gregory, incidental to his dogmatic inquiries. But even so he, too, can write (p. 601): εἰ δέ τις ἀπαιτοίη τῆς θείας οὐσίας ἑρμηνείαν τινὰ καὶ ὑπογραφὴν καὶ ἐξήγησιν, ἀμαθεῖς εἶναι τῆς τοιαύτης σοφίας οὐκ ἀρνησόμεθα . . . ὅτι οὐκ ἔστι τὸ ἀόριστον κατὰ τὴν φύσιν ἐπινοίᾳ τινι ῥημάτων διαληφθῆναι. ἐπεὶ οὖν κρεῖττόν ἐστι καὶ ὑψηλότερον τῆς ὀνομαστικῆς σημασίας τὸ Θεῖον [*numen* says the Latin translator] σιωπῇ τιμᾶν τὰ ὑπὲρ λόγον τε καὶ διάνοιαν μεμαθήκαμεν. ('But if one asks for an interpretation or description or explanation of the divine nature we shall not deny that in such a science as this we are unlearned. . . . For there is no way of comprehending the indefinable as it is by a scheme of words. For the Divine is too noble and too lofty to be indicated by a name: and we have learned to honour by silence that which transcends reason and thought.')

But another, long before Chrysostom—the 'heretic' Marcion—writing in a different situation, not within but on the fringe of the Church, had experienced the inconceivable aspect of the numinous and extolled it in words of an almost intoxicated fervour: 'O it is a marvel beyond marvels, enravishment, power, and wonder, that one can say nought about the Gospel, and think nought about it and compare it to nothing.'

It is remarkable to see how the several moments of the numinous in experience are constantly compounded and blended afresh so as to produce quite special and peculiar types of religion. In Marcion the original moment '*tremendum*' is silenced before the consoling power of the Gospel, in fulfilment of the word 'Perfect love casts out fear'. But there remains strongly and profoundly felt the 'wholly other', the ineffable and inconceivable, in his 'strange God', and in the first words of his treatise, whose 'violent ferment' (in Harnack's phrase) reveals the element of 'fascination',

The sense of the 'august' lives in the 'feeling of distance' in face of the 'strange God', and in that too we detect a light thrill that is the awe of the '*tremendum*' reawakened and returning in a nobler form.[1]

APPENDIX II

THE NUMINOUS IN POETRY, HYMN, AND LITURGY

Example of 'numinous' poetry.

From *Bhagavad-Gītā*, Chapter XI (Barnett's translation slightly altered).

In the *Bhagavad-Gītā*, Krishna, the embodiment of Vishnu— Vishnu himself in human form—instructs Aryuna in the deepest mysteries of his religion. Aryuna then desires to behold God himself in his own form, and his petition is granted. And now in Chapter XI there follows a theophany of terrific grandeur, which seeks to give a feeling of the unapproachable essence of the Divine before which the creature trembles and falls, by embodying the human and 'natural' means of terror, majesty, and sublimity. Aryuna stands in his war-chariot, about to enter the carnage of the battle against his brother Yudhishthira's enemies. Krishna is his charioteer. Aryuna tells him his request. 'Show to me thy changeless Self, Sovran of the Rule.' Krishna-Vishnu answers him :

7. Behold now, O Wearer of the Hair-Knot, the whole universe, moving and unmoving, solely lodged in this my body, and all else that thou art fain to see.

8. But for that thou canst not see Me with this thine own eye, I give thee a divine eye ; behold my sovran Rule.

9. Thus speaking, Hari (i. e. Vishnu), the great Lord of the Rule, then showed to Pritha's son his sovran form supreme,

10. of many mouths and eyes, of many divine ornaments, with uplifted weapons many and divine ;

11. wearing divine flower-chaplets and robes, with anointment of divine perfumes, compound of all marvels, the boundless god facing all ways.

---

[1] See Harnack, *Marcion*, 1921, p. 138,

12. If the light of a thousand suns should of a sudden rise in the heavens, it would be like to the light of that mighty being. . . .

14. Thereupon the Wealth-Winner (i. e. Aryuna), smitten with amazement, with hair standing on end, bowed his head, and with clasped hands spake to the God. . . .

17. 'I behold Thee bearing diadem, mace, and disc, massed in radiance, on all sides glistening, hardly discernible, shining round about as gleaming fire and sun, immeasurable. . . .

20. For this mid-space between heaven and earth and all the quarters of the sky are filled with Thee alone. Seeing this Thy fearful and wonderful form, O great-hearted one, the threefold world quakes.

21. These hosts of Suras come unto Thee; some, affrighted, praise with clasped hands. With cries of "Hail!" the hosts of Great Saints and Adepts sing to Thee hymns of abounding praise.

22. All the Spirits and Divine Powers that live in heaven and earth, in clouds and winds, in air and water, Daemons, Manes, Asuras, Saints, and Adepts, all gaze on Thee in amazement.

23. Looking upon Thy mighty form of many mouths and eyes, of many arms and thighs and feet, of many bellies, and grim with many teeth, O mighty-armed one, the worlds and I quake.

24. For as I behold Thee touching the heavens, glittering, many-hued, with yawning mouths, with wide eyes agleam, my inward soul trembles, and I find not constancy nor peace, O Vishnu.

25. Seeing Thy mouths grim with teeth, like to the fire of the last day, I recognize not the quarters of the heavens, and take no joy; Lord of Gods, home of the universe, be gracious!

26. These sons of Dhritarashtra all, with the hosts of kings, Bhishma, Drona, and the Charioteer's son yonder, and likewise the chief of our warriors,

27. hasting enter into Thy mouths grim with fangs and terrible; some, caught between the teeth, appear with crushed heads.

28. As many currents of rivers flow to meet the sea, so these warriors of the world of mankind pass into Thy blazing mouths.

29. As moths with exceeding speed pass into a lighted fire to perish, so pass the worlds with exceeding speed into Thy mouths to perish.

30. Thou devourest and lickest up all the worlds around with flaming mouths ; filling the whole universe with radiance, grim glow Thy splendours, O Vishnu !

31. Relate to me who Thou art in this grim form. Homage to Thee, chief of gods ; be gracious ! I would fain know Thee as First Being. . . .'

Thereupon Vishnu reassumes his friendly Krishna-form. Aryuna's petition to comprehend the incomprehensible is not granted him. It is forbidden to man, as Luther says, 'to soar into the height of Majesty'; he must confine himself to the Word of gracious Promise. Such a word is imparted. The tremendous chapter closes with the words which expositors take as the sum and epitome of the whole Gītā :

55. 'He who does what he does for Me alone ; who is given over to Me, who is devoted to Me, void of attachment, without hatred to any born being, O son of Pandu, comes to Me.'

The Numinous in Hymn and Liturgy.

A comparison of two poems may indicate the difference between a merely 'rational' glorification of the Godhead and one that also prompts to a feeling of the non-rational, the numinous, in its aspect of 'mysterium tremendum'. Gellert can sing of 'The Honour of God from Nature' powerfully and finely enough—

> Die Himmel rühmen des Ewigen Ehre,
> Ihr Schall pflanzt seinen Namen fort.

Here everything is bright, rational, and intimate up to the last verse :

> Ich bin Dein Schöpfer, bin Weisheit und Güte,
> Ein Gott der Ordnung und Dein Heil.
> Ich bin's ! Mich liebe von ganzem Gemüte,
> Und nimm an meiner Gnade teil.

But, beautiful as this hymn is, we do not encounter there the 'honour of God' in all its fullness. Some element is missing, and what this is we feel at once when we compare with this hymn that composed at an earlier date by E. Lange, 'To the Majesty of God':

> Vor Dir erbebt der Engel Chor,
> Sie schlagen Aug' und Antlitz nieder,
> So schrecklich kommst Du ihnen vor
> Und davon schallen ihre Lieder. . . .

o

> Denn Dein ist Kraft und Ruhm,
> Das Reich und Heiligtum,
> Da mich Entsetzen mir entreisset.
> Bei Dir ist Majestät
> Die über alles geht,
> Und heilig, heilig, heilig, heisset.

That goes farther than Gellert. And yet even here there is still something lacking, something that we find in the Song of the Seraphim in Isaiah vi. Even Lange, despite his 'numb amazement', sings ten long stanzas ; the angels sing a bare two lines. And he incessantly speaks to God in the second person singular ; whereas the angels speak before Yahweh in the *third* person.[1]

A liturgy unusually rich in numinous hymns and prayers is that of Yom Kippur, the great 'Day of Atonement' of the Jews. It is overshadowed by the 'Holy, Holy, Holy' of the Seraphim (Isa. vi), which recurs more than once, and it has prayers in it as wonderful as the *ubekēn tēn pachdekā* :

'So then, let Thy fear, O Yahweh our God, come over all Thy creatures, and reverent dread (*ēmātekā*) of Thee upon all that Thou hast made, that all Thy creatures may fear Thee and every being bow before Thee and that they may all become bonded together to do Thy will with all their heart, even as we know, O Yahweh our God, that Thine is the lordship, that might is in Thy hand and power in Thy right hand and Thy name exalted above all that Thou hast created.'

APPENDIX III

ORIGINAL NUMINOUS SOUNDS

FEELINGS and emotions, as states of mental tension, find their natural relaxation in uttered sounds. It is evident that the numinous feeling also, in its first outbreak in consciousness, must

---

[1] In point of fact one cannot always speak to God as 'Thou', and sometimes not at all. St. Theresa addresses God as 'Eternal Majesty', and the French readily use 'Vous' for 'Tu'. And Goethe came very near to the 'tremendum mysterium' when he said to Eckermann (Dec. 31, 1823) : 'People treat the name of God as though the inconceivable and wholly incomprehensible supreme Being were not far more than such as they. Else they would not say : "The Lord God," "the dear God," "the good God." Were they penetrated through and through by a sense of His greatness, they would be dumb and unable to name Him for very veneration.'

have found sounds for its expression, and at first inarticulate sounds rather than words ; but it is improbable that it devised special and peculiar sounds for itself. Analogous as it is to other feelings, it no doubt adopted the already familiar sounds expressive of the emotions of terror, amazement, joy, and the like. But it could, and sometimes did, put, as it were, a special stamp upon sounds coined for a different use. The German interjection '*Hu!*', for instance, expresses to-day invariably and exclusively, not terror in general, but terror accompanied by shuddering, i. e. numinous 'terror'. So, too, whereas *hus* in vulgar Arabic is, I am told, a sound expressive of soothing in general, the correspond-ing Hebrew sound *has* is only found in a numinous context. (Cf. Amos vi. 10 : 'Hold thy tongue (*has*), for we may not make men-tion of the name of the Lord.' Zeph. i. 7 : 'Hold thy peace at the presence of the Lord God.' Hab. ii. 20 ; Judges iii. 19; also Amos viii. 3.) Such a specialization of a common interjection has very possibly often come about. When the ecstatic Dervishes of Islam bring their 'Zikr' to an end, they break into ejaculations, such as 'Allah Akbar', which end finally in a protracted groan-ing *Hū*. This Hū has indeed been explained on rational grounds as the Arabic personal pronoun of the third person, 'He', i. e. Allah. But any one who has actually heard these ejaculations finds it hard to think of them simply as pronouns. Rather we have the impression that in this sound the numinous feeling is seeking to discharge itself.

This specialization is perhaps the clue to the understanding of the Sanskrit word *āścarya*, to which reference has been made more than once. Its derivation has been hitherto an enigma ; but one may conjecture that the explanation is in fact very simple, and that the word is just a compound of the two words *as* and *carya*. *Carya* = ' agendum ', that which is done or is to be done ; while *as* is a primitive sound to express the 'stupendum', the long protracted open vowel of wonder (ā, oh, hā), combining with the sibilant, which in all languages is used to express or produce a terrified silence (cf. Hist! Sh! Sst !). An '*āś-carya*'[1] would not then be properly and primarily anything conceptual at all, nor even a 'marvel', but simply ' that in the presence

---

[1] Compare the exactly parallel forms *ā-kāra*, *ahan-kāra*: and *vide* Söderblom, *Das Werden des Gottesglaubens*, 1916, p. 96, on the *Manitu* of the Indians.

of which we must exclaim "ās! ās!"'.   If this interpretation is correct, we can detect in this word just the original 'shudder' of numinous awe in the first and earliest form in which it expressed itself, before any figure of speech, objective representation, or concept had been devised to explicate it; it bursts forth crudely and vehemently in this primal cry and is unable to name its object otherwise than as a something before which such sounds must involuntarily be uttered.   Professor Geldner has kindly sent me a reference to a passage in the Kena-Upanishad (iv. 29) which seems to me to be an excellent confirmation of this and at the same time to illustrate how the primal numinous feeling did originally emerge as pure feeling, before any concept or concrete representation of it had come into being.   The fine, naïve old Kena-Upanishad aims at making perceptible to the disciple that before which 'all words turn back', and proceeds just as we do, by trying to produce in him an appropriate feeling-reflex by means of a simile.   The lines run:

> This is the way It (*sc.* Brahman) is to be illustrated:
> When lightnings have been loosened:
>   aaah!
> When that has made the eyes to be closed—
>   aaah!—
> So far concerning Deity (*devatā*).

What, then, is the *devatā*, the *Brahman*?   It is an *ā-caryam*, i. e. 'that in whose presence we must exclaim "aaah!"' And one cannot 'illustrate' the numinous character of this 'aaah' by any better analogy than that of the lightning here given.   The unexpectedness and suddenness of the lightning-flash, its dreadful weirdness, its overpoweringness and dazzling splendour, the fright and the delight of it, give it an almost numinous impressiveness, and indeed often do produce an actual numinous impression on the mind.

This reference of Professor Geldner's seems to me all the more significant from the fact that it appears to me to adumbrate quite a new method of solving the old puzzle of the 'Brahman', and what it means.   For this task philosophical speculation is too elevated, mere etymology too insufficient, a method.   What is necessary in order really to get at the heart of the matter is to have rediscovered and recaptured the *feelings* which this word originally connoted and which thrill through it.   And for this we have again a very instructive passage in that which, immediately preceding the one just quoted (Kena, iii. 15), at the same time serves to elucidate it. It is where the Devas catch for the first time an intimation of the 'Brahman'. They ask, in amazement, and yet obviously also in extreme eagerness : ' *Kim idam yakṣam ?* ' of which Deussen's trans-lation ' What marvellous thing (*Wunderding*) is this ? ' is too tame a rendering. It is more exactly : 'What un-thing (*Unding*) is this ? ' in the sense in which this expression is popularly used for a thing of which no one can say what it is or whence it comes, and in whose presence we have the feeling of the uncanny. ' *Yaksa* ', like ' *Unding* ', is sometimes a word for a ghost, and is originally the '*ungeheuer*', 'monstrous', in the sense of the un-canny, eerie, 'apparition', or spectre. And it is just as such that the 'Brahman' in this passage behaves. It does the things goblins and magical creatures usually do, vanishing suddenly like a true phantom at the climax of the transaction. Such feelings, which we meet at the commencement of the great Mysticism of Brahman, attend its course continually, and he who cannot recognize and detect their presence there cannot do more than reconstruct the meagre skeleton of concepts they have left behind. And the same thing, *mutatis mutandis*, holds good also for Western Mysticism.

Another original sound in which the numinous feeling is articulated is certainly the holy syllable '*om*'. It likewise has no sort of conceptual connotation. Like the particle *ās*, it is simply an articulated sound—no word, nor even a complete syllable, for the *m* in which it ends is not an ordinary 'm', but simply the long protracted nasal continuation of the deep 'o' sound. It is really simply a sort of growl or groan, sounding up from within as the quasi-reflex expression of profound emotion in circumstances of a numinous magical nature, and serving to relieve consciousness of a felt burden, almost physical in its constraining force. And this constraint and compulsion to expression are still recoverable to our feeling when we recapture this mood of submergence and absorption in the 'wholly other '.

This *Om* is exactly parallel to the similar sound in Sanskrit, *Hum*—like it, nothing but a numinous ejaculation, with probably no further significance.

It would be a task for the history and psychology of religion alike to examine the innumerable names of gods and demons, and perhaps also the various designations for ghost, soul, and spirit, with a view to seeing whether many of them may not simply have arisen from original numinous sounds and thus be parallels to the name *aścarya*, already considered.[1]

APPENDIX IV

'SPIRIT' AND 'SOUL' AS NUMINOUS ENTITIES

THE non-rational which we were looking for in the Idea of the divine was found in the numinous, and in our recognition of this we came to see that rationalistic speculation tends to conceal the divine in God, and that before God becomes for us rationality, absolute reason, a personality, a moral will, He is the wholly non-rational and ' other ', the being of sheer mystery and marvel. We had to turn to the feelings of horror and shudder and spectral haunting in order, by means of these caricatures of the authentic numinous emotions, to break through the hard crust of rationalism and bring into play the feelings buried deep down in our religious consciousness.

Now what is true of our apprehension of the divine is true also of its counterpart in the creature—soul and spirit. Gregory of Nyssa well says: ' Since one of the signs of the Divine Nature is its essential incomprehensibility, in this also must the copy be like the original. For were the nature of the copy comprehended, when the original was above comprehension, the copy would be a mistaken one. But, inasmuch as the nature of our spirit is above our understanding, it has here an exact resemblance to the all-sublime, representing by its own unfathomableness the incomprehensible Being of God.' Here, too, we need to break up anew

---

[1] K. Müller suggests that the divine name Yah, Yahū, may have had this origin. ' Euoios ', the secondary name of Bacchus, may also denote simply him in whose presence one ejaculates ' Euoi '. He could cite in his support Jelaleddin, who says in Divan 31. 8 : ' I know no other than Yahū.' This is here certainly nothing but ' one of the most familiar dervish cries ' (as the translator adds in a note, p. 282), and will then mean, in accordance with the usual rendering, ' O he ', or, as we rather suspect, simply ' O *hu* '. Nicholson puts ' Yahweh ' in brackets, without further justification. Cf. R. A. Nicholson, *Selected Poems from the Divani Shamsi Tabriz*, Cambridge, 1898.

our hardened and crusted feelings and to withstand the intellec-
tualizing tendency to which we are so prone in our doctrine of the
soul and its creation in God's image. For this divine image in
man also does not merely consist in the fact that he is reasonable,
moral, intelligent, and a person, but primarily in the fact that in
its profoundest depths his being is indeed for religious self-consciousness something numinous—that the soul is mystery and
marvel. This is how Mysticism apprehends it, and we can
understand at once why this is so from our definition of Mysticism
as the tendency to stress up to an extreme and exaggerated point
the non-rational aspect of religion. And what was already stirring in crude fashion at the earliest and lowest stage of numinous
feeling recurs at the most exalted level of Mysticism with after-
effects that colour the whole experience. In the mystic's praise
of the soul, and in that 'fundus animae' of which he tells the
mysteries, there echoes the 'stupor' before the 'wholly other'
that characterized the primitive belief in souls and even primitive
feeling of the presence of ghosts.

We said above (p. 124) that the most interesting point in the
primitive idea of soul is not the form given to it in fantasy,
multifarious in its variations, but the element of feeling—'stupor'
—which it liberates, and the character of 'mystery' and 'wholly
otherness' which surrounds it. This fact is obscured in the
measure in which the 'soul' becomes later the subject of myth,
fairy story, and narrative, speculation and doctrine, and finally of
psychological investigation. It then becomes more and more
something entirely rational ; its origin in magic and mystery
becomes overlaid with concepts, scholastic terms, and classifica-
tions. The Doctrine of souls or 'Ātman' of the Indian Sānkhya
system is the best example of this. But even this cannot entirely
conceal the fact that 'Soul' or 'Ātman' is *properly* the thing of
marvel and stupefaction, quite undefinable, outsoaring all conceptions, 'wholly alien' to our understanding. And this finds
wonderful expression in the verses of the Gītā, 2. 29, which we
transcribe here of intention in the original :

> Āścaryavat paśyati kaścid enam.
> Āścaryavad vadati tathaiva cānyaḥ.
> Āścaryavac cainam anyaḥ śrinoti.
> Śrutvā 'pyenam veda na caiva kaścit.

The sound of these verses suggests a magic formula, almost a conjuration, especially when they are heard intoned in the peculiar sacred sing-song in which such lines are commonly recited.   The note of magic and mystery is very palpable in them. As for the translation, it is usual to render *Āścaryam* by 'strange', 'wondrous', 'a thing of wonder' or 'marvel'; but we should perhaps catch the emotional accent in the lines more exactly as follows :

As 'wholly other' doth one gaze upon it (*sc.* Ātman).
He speaketh of the 'wholly other', who speaketh of the Ātman.
Something 'wholly other' hath he learned, who hath learned the Ātman.
Yet none, albeit he hath learned it, may come to know it.

But, however they be rendered into another language, there is living in these old phrases a profoundly numinous self-feeling, which still retains a trace of the 'stupor' before an apparition of spirits.   And it is continued where the Gītā (2. 25) designates the Ātman the '*acintya*', i. e. that which is incomprehensible by thought.   In this it is exactly like the 'fundus animae', the 'spark', 'Synderesis', or 'Inner Abyss' of our own Western mystics.   In both cases we have, surviving in an ennobled form, the primal awe and shrinking before the presence of '*āścaryam*' and '*adbhutam*', the haunting presence that prompts the earliest numinous feelings.   For, as an old mystic tells us, the soul and its bottommost depth lie hidden away, ineffable as God himself— 'so that no human skill ever attains to be able to know what the Soul is in its bottommost depth.   For that a supernatural skill is needed.   It is what is without a name.'   And 'the heights and depths which are disclosed in these Men can be grasped by no human sense or reason, for they surpass in their profundities all understanding'.[1]

Finally, it may be said that we catch a last reflection of the numinous wonder in the wonder, one might almost say in the eager curiosity, with which Augustine roves through the chambers of the soul, even when he is pursuing 'psychological' discussion. He feels that he has a story of marvel to tell when he describes the soul.   His psychology is half 'numinology'.   Cf. *Confessions*, x. 6–27.

The clearer insight into the inmost marvel of the soul is not set free as a sort of reflex : it comes in the experience as an uprush,

[1] Greith, pp. 70 and 80.

an irruption, a burst of illumination, 'like a flash', in the English phrase, as a 'sudden aperçu', in Goethe's. And so it easily shows the two elements; on the one hand there is an entry or penetration into consciousness of inspiration, sudden, unmeditated, once and for all achieved; and on the other hand there is a reminiscence (anamnesis), a recollection of something that was a familiar possession in the obscurity of feeling even before the moment of insight. Both of these elements are indicated in the old Kena-Upanishad, when (iv. 30), after speaking of the Brahman in the significant verses we have already considered (p. 196), the text goes on at once to speak of the Ātman, in words which may be rendered thus:

Now in respect to the Ātman:
It is as though something forces its way into consciousness
And consciousness suddenly remembers—
Such a state of mind illustrates the awakening of knowledge
    of the Ātman.

We may compare the saying of Plato, already quoted (p. 98 n.); and, finally, the words of Meister Eckhart:

'Upon this matter a heathen sage hath a fine saying in speech with another sage: "I become aware of something in me which flashes upon my reason. I perceive of it that it is something, but what it is I cannot conceive. Only meseems that, could I conceive it, I should comprehend all truth."' (W. Lehmann, *Meister Eckhart*, Göttingen, 1917, p. 243.)

And the 'obscure' Heracleitus says: 'Thou canst not discover the bounds of the soul albeit thou pacest its every road: so deep is its foundation.'

APPENDIX V

THE SUPRA-PERSONAL IN THE NUMINOUS

WE said above that the feeling of the 'wholly other' gives rise in Mysticism to the tendency to follow the 'via negationis', by which every predicate that can be stated in words becomes excluded from the absolute Numen—i. e. from Deity—till finally the Godhead is designated as 'nothingness' and 'nullity', bearing in mind always that these terms denote in truth immeasurable plenitude of being. Now this is also the origin of that tendency to let the conception of *personality* and the personal also be submerged in the same 'nothingness', a tendency which is in appearance so irreligious. We need not dispute that the denial of personality to God does often in fact denote a wholly irreligious attitude; mostly it is simply a disguised form of atheism, or betokens a desperate attempt to equate faith in God with belief in natural law and with naturalism. But it would be a huge error to suppose that anything of this kind is in the minds of the mystics when they set themselves to oppose the idea of personality in God. We shall be in a better position to understand what they are contending for if we take Mysticism—following our previous definition—as meaning the preponderance in religious consciousness, even to the point of one-sided exaggeration, of its non-rational features. What we have, then, is a sort of antinomy, arising from the inner duality in the idea of the divine and the tension of its more rational and its more non-rational elements. (The non-rational assumes thus an apparently *ir*rational character.) It is the 'wholly other' aspect of the numen, resisting every analogy, every attempted comparison, and every determination; so that it is here really true that 'omnis determinatio est negatio'.

Now this holds good not only in the case of the most lofty and reverent feelings, in which devotion and worship reach their consummation, but also in the case of that primary and elemental 'awe' of which we spoke on pages 129–132. Let us glance once more at the experience given in the story of Jacob at Bethel, there cited (Gen. xxviii. 16–17). If we use as a clue to it our own power of imaginative sympathy, introspection will show that even this experience contains a clear antinomy, a conflict of opposites. We said that the pure elemental 'awe' mirrored in Jacob's first words, 'How dreadful is this place!', is rendered explicit in the words that follow. The simple experience of 'awefulness' is *interpreted*—all but instinctively, and apart from reflection—and the interpretation is, in the English phrase, 'a presence', a real, present, and personal being. Now though we certainly feel that such an interpretation is needed and in some sense right, and that we should in Jacob's place have found no other to 'explicate' our feeling, yet we are no less certainly conscious of a counter-impulse in us which resists it, suggesting that, when all is said, such expressions as 'Being', 'Person', 'Thou', 'He', are strangely alien and repugnant to the very import of the experience.   Does this Power that impresses us with such awe admit of being comprised in such a firm outline, admit of question and answer in the second person ?   Is not this interpretation at first glance distinctly anthropomorphic?   The abstract English expression, 'a presence', is itself a good indication of this—for 'a presence' is simply felt, and the English usage of words is chary of saying anything more specific.   The 'Personalism' of the later developed mythology and the later developments of ordered worship (mostly practised on a wholly 'personalist' basis) have tended more and more to extrude this authentic and sensitive element of feeling from the religious experience ; and the 'daemon' or 'god', which they both contributed to shape, is not richer but poorer in content than the object of that primal 'awe', corresponding only to certain sides and aspects of it.   Before the 'gods' were the hard-outlined, clear-featured gods of the myths, they were 'numina', and, though the numen certainly gains something from subsequent mythology in definiteness and fixity of representation, it also certainly loses something of its original wealth of meaning in the process.   In drawing more near to earth and to humanity, it comes itself to acquire human traits, and, that this tendency may not be carried too far, it is necessary now and then to melt down, as it were, the human lineaments of God in the more elemental entirety of the original experience.   The numen has, no doubt, in itself personal features, which somehow enable the worshipper to refer to it by a pronoun, as 'he' or 'she'.   But, while the limits of the personal are at this stage still fluid, they cannot (any more than in the case of the more definite figure of the 'God') quite comprise the full import of the inapprehensible and unnameable, which presses out beyond them.

Thus already, at the outset, we find in the numen of primitive religious feeling that tension between the personal and the suprapersonal which recurs again in the maturer stages of the developing experience of God.   It is to be found next in the comparatively low level of 'the daemonic', where it is disclosed in an actual difference in the verbal forms employed.   The Greek δαίμων is indisputably a single, concrete, personal Being ; the δαιμόνιον, that, for example, of Socrates, is certainly none of these—neither concrete, nor personal, and hardly even to be called a being or individual entity. Yet in the impressiveness and devout awe which it suggests δαιμόνιον is, if anything, the richer of the two terms. In Indian terminology *raksás* is the concrete, personal, and masculine 'Daemon', but a transposition of the accent to the first syllable gives *ráksas* (the neuter), 'the daemonic', or rather demonic ; a word, perhaps, more charged with terror than is *raksás*; and the fact that the difference is merely one of accent shows very clearly how easily the one meaning passes into the other. But exactly the same thing is seen again at that highest stage, at which the unfolding of the numinous consciousness reaches its climax in India : *brahmán* is the everlasting Lord and God, the personal Brahmá ; while *bráhman* is the divine Absolute, the supra-personal Bráhma, an 'It' rather than a 'He'. And the two are bound together in indissoluble union as the two essential poles of the eternal unity of the Numen. And here, again, the closeness of their interconnexion is emphatically shown by the fact that they are denoted by one and the same word and distinguished by a mere change of accent and gender.

Now it is generally supposed that there is something peculiarly and specifically 'oriental' in this characteristic of Indian religion. But this is by no means the case. On the contrary, one may venture to assert that *all* gods are more than mere (personal) gods, and that all the greater representations of deity show from time to time features which reveal their ancient character as 'numina' and burst the bounds of the personal and theistic. This is obviously the case where the experienced relation of the worshipper to his god does not exclusively take the form of contact with a 'beyond' and transcendent being, but comes somehow as the experience of seizure and possession by the god, as being filled by him, an experience in which the god wholly or partially enters the believer and dwells in him, or assimilates him to his own divine nature, commingling with his spirit and becoming very part of him ; or, again, where the god becomes the sphere 'in which we live and move and have our being'. And what god has not in some sense had this character ? It is certainly true of the personal '*Īšvara*' of India, who, besides his personal character, pervades his 'Bhakta' as '*antaryāmin*', the immanent Indweller ; it is true of *Ahura-mazda*, who by his spirits does the same ; and it is true of Dionysus, Apollo, and Zeus. No less than the mere crude 'daemon' can the 'god' become πνεῦμα and permeate the soul of man. And in so far the notion of a 'god' passes beyond the sphere of social and personal ideas and breaks through the confines of the merely personal. *Persons* cannot strictly inter-penetrate, cannot become one inclusive of another. Such relations experienced between man and deity become altogether irrational, if we judge them by the standard of personality.

The Yahweh of the Old Testament is also more than a 'god' in the merely personal sense, for though it is a sign of his superior value to all tribal gods, that the personal traits are so incompar-ably more strongly marked in him, yet other and non-personal features are not lacking. We come up against these in groping fashion in the comparison made between God's dealings with men and the working of an inexplicable 'force' spontaneously released. But the second name of Yahweh, 'Elohim', is also a proof of their existence. Elohim is 'gods', in the plural; and 'in the begin-ning created (sing.) "gods" heaven and earth'. Our way to-day, when we try to escape from the too narrow confines of the notion of unitary personality applied to God, is to use either an abstract noun, 'deity' (*die Gottheit*), or an adjectival neuter expression, 'the divine' (*das göttliche*). In Israel the same groping instinct had recourse to the adoption or adaptation of a plural substantive form, which was yet made to govern a verb in the singular! There cannot be a more uncompromising expression of what we called the antinomy or conflict of opposites in the experience of the numinous. It is very similar when later *Shāmayim*, 'Heaven', becomes a name for God—to be used once as such also in the Gospel. It does not in the least signify an 'abstract' way of conceiving God; but rather the feeling that endeavours to escape from any too anthropomorphic conception. Above all does the God of Job burst the bounds of interpretation by mere persona-lity, as we have already seen. Moreover, Yahweh also is the numen which, blowing in the form of spirit, enters as 'ruach' and πνεῦμα into his chosen, mingling with their spirit, an *antaryāmin* in full completion.

And so, when we turn to the New Testament, we see that the 'Pneumatology' and doctrine of Immanence in Paul and John, which give such unmistakable expression to the supra-personal aspect of the divine as the 'Light' and the 'Life', do not mean a sudden irruption into religion of a wholly novel and alien element, but merely the complete realization of what was all the while potential in the character of Yahweh in his essence as a numen.

And what of the loftiest of all Christian claims, ' God is Love ' ? Usually we hear this saying without remarking how extraordinary it is. If we think of God in strictly and narrowly personal terms, He can indeed be ' He that loves ', ' the loving One '. But the God who is *Love*, who pours Himself out as love and becomes the love whereby Christians love, is something more even than this.[1] In fine, even our GOD is more than merely ' god '. And, when Meister Eckhart says that one must stand apart from God in order to find deity, his error is certainly grave, but it is one which we can easily conceive as springing from the very heart of religion.[2]

But it is very evident that the religious attitude in face of this supra-personal aspect of the numen must be different from the ordinary attitude in personal intercourse by petition, prayer, colloquy. These have all assuredly pertained to the essence of religion from the earliest times, yet from the beginning they were not the only forms of intercourse. The numen on its side ' has intercourse' with man in attracting him to it, seizing upon him, possessing him, breathing upon him, filling and permeating him. Its function is ἐνεργεῖσθαι, and on his side the man, the ἐνεργούμενος, is filled, possessed, made one with the numen. And what is true at the lower levels is true also at the highest. The Divine,

---

[1] There is an echo of this antinomy in the dispute of the Scholastics whether the love whereby we love is the 'Spiritus Sanctus', i.e. God Himself, or merely His ' donum '.

[2] We have seen that it is an indication of its superiority that in the Biblical conception of God the pole of the personal rather than of the impersonal is altogether preponderant. Taoism stands at the opposite extreme ; but it too is genuine and deeply felt religion, moving as it does wholly in the numinous. H. Hackmann says of it: ' Taoism originates in the contemplative speculation upon the secret of the world, the mystery of existence. Its basic instinct is to pay reverent and surmiseful heed to the marvellous forces operative in our phenomenal life, which give to its particular details system and connexion with the great unknown background of the universe. The word " mystery "—the *mysterium tremendum*—occupies a more central position in Taoism than in almost any other religion.... Here sounds a genuine note in the prodigious symphony of that life of the soul—the religious life—which searches and surmises a deeper unity and a firm foundation in the beyond behind the happenings upon earth.' (H. Hackmann, ' Die Mönchsregeln des Klostertaoismus ', *Ostasiatische Zeitschrift*, vii. p. 170.) For this whole question cf. the same author's essay: ' Über Objekt und Gebietsumfang der Religion,' in *Nieuw Theologisch Tijdschrift*, 1918.

experienced as 'light', 'fire', and πνεῦμα, cannot properly accost or be accosted. It is a penetrating glow and illumination, fulfilment, transfiguration—most of all where it is experienced as 'Life', or (what is but the intensification of this) as very 'Being'. One can make a petition *for* life, but not *to* life. One is simply quickened through and through by it; one cannot address it as 'Thou'. And so intercourse with the numen comprises a way other than that of personal intercourse, that of the 'mystic'. Each of the two, the personal and the mystical, belongs to the other, and the language of devotion uses very naturally the phrases and expressions of both commingled. They are not different forms of religion, still less different stages in religion, the one higher and better than the other, but the two essentially united poles of a single fundamental mental attitude, the religious attitude. In Luther's conception of 'faith' they are found in this relation openly manifested, where 'fides' denotes both 'fiducia' or trust—a term implying personal intercourse—and 'adhaesio', or intimate contact, a term essentially mystical.

It is in the light of this primal fact of religion that we must seek an answer to the question as to the general place of 'Personalism' and 'Supra-personalism' in religious history, and only so are we likely to avoid confounding this question with the question of Theism and Pantheism, with which it has nothing in common. In my books *Vishnu-Nārāyana* (pp. 59, 63) and *Siddhāntā des Rāmānija* (pp. 2, 80) I have referred further to the subject. And I have shown in a paper, 'Neues Singen' (*Christliche Welt*, 1919, No. 48), its important practical bearings for religious conduct and its expression in prayer and hymn. I reproduce the relevant passage :

'Our usual Prayers and Hymns confine themselves to the region which I call the "rational". They lack that element which I call the non-rational or the "numinous". But this is the other half of religion, its profounder and more mysterious background and basis. Yet only seldom has hymnody hitherto done justice to it. Consequently we are very deficient in the great and impressive "Hymns of Reverence", the hymns of the (grammatical) third person, and our hymns are almost entirely in the second person, "Thou", not "He". Now there is something lacking in this constant, direct, obvious mode of accosting God in the second person singular. The Seraphim in Isaiah vi do not venture on such an address, and many a glorious Ekteny and Litany of the older Liturgies follows their example. The creature

is simply unable to stand face to face with the Eternal without
interruption ; his vision cannot bear the perpetual sight of Holiness without an occasional screen.   He needs sometimes the
oblique as well as the straight, frontal approach, the indirect
relationship with face half averted and covered, as well as the
direct ; and consequently his utterance should not be so continually in the form of an address *to* God as to exclude prayerful and
thoughtful discourse *about* Him.   The same holds good of prayer
in general, not merely of hymns.   "Third person" hymns in
this sense are not necessarily less, but under certain conditions
may even be more genuine and first-hand utterances than those
which address God as "Thou".   There is a further consequence.
It is often thought that the designations of deity in impersonal,
neuter terms ("it"), rather than in terms of person and masculine
pronoun ("He", "Thou"), are too poor and too pale to gain a
place in our Christian thought of God.   But this is not always
correct.   Frequently such terms indicate the mysterious overplus
of the non-rational and numinous, that cannot enter our "concepts"
because it is too great and too alien to them ; and in this sense
they are quite indispensable, even in hymns and prayers.   It is a
defect in our devotional poetry that it hardly knows any other
image for the eternal mystery of the Godhead than those drawn
from social intercourse and personal relationship, and so it tends
to lose sight of just the mysterious transcendent aspect of deity.
Assuredly God *is* for us "Thou" and a Person.   But this Personal character is that side of His nature which is turned man-
ward—it is like a "Cape of Good Hope", jutting out from a
mountain range which, as it recedes, is lost to view in the "tene-
brae aeternae"—only to be expressed by the suspension of speech
and the inspiration of sacred song.'

So far we have spoken of the personal and supra-personal as
applied to the supreme, spiritual Being.   But what is true here is
no less true of that which was created in its image, our own
human soul or spirit.   In us too all that we call person and personal, indeed all that we can know or name in ourselves at all, is
but one element in the whole.   Beneath it lies, even in us, that
'wholly other', whose profundities, impenetrable to any concept,
can yet be grasped in the numinous self-feeling [1] by one who has
experience of the deeper life.

---

[1] We say 'numinous self-*feeling*', not 'numinous self-*consciousness*', as
Schleiermacher called it, who may be said to have re-discovered it.   The
ambiguity of his nomenclature, however, does not detract from the
importance of his discovery.

APPENDIX VI

THE MYSTICAL ELEMENT IN LUTHER'S CONCEPTION OF 'FAITH'

In connexion with the discussion of Luther's conception of faith on page 107, I would refer to my book, *Die Anschauung vom Heiligen Geiste bei Luther*, the chapter 'Geist und Glaube' (pp. 25–46), which includes the inquiry into Luther's conception of Faith and how far Faith for him is not merely confidence and trust (*confidere, fiducia*), but also a 'cleaving to God' in feeling and will (*adhaerere Deo*). And then let the reader study the noble little work of Albertus Magnus, *De Adhaerendo Deo*, to recognize the inner connexion of Luther with Mysticism in regard to his conception of faith, especially the 12th chapter, 'De Amore Dei quod efficax sit.' Luther says *nothing* of the impelling power of Faith to bring to new birth, to justify and to sanctify, that is not also said in this chapter of the 'Amor Mysticus'.

'Solus amor est, quo convertimur ad Deum, transformamur in Deum, adhaeremus Deo, unimur Deo, ut simus unus spiritus cum eo, et beatificemur cum eo.' [1]

Here 'amor' is the 'potent, active, creative thing that changes us and brings us to new birth'. 'Love', too, like Faith, is the 'affect' that knows no quiescence.

'Proinde nihil amore acutius, nihil subtilius, aut penetrabilius. Nec quiescit, donec universaliter totam amabilis penetravit virtutem et profunditatem ac totalitatem, et unum se vult facere cum amato. *Vehementer tendit* in eum et ideo *nunquam quiescit*, donec omnia transeat et ad ipsum in ipsum veniat.' [2]

The effect of this 'adhaesio' is thus exactly that which Luther also frequently describes:

'Quippe qui Deo adhaeret, versatur in lumine . . . qua ex re est

---

[1] 'It is Love alone whereby we are turned to God, and changed into the form of God, whereby we cleave to God and are made one with God, so that we are one spirit with Him and are beatified with Him.'

[2] 'For nothing is keener, nothing more subtle or more penetrating, than Love. Nor does it rest until it has penetrated the whole power and depth and entirety of its object, and its will is to make itself one with the loved one. It strives towards him with vehemence and so never has rest until it has passed through all things and reached him and entered into him.'

hominis in hac vita sublimior perfectio, ita Deo uniri, ut tota anima cum omnibus potentiis suis et viribus in Dominum Deum suum sit collecta, et unus fiat spiritus cum eo.'[1]

Luther calls this, in a still more violent expression, 'mit Gott ein Kuche werden' (to become kneaded into one cake with God).

It should at the same time be noted that in Albertus Magnus this 'amor' is already permeated through and through by Faith, Trust, Comfort, and the longing for certitude, and that for him no less than for Luther the 'Remission of Sins' stands as the first step in the 'ordo salutis', the order of salvation.   Thus:

'Sic scilicet in Domino Deo de omni sua necessitate *audeat plene totaliter confidere.*   Hoc ipso facto in tantum Deo complacet, ut suam ei gratiam largiatur et per ipsam gratiam veram sentiat caritatem et dilectionem, omnemque *ambiguitatem et timorem expellentem* in Deoque *confidenter sperantem*'[2] (*op. cit.*, ch. 5).

And so 'adhaesio' may come about just as well by means of 'faith': 'sed tantum fide et bona voluntate adhaerere Deo'[3] (ch. 6).

Here, too, are freedom from care and the assurance of consolation the things to be prized: 'et eius consolatione suaviter reficitur'[4] (ch. 7).

And the whole series of religious experiences, so often recurring in Luther, are already displayed in Albertus Magnus in their characteristic order:

'. . . peccatorum remissio, amaritudinis expressio, collatio dulcedinis et securitatis, infusio gratiae et misericordiae, attractio et corroboratio familiaritatis atque abundans de ipso consolatio, firmaque adhaesio et unio.'[5]

---

[1] 'He indeed who cleaves to God abides in light. . . . Wherefore is it man's loftier perfection in this life to be so united to God that the whole soul with all its strength and all its powers is gathered into its Lord and God and becomes one spirit with Him.'

[2] 'So then let (the soul) of its very necessity make the venture to trust wholly and completely in the Lord God.   In this very wise is the soul so pleasing to God, that He bestows His own grace upon it, and by that very grace it comes to feel the true love and affection which drives away all doubt and all fear and hopes confidently in God.'

[3] 'but only to cleave to God in faith and good will.'

[4] 'and by his consolation is (the soul) sweetly restored.'.

[5] 'The forgiveness of sins, the expelling of bitterness, the bestowal of sweetness and security, the inpouring of grace and of mercy, the attraction and the strengthening of friendship with Him and abundant comfort in Him, and a firm cleaving to Him and union with Him.'

But a complete judgement upon Luther's connexion with Mysticism will only be possible when all the manuscript remains of the popular mystical preaching of his time become known, which as yet lie undisturbed in our libraries.   They will show the background and setting of Luther's thought and phraseology, the soil out of which they grew, and how many similarities and analogues there are to the feelings to which Luther gives expression.   Were we unaware that the pamphlet *Of the Liberty of a Christian* was by Luther, we should probably count it among these writings. And in any case there are to be found within the limits of the so-called 'mystical' literature contrasts in mental attitude that go farther than that between this work of Luther's and that of Albertus Magnus from which we have been quoting.   And Luther is really far more akin to such a mystic as Meister Eckhart in his attitude than are either Plotinus on the one hand or, on the other, the crowd of God-enamoured monks and nuns, the 'doctores ecstatici' and 'seraphici', such as Ignatius and John of the Cross, Theresa and Madame Guyon.

But such comparisons as this are illuminating not only upon the question of the historical relation between Lutheranism and mystical religion, which is, after all, not a very important issue, but also upon the question as to the connexion between the two in their essential nature.   It has been said that for a Protestant to love Mysticism is mere dilettantism: if he is in earnest, he must become a Catholic.   But then 'Mysticism' is an ambiguous term. If we mean by it the melting transport of a transcendent quasi-nuptial rapture, then the assertion may be justified.   But the really typical 'moments' of mysticism—'creature-feeling' and 'union' —are not *less* but *more* possible upon the basis of Luther's 'fides' ('faith' as 'fiducia' and 'adhaesio') than upon the basis of the 'amor mysticus'.

Johann Arndt says at the commencement of his *Four Books of True Christianity* (ch. 5): ' By this heart-felt confidence and heart-felt trust man gives his heart to God utterly, reposes only in God, surrenders himself and attaches himself to Him, unites himself with God, becomes a sharer in all that is of God and of Christ, becomes one God with God.'   This is simply Luther's doctrine (his 'fides' as 'fiducia' and 'adhaesio'), clarified and raised to a higher power.   These expressions might well be found in Luther's *Of the Liberty of a Christian*—indeed their meaning is to be found there.   St. Paul says the same, only more forcibly still, in Gal. ii. 20 and 1 Cor. vi. 17.

But this question of the possibility of the transition from 'fides' to the experience of union is not to be definitely decided by a citation of texts from Luther or from the Bible, but by a consideration of what 'Faith' is in essence.   Faith is more than a conviction of the truth of the eternal verities.   It is a deeply felt state of tension with regard to them and of absorption in them; and, as 'trust', it is the most intimate feeling of nearness. But in all this it contains in itself the core of that which is meant by mysterious terms like 'union', something that is more than the 'knowledge' or the 'love' of the earlier mystic schools.   And this becomes still plainer to any one who has clearly recognized by deeper contemplation the profoundly non-rational elements to be found in the very act of faith.

APPENDIX VII

'SIGNS FOLLOWING'

(I GIVE here a passage from my *Leben und Wirken Jesu* relevant to this subject, touched upon on p. 176.)

Jesus begins his work on the shore of the Sea of Galilee, and the Gospels present us with its main features unmistakably.   He preaches in the synagogues, in the houses of his friends, on every sort of occasion at table and under the open sky, now sojourning in one spot, now journeying from place to place.   His fame is spread abroad especially by means of the mysterious gift of healing which is active in him.

What are we to say of this?   The Jesus who works the miracles in the Synoptic narrative is, as we saw above, not the wonder-worker *par excellence*, of whom we read in St. John's Gospel or whom the traditional view presents to us.   But even in those passages which can be least impugned by criticism there is something incommensurable with our rational standards in the setting in which we see his figure, and this gift of healing is an example of it.   The narratives of these acts of healing stand out with such an assured and plain simplicity, with a clarity so wellnigh disconcerting, that they cannot be the fabrications of legend. We have only to read the sober account—it is almost like an official report—of the healing of Peter's wife's mother (Mark i. 29–31), or that of the healing of the man with the palsy (Mark ii. 1–12), with its concreteness of detail. And it is the same with many other cases. The story of the centurion of Capernaum, and Jesus's astonished wonder at the faith of this Gentile; the story of the woman of Canaan, and of how Jesus, at first reluctant, comes to be inwardly won over; this is not the way of imagination and legend. Moreover, there is the fact that we encounter exactly similar occurrences among the early Christian communities. Even if we are ready to impugn the accounts of Jesus's miracles of healing in the Gospels, we cannot impugn the accounts in the Pauline epistles of the same thing as happening among the Corinthians, Galatians, and Romans, and to Paul himself. Here they stand in the full light of history and with the fullest testimony of history. It is quite evident that both Paul and the first Christian communities were firmly convinced that they had the 'charismata', the 'gifts', among them. St. Paul gives, in 1 Cor. xii. 4–11, a formal catalogue of these, in which the gifts of healing the sick and of the exercise of super-normal physical power and other abnormal psychical gifts take their place alongside the gifts of tongues and prophecy. No doubt he says (1 Cor. xiii) that something is higher and more precious than all 'gifts', namely, the simple Christian virtues of Faith, Hope, and Love, and Love 'the greatest among these'. But it is implied thereby that those other gifts too are a reality and a present possession. He has them in himself and frequently exercises them, and in every Christian congregation they make their appearance. In fact we have sure historical warrant for holding that 'gifts' of this kind were in evidence for a long time beyond the borders of the early Church—just as, for that matter, we have similar warrant for recognizing that analogous phenomena have been since observed in other than Christian surroundings. Will this mysterious region one day be clearly revealed to us? We can at any rate say this: that our procedure is very uncritical if we propose to rule it out as non-existent simply because it does not square with our current conceptions of 'agreement with the natural order'.

Now the fewer the preconceptions which we bring to our reading of the narrative-material of the Gospels, as reviewed and guaranteed by a thorough criticism, the stronger becomes the impression that in Jesus these powers were present with a rare potency. We have in a sense a key to the matter in the peculiar predisposition and endowment for their calling which marked the great prophets of the Old Testament. What characterized them really was not omniscience and not the capacity of predicting a future many hundred years distant: it was beyond question in many cases a unique power of forefeeling and foreboding impending supernormal occurrences that threatened to break in upon the natural course of events. This gift we have held to be not something 'supernatural' and miraculous in the old sense of the word, i. e. something that falls altogether outside all analogies of what happens elsewhere; on the contrary, analogies in plenty for this extraordinary prophetic gift are to be found in the phenomena of clairvoyance, presentiment, second-sight, &c. Now it is possible that the gift of healing of Jesus which appears so puzzling was 'merely' a heightened and intense form of capacities which lie dormant in human nature in general. But for a manifestation of the influence exerted by the psychical upon the physical we need in fact go no farther than the power of our will to move our body —the power, that is, of a spiritual cause to bring about a mechanical effect. There assuredly is an absolutely insoluble riddle, and it is only the fact that we have grown so used to it that prevents it from seeming a 'miracle' to us. But, this granted, who can pronounce beforehand what intenser and heightened manifestations of this power may not be possible? Who can presume to determine what direct results a will may not achieve which, wholly concentrated and at one with itself, rests altogether upon God? We have had in recent years many indications of parallels and analogies to the miraculous power of Jesus in the newly-discovered methods of suggestion and hypnotism, in telepathy, 'action at a distance', and (in my opinion) animal magnetism. All these suppositions may be accepted without misgiving, only with this addition, that what Jesus did passed gradually far beyond anything known to us in these fields; and moreover, that Jesus' whole power grew out of his consciousness of his mission, and his will, unusually strong as it was, drew its strength only from his religious and moral consciousness, from the fact that he was rooted and grounded in God.

If it be granted that Jesus really had an abnormal power in action, it is evident that this very fact would stimulate rumour and imagination to exaggeration and embellishment and invention of miraculous incident. It is evident that we may quite properly approach the miracle narratives with a certain expectation of finding such features in them; and that it will not do, in face of some sheer prodigy, to rest content with 'the mysterious gift' as a solution to every difficulty. Thus a raising from the dead, as that of Lazarus, or a changing of water into wine (both stories only in St. John), is excluded from the region of the historically conceivable and admissible. And there is in the Synoptists also matter enough that passes these limits, e. g. the walking on the sea, the feeding of the five thousand, the tale of the Gadarene swine. When such stories have been deducted, then practically all that is left in the Synoptic narrative are cases of healing, though of course some of these are of an astonishing character. There are also two cases of raising from the dead— that of Jairus's daughter and that of the young man of Nain. Criticism will be inclined to reject these. It must, however, be granted that there is a real difference between these stories and that in St. John of the raising of Lazarus. Jairus's daughter had not lain three days in the grave, like Lazarus; she had only lost consciousness a short time before the miracle. Where is the margin that divides complete death from the last faint glow of the spark of life, very likely already passed into unconsciousness? May not he who by his will had power to restore a consciousness confused by madness have had also the power to arrest a consciousness just vanishing over the borders of life, and even awaken again in the body one that has but just vanished? Here the account is strikingly concrete. Even the very words Jesus uses to awaken the girl as uttered in Aramaic—'Talitha Cumi' —are still given in the Aramaic form by the Greek narrator. There is nothing grandiose or theatrical, as is customarily the case with a miracle designed for display. Jesus only admits the most intimate even of his disciples, and the whole incident closes with the soberly practical injunction to give the newly restored child food, and with the direct prohibition to talk further about the event. We have only to compare with this the raising of Lazarus; here is the exact opposite, a genuine miracle of display. The wonder-worker designedly delays his arrival, so that a miracle becomes necessary ; the whole proceeding, with its solemn *mise-en-scène*, takes place in public, and is accompanied by a prayer, which is at the same time a sort of address to the surrounding spectators. The act is to be performed expressly ' because of the people which stand by '. This is how a miracle-narrative looks when it is the offspring of literary art. The raisings from the dead given in St. Mark are quite other than this, and consequently a circumspect criticism may perhaps in their case suspend judgement.

APPENDIX VIII

SILENT WORSHIP

Still-born Silence, thou that art
Flood-gate of the deeper heart.

I TAKE these lines [1] from a little Quaker book on *Silent Worship* [2] which, recently translated into German, should give the German public a good impression of the worship of silent waiting upon God which has been a feature of the Quaker community from the days of George Fox up to the present day. It is the most spiritual form of divine service which has ever been practised, and contains an element which no form of worship ought to be without, but which, as has been hinted on a former page, is unduly neglected in our Protestant devotional life. We must learn it once again from the Quakers, and thereby restore to our divine service a spirit of consecration the loss of which has cost it dearly.

I

Devotional Silence may have a threefold character. There is the numinous silence of Sacrament, the silence of Waiting, and the silence of Union or Fellowship.

1. The first of these is that silence meant in the verse of the Prophet (Hab. ii. 20), ' Let all the earth keep silence before him.'

---

[1] They are quoted from Charles Lamb's essay, 'A Quakers' Meeting ', (*Trans.*)
[2] *Silent Worship : The Way of Wonder*, by Violet Hodgkin.

Such impressive moments of silence were known not only in the worship of Israel but in that of other peoples. They are the culminating sacramental point in the worship, denoting as they do the instant when 'God is in the midst', experienced as 'numen praesens'. All the preceding part of the service is but a preparation for this, a preparation for the moment of which the words hold good, 'Das Unzulängliche, hier wird's Ereignis,' 'the Insufficient here becomes Event'. For what was previously only possessed in insufficiency, only longed for, now comes upon the scene in living actuality, the experience of the transcendent in gracious intimate presence, the 'Lord's Visitation of His people'. Such a realization is Sacrament, and what occasions it, attends, or prepares for it, must be termed sacramental. Such a silence is therefore a sacramental silence. It was found in the forms of worship of ancient Israel, and it is found to-day in the Roman Mass, in the moment of 'transubstantiation'.

2. Next there is the silence of *Waiting*. The meaning of this is primarily other than sacramental. When the Quakers assemble for a quiet time together, this is first and foremost a time of waiting, and it has in this sense a double value. It means our submergence, i. e. inward concentration and detachment from the manifold outward distractions ; but this again has value as a preparation of the soul to become the pencil of the unearthly writer, the bent bow of the heavenly archer, the tuned lyre of the divine musician. This silence is, then, primarily not so much a dumbness in the presence of Deity, as an awaiting His coming, in expectation of the Spirit and its message. But it passes over naturally into the Sacramental Silence of which we have spoken. And in fact 'Silent Worship' may remain without words from first to last—it may exclude all *utterance* of the Spirit's message in vocal form, and in that case the worshippers part, as they met, without any audible exhortation or thanksgiving. Yet the worship need not have been in any way defective, for the silence may have been a direct 'numinous' experience, as well as a waiting upon God. The Eternal was present in the stillness and His presence was palpable without a word spoken. The solemn observance of silence became a Sacrament.

3. The consummation of the Sacrament is the achievement of unity, i. e. fellowship and *Communion*. This third silence is the completion of the waiting and the sacramental silences. The Silent

Worship of the Quakers is in fact a realization of Communion in both senses of the word—inward oneness and fellowship of the individual with invisible present Reality and the mystical union of many individuals with one another. In this regard there is the plainest inward kinship between the two forms of worship which, viewed externally, seem to stand at the opposite poles of religious development, viz. the Quaker meeting and the Roman Catholic Mass. *Both* are solemn religious observances of a numinous and sacramental character, *both* are communion, *both* exhibit alike an inner straining not only ' to realize the presence' of God, but to attain to a degree of oneness with Him.

II

'Silent Worship', in the fully-formed character in which the Quakers practise it, is not possible in a 'Church', as we understand the word to-day, but only within the narrower limits of a more intimate 'Brotherhood of the Spirit'. May God grant that such a brotherhood may one day arise among us, not as a sect or a Church alongside our other Churches, but as a circle of self-dedicated enthusiasts, who have rediscovered the ancient heritage of the early Church—the Spirit and its sevenfold gifts!

But if the Quaker Silence is excluded, still less is any imitation of the Sacramental Silence in the form of the Catholic Mass possible in our Protestant services. All that tends in this direction is bound to go astray. The Communion Service does, it is true, celebrate Christ's Passion, that event which in all world history is the numinous event *par excellence*, the entry of the divine in fullest and loftiest presence upon the human scene. But the Communion Service is emphatically not a Mass, and the Mass has grown to be a distortion of its true form. The Communion Service is, in the original intention of its first celebration or institution, not a piece of public ceremonial at all, far less a drama to be performed by one or at most a few participants in the presence of spectators, but a tender mystery, restricted to a fellowship of brothers, pertaining to a special time and hour, and needing particular preparation—in short, something that should be precious and rare. For Protestants it is to be kept entirely apart from the regular and congregational Divine Service, and should be reserved for particular feasts, for celebration at evening or in the night stillness. It ought to be withdrawn altogether from the use and wont of every day and become the most intimate privilege which Christian worship has to offer.

But though these two means are excluded, it is yet possible to find another way to introduce Silent Worship into our ordinary Sunday services, and so to give these a consecration which is as yet lacking to them. We can make the service culminate and find its climax in a short period of silence, which shall be at once the silence of sacrament and the silence of waiting, and which may become, at least for the more practical, also a realization of union. We may devise an opportunity of silent dedication which will avoid the ceremonial apparatus and mythology of the doctrine of 'Transubstantiation', and yet in its simplicity and pure spirituality may be more deeply sacramental than the Mass, for which many are again beginning to crave. We have only to follow the indications afforded by the example of the 'Silent Worship' of the Quakers.

Where lies the essence of the sacramental? It is in fact—in the expression of the English High Churchmen—the 'real presence', the real presence of the transcendent and holy in its very nature in adoration and fellowship, so as to be laid hold of and enjoyed in present possession. No form of devotion which does not offer or achieve this mystery for the worshipper can be perfect or can give lasting contentment to a religious mind. And it is just because our usual Divine Services fall short in this that we see to-day again—quite comprehensibly—such a ferment and stirring of all sorts of uneasy ' High Church ', ' Ritualistic ', and ' Sacramental ' movements.

But—we may well be asked—has it any meaning to ask for ' the presence of the divine ' ? Does not that Sacramental idea at once cancel itself, when thought out? Is not God 'omnipresent' and 'really present' always and everywhere?

Such a view is often put forward, and with a confident air of assurance which is in sharp conflict with the testimony of genuine religious experience; so much so, indeed, that one is tempted to venture a very blunt reply to it. We say, then, that this doctrine of the omnipresence of God—as though by a necessity of His being He must be bound to every time and to every place, like a natural force pervading space—is a frigid invention of metaphysical speculation, entirely without religious import. Scripture knows

nothing of it.   Scripture knows no 'Omnipresence', neither the
expression nor the meaning it expresses; it knows only the God
who is where He wills to be, and is not where He wills not to
be, the 'deus mobilis', who is no mere universally extended
being, but an august mystery, that comes and goes, approaches
and withdraws, has its time and hour, and may be far or near in
infinite degrees, 'closer than breathing' to us or miles remote
from us.   The hours of His 'visitation' and His 'return' are rare
and solemn occasions, different essentially not only from the
'profane' life of every day, but also from the calm confiding
mood of the believer, whose trust is to live ever before the face of
God.   They are the topmost summits in the life of the Spirit.
They are not only rare occasions, they must needs be so for our
sakes, for no creature can bear often or for long the full nearness
of God's majesty in its beatitude and in its awefulness.   Yet there
must still be such times, for they show the bright vision and completion of our sonship, they are a bliss in themselves and potent
for redemption.   They are the real sacrament, in comparison with
which all high official ceremonials, Masses, and rituals the world
over become the figurings of a child.   And a Divine Service would
be the truest which led up to such a mystery and the riches of
grace that ensue upon the realization of it.   And if it be asked
whether a Divine Service is able to achieve this, let us answer
that, though God indeed comes where and when He chooses, yet
He will choose to come when we sincerely call upon Him and
prepare ourselves truly for His visitation.

APPENDIX IX

A NUMINOUS EXPERIENCE OF JOHN RUSKIN

My attention has been called by Professor Deutschbein to the following passage in Ruskin, in which he recounts experiences of his youth that repeatedly recurred. They are purely numinous in character and wellnigh all the 'moments' which we discovered reappear here quite spontaneously. I give the passage without detailed comment:

'Lastly, although there was no definite religious sentiment mingled with it, there was a continual perception of Sanctity in the whole of nature, from the slightest thing to the vastest; an instinctive awe, mixed with delight; an indefinable thrill, such as we sometimes imagine to indicate the presence of a disembodied spirit. I could only feel this perfectly when I was alone; and then it would often make me shiver from head to foot with the joy and fear of it, when after being some time away from hills I first got to the shore of a mountain river, where the brown water circled among the pebbles, or when I first saw the swell of distant land against the sunset, or the first low broken wall, covered with mountain moss. I cannot in the least describe the feeling; but I do not think this is my fault, nor that of the English language, for I am afraid no feeling is describable. If we had to explain even the sense of bodily hunger to a person who had never felt it, we should be hard put to it for words; and the joy in nature seemed to me to come of a sort of heart-hunger, satisfied with the presence of a Great and Holy Spirit. . . . These feelings remained in their full intensity till I was eighteen or twenty, and then, as the reflective and practical power increased, and the "cares of this world" gained upon me, faded gradually away, in the manner described by Wordsworth in his "Intimations of Immortality".' (*Modern Painters*, Popular Edition, vol. iii, p. 309. George Allen.)

Schleiermacher calls such an experience 'intuition and feeling of the infinite'; we give it the name 'divination'. Schleiermacher was right in saying that even greater than all this divination in the sphere of nature is divination in the sphere of history. Will not a Ruskin arise to divine and reveal the non-rational and 'numinous' character of our own epoch?

APPENDIX X

THE EXPRESSION OF THE NUMINOUS IN ENGLISH [1]

ALTHOUGH it could hardly be disputed that the German philosophical vocabulary is superior to the English both in fullness and in precision, in regard to the subjects discussed in this book our language does not seem to be altogether at a disadvantage. Indeed, the English wealth of synonyms has presented the translator with an embarrassment at the very outset. In place of the single German adjective *heilig*, with its derivative noun and verb, we have the words *sacred* and *holy, sacredness, holiness* and *sanctity, hallow* and *sanctify. Gottheit* again gives us a triad of synonyms, *deity, divinity, Godhead.* Each of these alternatives is probably the most appropriate rendering in some special context, and in choosing any one of them we are bound to sacrifice subtle differences in meaning which would be suggested by the others, and which are perhaps implicit in the single German equivalent. The deciding factor in the choice of *holy* rather than *sacred* as the regular rendering of *heilig* was the fact that it is the Biblical word, found especially in those great passages (e. g. Isaiah vi) of which this book makes repeated use, and which seem central to its argument. *Holy* will be felt, I believe, to be a distinctly more 'numinous' word than *sacred*: it retains about it more markedly the numinous atmosphere. And although, as is urged in the text with perhaps still more reason of its German equivalent, it refers mainly to the higher levels of religious experience at which the numinous has been interpreted in rational and moral terms, and therefore means to us mainly *goodness*, the word 'holy' is found also in contexts where this more exalted meaning is excluded, and where it is simply the numinous at an early and savage stage of development. The well-known lines from Coleridge's *Kubla Khan* give an example of such a use:

> A savage place ! as holy and enchanted
> As e'er beneath a waning moon was haunted
> By woman wailing for her demon-lover !

This is a finely numinous passage, but it is the numinous at the primitive, pre-religious, 'daemonic' level : it conveys nothing of

[1] Added by the translator.

sanctity. For, while the daring use of 'holy' in this context may be just permissible, we reserve 'sanctity', if I mistake not, for the more restricted and elevated meaning.

Apart from these words it would appear that the English language is in general rich in numinous terms. Dr. Otto has himself noted (p. 14) that the English 'awe' has a numinous suggestion lacking in the German 'scheu', and (p. 131 n.) that 'haunt' has no precise German equivalent in all its range of significance. And besides 'uncanny' (a more or less exact rendering of *unheimlich*) I have made use of words like *weird* and *eerie*, which convey the indefinable numinous atmosphere unmistakably. The old word *freit* (a supernatural intimation or sign) may be another such; and possibly the obsolete verb-form *oug*, which gives us *ugly*, may have conveyed originally a suggestion of unnatural, uncanny, daunting or repulsion. It should be noticed that these numinous words are all (except 'awe') concerned *primarily* with the 'cruder' and more primitive forms of the experience : they are not in the first instance *religious* words in the higher sense, though, unlike such words as *grue, grisly,* and *ghastly,* they can be used with a loftier and more ennobled, as well as with a lower and more primitive meaning. And it can, finally, be hardly an accident that they all, or nearly all, are northern in origin. A peculiar susceptibility to numinous impressions—what Dr. Otto would call a peculiarly sensitive faculty of 'divination'—would seem, indeed, to be a characteristic of the North British. Such phenomena as those of Clairvoyance and Second-sight would seem to make for the same conclusion.

Apart from the expressiveness of single English words, it would be easy to amass from English poetry and prose alike passages (like that from Coleridge already quoted) illustrative of the different elements in numinous apprehension which have been discussed in this book. I venture to give three further citations.

On page 193 the contrast between the piety in which the 'rational moments' predominate and that in which a more numinous feeling is to be noted is illustrated from two German hymns of praise.

The same antithesis could hardly be shown more clearly than by the contrast between two poems familiar to every English reader, Addison's hymn based on Psalm xix, and Blake's poem 'The Tyger'. Both poets are hymning the Creator as revealed in

his creation, but the difference of temper is unmistakable. On the
one hand there is the mood of tranquil confidence, serene dignity,
thankful and understanding praise; on the other, a mood of
trepidation, awed surmise, the hush of mystery, in which rings
none the less a strange exultation.

> The spacious firmament on high
> With all the blue ethereal sky,
> And spangled heavens, a shining frame,
> Their great Original proclaim.
> The unwearied sun, from day to day,
> Does his Creator's power display
> And publishes to every land
> The work of an Almighty hand.
>
> Soon as the evening shades prevail
> The moon takes up the wondrous tale
> And nightly to the listening earth
> Repeats the story of her birth;
> While all the stars that round her burn,
> And all the planets in their turn,
> Confirm the tidings as they roll
> And spread the truth from pole to pole.
>
> What though in solemn silence all
> Move round the dark terrestrial ball;
> What though no real voice or sound
> Amid their radiant orbs be found?
> In reason's ear they all rejoice,
> And utter forth a glorious voice;
> For ever singing as they shine:
> 'The hand that made us is Divine.'

This is, confessedly, *rational* piety; it is 'reason' that listens to
nature's hymn of praise.   As such it is characteristic not only of
a certain type of mind, but of the particular age in which it was
written.   And the contrasted numinous note can hardly be missed
in Blake's wonderful verses:

> Tyger, Tyger, burning bright
> In the forests of the night,
> What immortal hand or eye
> Could frame thy fearful symmetry?
>
> In what distant deeps or skies
> Burnt the fire of thine eyes?
> On what wings dare he aspire?
> What the hand dare seize the fire?
>
> And what shoulder and what art
> Could twist the sinews of thy heart?
> And, when thy heart began to beat,
> What dread hand and what dread feet?

What the hammer ? What the chain ?
In what furnace was thy brain ?
What the anvil ? What dread grasp
Dare its deadly terrors clasp ?

When the stars threw down their spears,
And watered heaven with their tears,
Did he smile his work to see ?
Did he who made the lamb make thee ?

Tyger, Tyger, burning bright
In the forests of the night,
What immortal hand or eye
Dare frame thy fearful symmetry ?

The remark of the author on page 221 suggests my last quotation. Wordsworth, in the tenth book of *The Prelude*, recounts the profound impression made upon him by the terrific events in which the French Revolution culminated. Then, as now, outward convulsion and catastrophe had their inward counterpart in spiritual tumult and overthrow, in widespread disillusionment and despair. And Wordsworth tells us in effect how the very tremendousness of the time, its 'portentousness', became to him a revelation of the sustaining presence of the holy and the divine (see *The Prelude*, x. 437–469) :

... 'So, with devout humility be it said,
So, did a portion of that spirit fall
On me uplifted from the vantage-ground
Of pity and sorrow to a state of being
That through the time's exceeding fierceness saw
Glimpses of retribution, terrible,
And in the order of sublime behests :
But, even if that were not, amid the awe
Of unintelligible chastisement,
Not only acquiescences of faith
Survived, but daring sympathies with power,
Motions not treacherous or profane, else why
Within the folds of no ungentle breast
Their dread vibration to this hour prolonged ? ...
Then was the truth received into my heart,
That, under heaviest sorrow earth can bring,
If from the affliction somewhere do not grow
Honour which could not else have been, a faith,
An elevation, and a sanctity,
If new strength be not given nor old restored,
The blame is ours, not Nature's.'

Q

INDEX

PRINTED IN ENGLAND AT THE OXFORD UNIVERSITY PRESS
BY FREDERICK HALL

CPSIA information can be obtained
at www.ICGtesting.com
Printed in the USA
LVHW111519181219
640938LV00003B/284/P